P9-CFI-406

TAINTED TRUTH

The Manipulation
of Fact
in America

Cynthia Crossen

SIMON & SCHUSTER

New York   London   Toronto   Sydney   Tokyo   Singapore

SIMON & SCHUSTER
Rockefeller Center
1230 Avenue of the Americas
New York, New York 10020

Designed by Barbara Marks

Manufactured in the United States of America

1   3   5   7   9   10   8   6   4   2

Library of Congress Cataloging-in-Publication Data
Crossen, Cynthia.
Tainted truth : the manipulation of fact in America / Cynthia Crossen.
p.   cm.
Includes bibliographical references and index.
1. Mass media—United States—Objectivity.   I. Title.
P96.O242U63   1994
302.23'0973—dc20   94-5525
CIP
ISBN: 0-671-79285-7

ACKNOWLEDGMENTS

Hundreds of people from the fields of business, academia, medicine, government, public policy, journalism and law contributed to this book. After almost twenty years as a journalist, I am still gratified to find that so many people will selflessly share their intelligence and time with strangers in the name of knowledge.

Reporters at the *Wall Street Journal* are blessed with some of the best editing in journalism today. I gratefully acknowledge the assistance and encouragement of the many editors who contributed to my original story for the *Journal*, from which this book grew. These include John Bussey, my editor on page one; Dan Kelly, deputy page-one editor; Jim Stewart, page-one editor; Byron Calame, deputy managing editor; and Paul Steiger, managing editor.

Bruce Levy is one of the great, unsung heroes of the *Wall Street Journal*, a researcher who not only has a remarkable memory for what has been written but can intelligently, quickly, and cheerfully retrieve it. Liz Yeh of the *Journal*'s library also helped me track down some obscure material with patience and good humor.

My editor, Dominick Anfuso, and my agent, Richard Pine, were enthusiastic and faithful companions in my project.

Jane Berentson, my friend and editor, gave me the spiritual and editorial lift I frequently needed, as well as thoughtful comments on my manuscript.

Larry Rout, friend, editor and mentor, read my first draft and pulled no punches. His unflagging curiosity about my subject pulled me through moments of doubt; his criticisms helped me to focus my ideas and sharpen my prose.

Finally, I thank my husband, James Gleick, without whom this book would not have been written. From the beginning, he believed that the subject of corrupted truth was a story, and the story was a book. His dedication to this work —his editorial suggestions, enthusiasm and sense of outrage at what has happened to so much research—was an inspiration to me.

For Jim and Harry

CONTENTS

CONTENTS
10

CHAPTER ONE

The
Study
Game

Thou shalt not sit
With statisticians nor commit
A social science

—W. H. AUDEN

I want to know the truth. I want some numbers.

The Princeton, New Jersey, office of the Gallup Organization seems like the right place to start. Harry Cotugno and Eileen McMurray, two veterans of the survey research business, meet me in the firm's nouveau colonial conference room. Cotugno and McMurray are responsible for Gallup's "client-initiated, public-release" business. That's me.

I am researching a book about information, I explain. I believe that numbers are powerful and credible persuaders, and I want to test that hypothesis. How much do people believe polls, surveys and studies? When people read that eating five big oat bran muffins a day will prevent heart disease, do they believe it? When they hear that 64 percent of Americans do not think Barbie should leave Ken, do they believe it? When they hear that more women believed Clarence Thomas than Anita Hill, or that Styrofoam cups are as good for the environment as paper cups, do they believe it? If all information is not equally believable, how is the good distinguishable from the bad?

My questions take the Gallup team aback. Gallup, still among the most prestigious names in the research world, produces information for major businesses and institutions, information that goes to the bottom line. What I am asking may not be answerable by survey research. My questions are broad and theoretical. Do I mean information contained in advertising? Do I mean the contents of the *National Enquirer?* Do I mean a fact disseminated by the American Medical Association or one disseminated by Procter & Gamble? Do I mean statistics about health or about political candidates?

All of these. I mean all the information that comes to people in the form of numbers or facts by any means and with any intent. I mean the nuggets of knowledge that have replaced anecdote, hearsay, imagination and history as the fodder of so much modern discourse.

Now Cotugno and McMurray look uncomfortable. Gallup typically tries to answer more concrete inquiries, such as whether Americans want to keep the penny (Yes! said 62 percent in a Gallup survey sponsored by the zinc industry) and whether people who use cellular telephones are more successful in business (Yes! said seven of ten cellular phone users in a survey sponsored by Motorola). Survey questions must be narrow, precise and comprehensible to the common person. To pin down specific questions about information, McMurray suggests we look for precedents. Earlier research on the subject might suggest some questions for us, and a changing trend is good for a story.

In Cotugno and McMurray's world, the more general the question, the less useful the answer. There is an old saying in the survey research business: Ask a question, and you will get an answer. But if the answer cannot be used to make a business decision or attract media interest, what good is it? They do not offer knowledge for the sake of knowledge; they sell strategic information. For a Gallup "omnibus" survey, in which several small clients share the cost of the research, Cotugno and McMurray will ask just about anything. But first they want to know: What will we learn from these questions about statistics, credibility and truth?

◆

PEOPLE KNOW HOW TO DISCOUNT some kinds of information. We usually would not take too seriously a claim by the maker of Quick 'n Crispy Crinkle Cut Fries that "In a nationwide taste test, you preferred the crispiness of Quick 'n Crispy Crinkle Cut Fries, 3 to 1." Similarly, when the *National Examiner* publishes a story saying, "You can slash your cholesterol level [as much as 30 percent], strengthen your heart and add years to your life with a daily can of 7UP," many people would, rightly, not stop taking their cholesterol medication. We tend to give more weight to surveys, studies and polls reported in the *New England Journal of Medicine*, *Time* magazine, the *New York Times*, the network news shows or the *Wall Street Journal*. Yet even forums like these have been slow to recognize how dubious is much of the research they publish.

People know enough to be suspicious of some numbers in some contexts, but we are at the mercy of others. We have little personal experience or knowledge of the topics of much modern research, and the methodologies are incomprehensibly arcane. Nevertheless, we respect numbers, and we cannot help believing them. Numbers bring a sense of rationality to complex decisions—the ones we once made with common sense, experience and intelligence.

Yet more and more of the information we use to buy, elect, advise, acquit and heal has been created not to expand our knowledge but to sell a product or advance a cause. If the results of the research contradict the sponsor's agenda, they will routinely be suppressed. Researchers have become secretive and their sponsors greedy. The media, which can usually get the raw numbers if they want them, are stingy with data because data are boring, and so many journalists are themselves innumerate.

In supermarkets and drugstores, privately sponsored research now acts as our doctor, parent and pharmacist; in the courtroom, studies, surveys and polls are lawyers; they are advocates in legislatures, and propagandists in advertising and marketing. In public opinion, polls and surveys have formed a weird loop in which one's own beliefs are increasingly shaped by the beliefs of a few hundred strangers. So integral to our lives has sponsored information become that we have invented a new vocabulary to describe it: infomercial, infotainment, factoid, advertorial, docudrama. But these are only the forms that admit to being a blend of fact and fancy. Much sponsored research still wears the guise of neutrality.

Buying and selling information to advance private agendas is only one way our sense of truth is warped. There is also a growing sense that nothing can be asserted to be true unless it is backed by statistical research, even if it is completely obvious. Is a study really required to show that hospital patients are more satisfied if their doctors and nurses are nice to them? Such a study, carried out at several U.S. hospitals, tried to measure the effects on patients of being smiled at, helped to read their charts and not awakened in the middle of the night for tests. The results: Patients felt happier and healthier.

Another assault on the truth comes in the form of information trivia—the explosion of facts about everything, no matter how banal. Because this information usually comes in the form of numbers, all of it, regardless of its significance, looks and sounds similar. Studies about heart disease or pesticides answer questions with precise numbers; so do studies about nose-picking. A 1993 study done by the Southern Baptist Convention found that 46.1 percent of people in Alabama risk going to hell. A 1991 Roper study showed that one of fifty adult Americans—3.7 million—may have been abducted by a UFO. The 6,000 people surveyed were asked if any of a number of experiences had ever happened to them. If they said yes enough times, that strongly suggested UFO abduction. On the list were things like having seen, as a child, a terrifying figure in your closet, or having found puzzling scars on your body. The survey contained a control question designed to weed out people who will say yes to anything. It was: "hearing or seeing the word TRONDANT and knowing that it has a secret meaning for you." Eighteen people said that had happened to them more than twice.

◆

THAT NUMBERS CAN—AND DO—lie surely comes as no shock to anyone who lives in the United States, where statistical manipulation has a long and rich history. The 1840 Census was a cesspool of error, fraud and political machination largely driven by the slavery debate. Much of the battle over Prohibition was fought with finagled statistics. In one particularly deft bit of strategic statistics, a Prohibitionist group neutralized the efforts of an outspoken critic of Prohibition, Pierre du Pont of Delaware. Du Pont had sent out a questionnaire to state residents hoping to prove they wanted to drink. Using newspaper ads, dry groups urged drys not to respond to the questionnaire. Without their responses, the result of the survey was 97 percent against Prohibition. That so obviously did not represent the truth that the survey was rendered worthless.

Other common twisting of statistics includes wartime casualty figures—America's Defense Intelligence Agency es-

"Million Man March"

NIFTY

NUMBERS

timated 100,000 Iraqi soldiers died in the Persian Gulf War; other sources have put it at 8,000—and crowd counts of political demonstrators, which during the Vietnam War varied by hundreds of thousands depending on the counter's politics. But now more than ever, manipulated statistics can be seen in other areas of life. Advertisers are regularly sued for using misleading or unsupported data. Disaster figures, usually made in the hysteria of the immediate aftermath, are almost always wrong; estimates of damage in the massive 1991 Oakland, California, hill fire began at $5.2 billion and ended at $1.5 billion. The American Cancer Society has declared that women's risk of breast cancer is one in nine. In fact, there are many differing estimates, most of them lower, including that when a woman is under fifty, her chance is probably about one in 1,000; even when she is in her early eighties, her chance is not one in nine. The risk of breast cancer rises as a woman ages, so one in nine is the cumulative probability starting the day a girl is born and ending at an age so advanced—somewhere between 85 and 110, depending on whose figures you believe—that she'll probably already be dead of something else. Economic statistics are so soft they are almost liquid, and few know how to read them anyway. Consider these two headlines based on the same government data: "White-Black Disparity in Income Narrowed in 80's, Census Shows" (the *New York Times*, July 24, 1992) and "Income Equality Gap Widens for Minorities" (*USA Today*, July 24, 1992). Two headlines show how definitive political polls are: "Dave Fades with Hispanics: Poll," stated the *New York Post* about the city's then-mayor, David Dinkins. Using the same numbers, the *Daily News*'s headline read, "Latinos Back Dave: Poll."

A few scholars have begun to waken to the increasingly disturbing trend of inaccurate and corrupt information. "Fraudulent activities pervade all forms of official information we have studied," wrote Jack D. Douglas, then a sociology professor at the University of California at San Diego. "Sonar reports, body counts, efficiency reports, preparedness reports, population (census) studies, crimes reported to the police, university personnel records, and all the others involve many fraudulent practices . . . prefiguring, file building, unrepresentative glossing, unrepresentative windowing, outright lying, and many other forms of deceit."

Politicians use so many bad statistics they have become famous for them. Ross Perot's straight-talking television commercials were filled with false facts—Taiwan is spending $600 billion a year on public investment programs, Perot claimed, trying to shame America for its $150 billion program. The truth: Taiwan is spending $50 billion a year for six years. Bill Clinton claimed that 80,000 lobbyists were lining the corridors of Washington—a figure that originated with a university professor who admitted it came "off the top of my head." The real number is between 6,000 and 20,000. In the 1992 presidential campaign, George Bush tossed around a figure for how much lawyers cost America. "He mentioned a specific number of billions, which I instantly forgot after checking the amount of brain space still available for storing fraudulent statistics and finding none left," wrote the columnist Russell Baker. Nonetheless, the number was widely reported.

We are skeptical about statistical and factual information, but not as skeptical as we think. The sheer volume of research we are exposed to in our daily lives is formidable and growing. Every day's newspaper teems with references to studies, surveys and polls: studies about health (Does coffee raise cholesterol levels? Should young women have mammograms?); presidential popularity polls; "lifestyle" surveys, on how people work, eat, relax; policy studies, showing the environmental or political effects of a course of action; pharmaceutical studies that promise another breakthrough in fighting disease; and advocacy studies showing the worsening plight of a group that needs help.

The psychology of researchers themselves—mostly without reflection or self-awareness—has undergone a profound change over the past decade, and many researchers' ethical standards have drifted from the scientist's toward the lobbyist's. Researchers have almost given up on the quaint notion that there is any such thing as "fact" or "objectivity." Although their tools have never been faster, more efficient or more accurate, the path to truth is blocked by a financial obstacle—the escalating funding power of private interests—

and an intellectual one. That is their growing understanding that the main subjects of their research, human beings, are even more unpredictable than they had known.

Nothing is certain about people: Their height changes during the day, their hormones by the season. Their bodies and minds are unique and inconstant. Since there can never be true certainty, there must be a new kind of objectivity. Scientists never believed the road to truth was a straight line, or that the most recent study was the final word. But they at least believed the search for knowledge was progressive and cumulative. Now some scientists are not so sure. Perhaps instead of a jagged line leading toward certainty, the truth could be better achieved by the creation of many semi-certainties competing for people's credulity. These research-ers—and a growing number of other people—believe the world has become too clever and sophisticated to embrace positivism, the belief that objective knowledge really exists. In some fields, a new credo of many truths, called postpositivist critical multiplism, is replacing it.

The belief that no piece of information can tell the truth (and its frequent concomitant: So do not worry about inconsistencies and contradictions) has trickled into many parts of the research business, which is, after all, a business. "Truth usually lies in the preponderance of evidence from a multiplicity of polls using divergent approaches," concluded Thomas E. Mann and Gary R. Orren in their book *Media Polls in American Politics*. Along with this philosophy comes another convenient idea that just because studies are different does not mean one is good and another bad. Mann and Orren call that "no-fault variability," a real boon to the disputatious world of research.

The proposition that there is no such thing as objective reality is easier on researchers than on consumers of information. For researchers, it means the standard of proof is whatever can be defended, and absent outright fraud, there is no real way for anyone to disprove any particular set of findings. For the rest of us, it means that we who lack the tools, expertise and confidence to judge most information must delicately weigh results against motives before we believe anything. We are left adrift in doubt, losing our grip on

one of our most potent tools: numbers. "As dupes we know
what as liars we tend to blur," Sissela Bok has written. "That
information can be more or less adequate; that even where
no clear lines are drawn, rules and distinctions may, in fact,
be made; and that truthfulness can be required even where
full 'truth' is out of reach."

◆

BEHIND THE EXPLOSION OF CORRUPTED information is, first,
money. For a few decades after World War II, scientific research was sponsored primarily by the government and academic institutions, which let researchers ask and answer
questions largely free of commercial or partisan influence (although many academic researchers worked for the military).
But in recent years the pool of scientists looking for work has
grown while state and federal government research budgets
have flattened. Universities themselves face declining revenues and higher costs. Private companies, meanwhile, have
found it both cheaper and more prestigious to retain academic, government or commercial researchers than to set up
in-house operations that some might suspect of bias. Corporations, litigants, political candidates, trade associations, lobbyists, special interest groups—all can buy research to use
as they like. Freedom of the press, the critic A. J. Liebling
once said, belongs only to those who own one. In the information business, truth has come to belong to those who commission it.

The commercialization of research means that the number of independent voices in our society is dwindling. Every
university professor, researcher or doctor who sells his soul
to self-interested sponsors comforts himself with some ratio-
nale: "*I* can accept this money without compromising my
independence; *my* ethics are intact; *I* won't be biased." But
it is never so. "[F]ew doctors accept that they themselves
have been corrupted," wrote Michael D. Rawlins in the medical journal *Lancet*. "Most doctors believe that they are quite
untouched by the seductive ways of the [drug] industry's marketing men. . . . The degree to which the profession . . . can
practise such self-deceit is extraordinary. No drug company

gives away its shareholders' money in an act of disinterested generosity. . . . The harsh truth is that not one of us is impervious to the promotional activities of the industry, and that the industry uses its various sales techniques because they are effective."

Without the unpaid voices of these researchers, no one speaks disinterestedly. "Say you're sick and you want to buy some drugs," said David Noble, a historian and author. "The drug industry can provide you with a wealth of information about the drugs. You know what you're reading is part information and part advertisement, and that it's important to distinguish the two. So you try to get an independent evaluation. Where are you going to get it? The universities in theory are the only institutions in our society that supply information on a disinterested basis. But in fact, the universities are bought. If someone comes from Squibb, caveat emptor. But here, you're disarmed, which is precisely what the clients are seeking. The universities are going to lose their credibility, and I think that's tragic."

Others who worry about the overlap between business and academia wonder whether it will change the whole course of scientific inquiry. Will applied research drive out basic research? Will the proprietary needs of the sponsor overwhelm traditions of science like openness? Will the large, powerful and affluent dictate what subjects are researched, and will there be any accountability to anyone else? Will scientists cling to their positions even more defensively than usual, since abandoning them could mean losing not just face but money?

Privately sponsored research also exacerbates the problem of overreporting positive results and underreporting negative ones. In science, positive does not necessarily mean good; it simply means the results are statistically significant; in other words, they could not be attributed to chance alone. Negative means that nothing happened or that whatever happened could have happened by chance alone. Commercial sponsors obviously want to publicize only positive results that make their product look good; results that make their product look bad, or no results at all, they almost never want to talk about. Nor, for the most part, do researchers, journals or the news media. The overemphasis on positive results reaches down to many of today's students, who say, if their hypothesis is not supported by their results, "My research didn't work." Furthermore, the increasing stratification among research scientists means junior and senior scientists are less likely to work shoulder to shoulder in the lab, where the traditions and ethics of science have long been conveyed by example. "There has been a tremendous influx of new people who weren't grounded in the traditions of scientific thinking," lamented Jack Douglas. "It's getting harder to be an honest scientist."

◆

THE SUBJECT OF INFORMATION HAS BEEN researched many times, although, as it turns out, none of the research asked the precise questions I have in mind. A batch of studies about newspaper credibility came out in the mid-1980s during one of the regular flare-ups of criticism by political conservatives that the media are liberal. In 1985, the Times Mirror Company sponsored a study on the credibility of thirty-nine news organizations and personalities, from Walter Cronkite (most believable) to the *National Enquirer* (least believable, just edging out *Rolling Stone* magazine). In a 1989 study on public attitudes toward the press, Pope John Paul II was identified as the most believable leader, and Mikhail Gorbachev the least—less believable even than Geraldo Rivera and Donald Trump. Studies have compared the credibility of various categories of media—newspapers, magazines, television. Louis Harris did a study, "The Road After 1984," which showed a population concerned about "information abuse"—primarily technological invasions of privacy. All of these studies share a flaw: People can't be trusted when they say they believe someone.

Studies have also been done on the psychological aspects of credibility, like the "Dr. Fox effect" research of the early 1970s, in which an actor was programmed to teach material he knew nothing about. A majority of the audience of well-educated professionals found the distinguished and authoritative Dr. Fox stimulating and interesting; one member of the audience even claimed to have read something Dr. Fox had written. The researchers concluded that even well-educated audiences cannot necessarily detect propaganda or false information.

"You can't separate the medium from the message," warns Albert E. Gollin, director of research for the Newspaper Advertising Bureau.

I do not want to. I want to ask about credibility across all disciplines, all media, all sources. But I doubt that I have a question worth asking yet.

Asking the right question is the pillar of good science, both social and other, as well as a source of endless debate and despair among researchers. In survey work, the perfect question has become the Holy Grail, forever out of reach. Researchers dedicate themselves to the question, experimenting with words to create the perfect inquiry—a question that does not presume, lead or color. But, as many of the attendees of the 1992 conference of the American Association for Public Opinion Research, a trade organization of survey research, knew, there will never be a truly neutral question.

Researchers know one thing about questions: However precise and neutral they seem to be, they often have unpredictable effects—response effects, researchers call them. Response effects arise from the quirkiness of language and the complexities of human emotion—pride, embarrassment, self-righteousness, contempt or any of the hundreds of other strings that play when one person speaks to another. Even under ideal circumstances, when asked to remember something recent and concrete, recall is often different from fact. What time did you go to bed the night before last? What is your license plate number? What did you do last Sunday? What color shirt is your spouse wearing today?

Because modern polls ask busy adults to answer dozens, sometimes scores, of questions on a variety of topics, respondents often feel they have to give their answers quickly. The respondents reason that the interviewers could not possibly be asking for a precise answer because they are leaving no time to compute it. So they take a guess. Unfortunately, a guess is a guess, and people tend to guess in a self-serving way.

TV scale!"

A classic example of the way people's egos distort fact is a poll about television viewing. Two groups of people were asked how much they watched a day. Both groups were given scales from which to choose. One scale started at less than thirty minutes of television a day and ended at more than two and a half hours. The other scale had a much higher minimum—less than two and a half hours—and the maximum was more than four and a half hours. In the first group, only 16.2 percent admitted to watching the greatest amount of television—more than two and a half hours. But in the second group, more than double that number said they watched at least two and a half hours. Whatever the truth, people did not *✗1.* want to be on the high end of the scale.

And that is a question of fact. When there is an emotional or political component—questions about race, religion, abortion, sex—recall is an even faultier connection from the churning stew of the mind.

The imprecision of language exacerbates the problem. Single words that mean the same thing can convey wildly different ideas. Taxes or revenues? MX missile or Peacekeeper? Pro-choice or pro-abortion? Welfare or public assistance? Department of War or Department of Defense? There are "magical qualities" in the phrase "to maintain world peace," one pollster noted; the linguist S. I. Hayakawa called some words "purr-words," and others "snarl-words." A young monk was once rebuffed by his superior when he asked if he could smoke while he prayed. Ask a different *first* question, a friend advised. Ask if you can pray while you *grilled* smoke.

Responses can also be dramatically different depending on whether people are given options from which to choose or simply say whatever comes to mind. In one survey, respondents were asked what is the most important thing for children to learn to prepare them for life. When given a choice of five options, 62 percent chose "to think for themselves." But when given the open-ended question with no options, only 5 percent gave that answer.

Meanwhile, there is a person asking the questions who may seem, to those being interviewed, as a judge of knowledge or character. That can tempt respondents to sound more sure than they really are or even to lie to seem more informed. In 1947, a researcher named Sam Gill asked people their thoughts on the entirely fictitious Metallic Metals Act; some 70 percent opined about it. When the American Jewish Committee studied Americans' attitudes toward various ethnic groups, almost 30 percent of the respondents had an opinion about the fictional Wisians, rating them in social standing above a half-dozen other real groups, including Mexicans, Vietnamese and African blacks.

There are also times when a question written in a remote and sterile office clashes with a complex and ungraspable reality. "You sit in a lady's living room, look through cracked, broken-out windows at blocks and blocks of gutted has-been homes," remembered a researcher. "You walk across a sagging creaking floor, and look into narrow eyes peering at you from beneath a dresser. Not a dog, nor a cat—no, a child. Now you ask the big question in the neighborhood problem section: 'Have you had any trouble because of neighbors not keeping up their property?' " Passion, too, is rarely captured by surveys or polls. A cartoon by Lee Lorenz pictures a polltaker standing outside an apartment door, talking to a hefty man. On his T-shirt, in big bold letters, are the words NUKE EM. "Suppose we just put you down as believing eternal vigilance is the price of liberty," the polltaker says.

The growing understanding of the problem with the question has been a setback for survey researchers, but it is not good news for everyone else, either. In one study, researchers asked people to make a hypothetical choice between two treatments for lung cancer—surgery or radiation. Everyone received statistical data on the effectiveness of the two therapies, but the data for one group were stated in terms of survival and for the other in terms of mortality. For example, the "survival" group was told that "Of 100 people having surgery, 90 will live through the surgery, 68 will be alive at the end of the first year, and 34 will be alive after five years. Of 100 people having radiation therapy, all live through the treatment, 77 will be alive at the end of the first year, and 22 will be alive at the end of five years." The "mortality" group was told this: Of 100 people having surgery, 10 will die during the treatment, 32 will have died in a year, and 66 will have died by five years. Of 100 people having radiation therapy, none will die during treatment, 23 will die by one year, and 78 will die by five years.

Presented the first way—in terms of survival—only 18 percent chose radiation therapy over surgery. But presented the second way, in terms of mortality, more than twice as many people—47 percent—chose radiation therapy over surgery. The statement that "none will die during treatment" seemed to loom much larger than long-term survival even to doctors and business students, two groups who should be able to sort out statistics from the words "live" and "die."

If all this was not already discouraging, researchers now know that the order in which questions are asked is as critical as the wording of any of them. Consider these two questions, artifacts of 1950. The first: Do you think the United States should let Russian newspaper reporters come here and send back whatever they want? The second: Do you think Russia should let American newspaper reporters come in and send back whatever they want?

If people were asked the first question first, only 36 percent of them said the U.S. should allow Russian reporters in. But if they were asked about American journalists first, they had to, at least subconsciously, think about fairness, and more than twice as many people—73 percent—said the Russians should be allowed in.

Researchers have tried to reduce this problem, the so-called context effect, by experimenting with "buffer" questions, which are asked between items on the same topic. In one experiment on buffer questions, people were asked to say something—anything—about what their U.S. representative had done for his or her district. Then they were asked if they follow politics a lot, some or not that much. If they had not been able to think of much to say about their congressman, it was hard for them to pretend to themselves they followed politics. No number of buffer questions about unrelated topics, up to 101, seemed to let most people off that psychological hook.

But a single buffer question on the same topic did the trick. That intervening question asked people to evaluate the quality of their representative's public relations work. Now people who knew nothing about their representative could blame it on his or her public relations efforts, an alternative explanation for their lack of knowledge.

If any question would seem straightforward, it is a simple comparison: Compare this to that. But even this turns out to be loaded. A German research team has shown that you can get dramatically different answers depending on whether you ask someone if tennis is more or less exciting than soccer or if soccer is more or less exciting than tennis. (This might also hold true if someone is asked whether Clinton would be a better or worse president than Bush or vice versa.) The theory is that when people are asked to compare tennis to soccer, they focus on the features of soccer and then mentally check to see if those features are also in tennis. People would not remember the unique features of tennis, because they are not brought to mind by soccer.

The well-known difficulties of asking and answering questions have become opportunities for sponsors of research. The wording of questions, their order, the intonations, the pacing—all are so subtly persuasive that they can look innocent even though they have been consciously manipulated. The pitfalls of the researcher's craft have also become the tools of its corruption.

◆

I SEND GALLUP A COPY of five questions I have written about credibility and information. They are:

1. Are you more likely to believe a claim when you hear it is backed by a "scientific study"?

2. Do you think you could find a scientific study to say just about anything?

3. Given that no one can agree on much these days, do you think there's any such thing as an absolute truth?

4. Do you think people are overwhelmed by information, or do you think that the more information people have the better off they are?

5. Do you think most of the information you hear that came from consumer surveys, public opinion polls and scientific studies is probably right, or are you skeptical about it?

Omnibus surveys vary little from company to company, despite the companies' sales pitches asserting otherwise. Gallup's is among the most expensive—$1,500 for one closed-end question—but otherwise it is standard survey research —1,000 interviews, either by telephone or in person, of randomly selected adults eighteen or older in the forty-eight mainland states (Alaska and Hawaii are too expensive to survey by telephone), projectable to the nation, tabulated by standard demographics. For half that price you could get onto Bruskin/Goldring's OmniTel, where, as the brochure says, "you can be sure that your results will not be affected by position bias." That means the interviewers shake up the order of the questions so your perfume question will not follow someone else's deodorant question in every one of the 1,000 interviews.

ICR's Excel survey is better than others, said ICR's Fred Soulas, because Excel interviews are done on both weekdays and weekends, and they have a better call-back rule (up to three attempts). Opinion Research's Caravan is better, said the company's Judy Lescher, because they do everything in-house, and their interviewers are very strictly controlled.

The Roper Organization's limo-bus ("the limousine of omnibus surveys") goes door-to-door, an increasingly rare method of collecting data. Telephone interviewing is quicker, but the sample tends to be more affluent; lower income people are less likely to answer a stranger's questions on the phone, and some people find it easier to hang up than to slam the door in the face of a kindly middle-aged woman. For most omnibus work, speed is of the essence; five days from beginning to end is not unusual, and overnight is not unheard of. Although research companies will help their clients shape a question so it is more useful to them, anything, for the most part, goes. "We're the chauffeur, and what they do in the backseat is their business," said Tom Miller of Roper.

To protect its name, which commands premium rates in a very competitive field, Gallup has rules about the way its research can be used. It cannot, for example, be mentioned in paid advertising. A Gallup survey must be publicly released in its entirety or not at all, and the results must be made available to anyone on request. Publication of survey results must include the exact question wording, dates of interviewing, sample size, interviewing method, definition of the survey population and size of sampling error. Gallup generally reserves the right to review all press releases or, in the case of this book, what I write about its survey results. (Should Gallup not approve of what I or other clients write, its policy is simply to issue its own news releases.)

◆

ALTHOUGH THE SURVEY BUSINESS HAS exploded in the past few decades, making research a commodity that even an individual can afford, Americans have been charting their course with numbers since the birth of the nation. In the New World, where people had fled to escape the authoritarianism of churches and states, political decisions would be made by common men and women who had come to a reasoned judgment. Since each person's opinion would be equally valid, the more people who believed something, the more likely it was to be right. Or as the French proverb put it, everybody knew better than anybody. In the ideal democracy, leaders would take an accurate poll every minute and rule accordingly. Empirical knowledge of all kinds was essential for determining the common good.

The faith in knowledge and the majority still holds, perhaps even more strongly today. In times of crisis like Watergate or war, polls tell our leaders it is time to resign or give them an encouraging pat on the back. Few leaders seem capable of pulling together a working consensus from the shrill public discord about health care, gun control, abortion, drugs, pollution, racism or welfare; today the only consensus about many issues is the artificial one produced by polls and surveys. Other traditional repositories of information and guidance, like the family, churches and schools, have lost their authority. Today the first question commonly asked of political candidates is not their opinion on an issue but their opinion of the latest polls. Political commentators, who are paid to make judgments, sometimes refrain from expressing their opinions, saying, "Let's wait until we see the polls." Yet vast parts of the research industry have no barriers to entry, and no higher authority certifies or censors information. For better and worse, almost all of it is protected by the First Amendment.

So important are surveys and polls that on many questions Americans believe our leaders should blindly follow the polls, ignoring their own common sense or judgment. To cite a study, the Roper Organization asked almost 1,000 people on which of the following three influences the votes of elected officials should be based: experts and leaders, the will of the majority or the officials' own consciences. Another roughly 1,000 people were asked the same question with one change: The term "public opinion polls" replaced "will of the majority." On every topic, from reducing the deficit to a woman's right to abortion, people said leaders should pay less attention to their own beliefs than to the will of the majority. On most topics, people also said officials should pay less attention to leaders and experts than to the majority. When the term "public opinion polls" replaced "will of the majority," the results were the same.

Most researchers are trained as scientists. To be published in prestigious journals they must lay out their hypotheses and experiments in such detail that other scientists have the weapons to attack them. If the work is carelessly or fraudulently done, they will probably hear about it, or it will sink into oblivion. It is possible, however, to produce tainted research well within ethical and professional barriers. In survey research, the effect of a poorly worded question might be debatable, but few would call it corrupt. If the sample of a poll is poorly selected or too small, it might be considered flawed, but probably not fraud. If a biomedical researcher chooses not to use a placebo because the tested drug looks better without one, that might be a questionable judgment but not evidence of malfeasance. Between dishonesty and honesty in research there is a sprawling gray area.

At each step from hypothesis to conclusions, there are intellectual choices. Who are the subjects of the research— men or women, young or old, sick or well? Are they randomly selected, or are they chosen because they share a certain trait? Over what period of time does the research take place

—a few days, months, a year, a decade? Are subjects approached by telephone or in person? Who monitors the behavior or language of the subjects, and what assumptions are made when analyzing the data? How are the results disseminated? Each choice has consequences, some known and some not. It is here that researchers can push or pull a study in some direction that will please the sponsor but not threaten their scientific integrity.

Computers have become indispensable tools for modern researchers, and often tools for mischief. Computer models give the illusion of neutral precision, but they are actually quite tractable. Computers also exacerbate the polarization of researchers and everyone else. Some kinds of research—biomedical, for example—have always been outside the ken of most people. Today, as computer models have become more complicated, the gulf between the producers and the consumers of studies has become true of other research. Dressed up in complex tables and graphs that measure, usually pointlessly, to the tenth or hundredth of a decimal point, the packaging of information often makes it seem even more intimidating than it is. The only people who can quickly analyze most research are the people who do it. That practically guarantees an uncritical reception from press and public.

Once a piece of commissioned research leaves the scientist's door, it can be used by whoever paid for it in whatever way they want. There are two primary ways to lie, wrote Paul Ekman in his book *Telling Lies:* to conceal and to falsify. If the results of the study do not support its sponsor's agenda, the sponsor can simply bury it, creating the "file drawer" bias that skews published research to the positive. If the results are good, the sponsor can peddle the study to the media, sending it out in slick packages, sometimes even including eight-by-ten glossies of the scientists. Research sponsors write news releases that distort or magnify the study's findings. "There's good news for the 65 million Americans currently on a diet," said a news release for Nutri/System, reporting a study showing that people who lose weight can keep it off. The study consisted of interviews with twenty dieters, all graduates of the program who had previously endorsed it in the company's advertising.

The news media play a crucial role in misinforming people about studies, surveys and polls. Journalists rarely try to pull apart the inner workings of a study. Their editors, increasingly uncomfortable making news decisions about complex issues by instinct or common sense, may have demanded statistics to prop up a story. Reporters and editors, sensitive to accusations of bias, appreciate the apparent neutrality of numbers.

It is even more dangerous when newspapers and television programs commission their own studies—purveyors of information buying information to purvey. The NBC show *Dateline NBC* described as "unscientific" a crash demonstration of a General Motors truck whose gas tank was allegedly defective. That was before network executives realized that the study was not only unscientific—it was rigged. The consulting firm NBC had commissioned to do crash tests, the Institute for Safety Analysis, did not have even a veneer of neutrality. It frequently provided evidence in personal-injury actions against automobile companies, including General Motors. For its *Dateline* client, the researchers strapped model rockets to the bottom of one truck to insure it would produce a picturesque fire. It was not until a GM lawsuit was filed that NBC would admit that it had distorted information for its own self-interest.

The studies, surveys and polls that the news media do for themselves are not typically so tainted, but it is routine to make studies seem more dramatic and definitive than they are, and to cover up the indecision and subtleties inherent in most public opinion. Sellers of news do not like research with no results. If a public opinion poll is judged to be boring, regardless of whether it is a valid picture of opinion, it may be discarded in the file drawer. "That's what surveys do, they basically manufacture news," said Tom Miller of Roper.

At the end of the information chain are the consumers, most of whom didn't take even a basic statistics course. If students did venture into statistics, many were driven away by the horrendous difficulty of the courses, with their interquartile ranges and product-moment coefficients, designed for statistics majors rather than people who need a working knowledge of the subject. The result is that most consumers,

voters and leaders have neither the confidence nor the tools
to judge research. They may agree that it is easy to lie with
statistics but, like the statistician Frederick Mosteller, they
probably also think it is easier to lie without them. Today it is
pretty much a toss-up.

◆

GALLUP'S RESPONSE TO MY QUESTIONS is simply to put them into
survey language. In an earlier telephone conversation, we
have already agreed to drop my fourth question, about information overload. Gallup has distilled my four questions into
three:

    1. I am going to read some factors that might
help you to decide whether or not a story you hear
or read is true. As I read each, please tell me to
what extent, if any, this information might help you
to believe the story is true. First, to what extent
would (READ AND ROTATE A-C) increase its
credibility—a great deal, to some extent, not too
much or not at all?
____References in the story to scientific research
____Statements by known experts
____Statistics that back up the story
[Read and rotate means that the three factors will
be read in rotating order to minimize possible position bias.]
    2. I am going to read you some statements.
For each, please tell me whether you agree completely, mostly agree, mostly disagree or disagree
completely (READ AND ROTATE).
____You can find a scientific study that proves just
    about anything you want to prove.
____There is no such thing as absolute truth.
____You can be confident that when a newspaper
    publishes the results of research, the informa-
    tion is accurate.
    3. How much confidence do you have in the
truth and accuracy of information from the follow-

ing sources? Would you say you are very confident
that the information is true and accurate, some-
what confident, not too confident or not at all con-
fident? (READ AND ROTATE A-C, REPEAT
RESPONSE CATEGORIES AS NECESSARY)
____Consumer surveys that show how many people
    like a particular product
____Public opinion polls that show how people feel
    about political and social issues
____Scientific studies that describe the causes of
    diseases

McMurray of Gallup said converting my questions to a
survey format was relatively simple, the biggest catch being
in the first question, where I ask about whether statistics,
opinions from experts or scientific research might affect the
credibility or believability of information. "Believability" is a
mouthful for an interviewer, but McMurray worried that the
general public might not understand "credibility." I wondered about using the word "accurate" rather than "true,"
which McMurray and I agreed meant different things although we could not precisely describe the distinction. The
dictionary was not much help: It defines "accurate" first as
"free from error" but then as "conforming exactly to truth."
    With these minor changes, the questions go on their way
—to a few old Gallup hands for reactions and to members of
a public-release committee, made up of members of the Gallup family, someone from the company's media group and the
editor of the Gallup Polls. The price for asking the three
multipart questions.to enough people to be projected to the
entire population of the U.S. is a bargain at $4,500. Interview-
ing is set to begin within a few weeks.
    Although some of Gallup's business is still conducted in
Princeton, the town to which its founder, George Gallup,
moved the firm in the 1930s, interviewing for its surveys is
done almost exclusively in Nebraska. That is because in 1988
Gallup, then running in the red, was acquired by a Lincoln-
based market-research company called Selection Research,
which trimmed the Princeton staff and consolidated several
divisions back home. Reflecting a broader change in the poll-

ing industry, Gallup has shifted its emphasis from social trend research to more lucrative market research. It continues to publish its regular Gallup Poll, which is syndicated to newspapers around the country. But a much higher percentage of Gallup's survey work is done for commercial clients than in the past, and Gallup's name can be seen on many pieces of research used to advance an agenda.

Like most modern survey research firms, Gallup does its interviewing on a Computer-Assisted Telephone Interviewing, or CATI, system. These speedy phone and computer stations flash questions onto the screen in the appropriate order, relieving the interviewer of the job of shuffling through a bunch of papers to find the question that logically follows the answer to the last one. As the interviewers record the answers on their computers, the results go simultaneously into a central computer, which tabulates the responses even as the interview continues. In a control room, supervisors can pick up the phone and silently monitor the interviews to make sure the interviewers are working hard and competently and the questions are comprehensible.

Gallup's interviewers, like those at most survey research firms, tend to be women, although that is changing. In the early days of survey research, interviewing was an attractive job for women. It was often part-time, and it could be done from home. The research industry also believed that women were better interviewers than men. "People are really less reluctant to talk with a woman," said George Gallup, "and women are much more conscientious."

Persuasiveness and the ability not to take rejection personally have always been crucial assets of interviewers, and that is even more true now. People are harder to reach, and they have less time for sharing their opinions with strangers. The Republican poller Richard Wirthlin said Mormons are ideal interviewers. These young people in Provo, Utah, have already been on two-year missions to bring converts into the church, Wirthlin said. They are used to approaching strangers, and they know how to handle rejection.

The miracle of statistics is that 1,000 people, and sometimes even fewer, *can* speak for 250 million, just as a tube of blood or a sip of wine can tell the whole story of the body or the bottle. On the other hand, if the sample is poorly drawn, increasing the number of people in the sample from 1,000 to 10,000 or even to 50,000 will not make the results any more accurate. With dropping response rates, it usually takes many more than 1,000 calls to get the 1,000 interviews needed to make the results projectable to the national population. When the percentage of people willing to answer survey questions drops to 65 percent and lower, as it increasingly does, researchers get worried. For one thing, making more phone calls to get the same number of responses is expensive. But researchers also believe lower response rates may skew randomness, a critical tool of their trade. How representative is a sample of people who will agree to a fifteen-minute interruption in the middle of their busy day?

The interviewing for my survey is done over six days in February 1993. The telephone numbers are "random digit dial" samples that are bought from a company called Survey Sampling. Throwing darts at a telephone directory would not produce a random nationally projectable sample, because so many households do not list their telephone numbers. Another slice of listed numbers reach empty houses, and many newly occupied houses are not listed yet. Survey Sampling generates numbers by taking known area codes, known telephone exchanges (the first three digits of a seven-digit number), known "bank" numbers (the fourth and fifth digits) and then randomly generating the last two digits.

For my survey, the interviewers, who are calling either on weekday evenings or on weekends, ask first for the youngest man eighteen years or older who is home. If no man is home, the interviewer asks for the oldest woman at home. A quota is set so that half the interviewees are male and half female. If no one is home or the phone is busy or someone cannot talk, the interviewer will try the number twice more at different times of day to try to complete an interview.

The data are entered into a computer, which tabulates the answers by sex, age, education, region and income. If I were willing to pay more, Gallup would do more elaborate tabulations; as it is, the company sends me a handsomely bound report of my study, which they have named "The Public and the Media: Factors in Believability and Attitudes Toward Information." The margin of error for the entire sample is plus or minus 3 points at a 95 in 100 confidence level. That means the chances are 95 in 100 that the sampling error will be no larger than 3 points. I do not use the breakdowns by gender, age and geography, where the margin of error would be higher.

◆

THE RESULTS OF MY SURVEY show exactly what I expected—even hoped: a public that is, paradoxically, both trusting and skeptical of information. The survey suggests that people are, at least in their own opinions, skeptical about information, agreeing that there are scientific studies to prove just about anything. But it also suggests that references to scientific studies, political polls and consumer surveys make people trust the information more.

Seventy-six percent of the respondents agreed either completely or mostly with the statement that you can find a scientific study that proves just about anything you want to prove. Yet 86 percent said references to scientific research in a story increased its credibility somewhat or a great deal; 82 percent said statistics increased a story's credibility; and 81 percent believed statements by known experts make a story more believable.

Different kinds of research elicited different responses, suggesting that people already adjust their credibility depending on the type of research. For example, 63 percent of the respondents said they were confident in the truth and accuracy of consumer surveys showing how many people like a particular product. Only 54 percent said they were very or somewhat confident in the results of public opinion polls. But a sizable 81 percent said they were very or somewhat confident in scientific studies describing the causes of diseases.

I did not need Gallup, of course, to tell me that people believe studies, surveys and polls. But it is difficult to assess, socially, politically or economically, the cost of this trust to people's lives. If they are swayed by tainted information despite themselves, the consequences range from trivial to profound. Maybe they bought the wrong car; unless it was a Corvair, what real difference did it make? Maybe they ate more oat bran or drank less coffee—probably inconsequential, even beneficial—to either their longevity or happiness. But maybe they elected the wrong mayor, governor or even president. Maybe they got the wrong treatment for their disease; maybe they did not stop smoking; maybe they starved themselves on diet pills; maybe they exonerated a polluter or acquitted a murderer; maybe they lost their life savings; maybe they could not solve their society's gravest problems.

The loss of our numbers may be irrevocable. We want numbers, but we mistrust them, and the clash of those feelings makes people feel both vulnerable and cynical. We need to reclaim the purity of our numbers, or we will all be the losers. Without them, we are feeling our way through the landscape with neither map nor compass.

◆

THERE IS MUCH GOOD RESEARCH being done today, and it has resulted in extraordinary human progress on many fronts. In each kind of research—studies, surveys and polls—there are many ethical professionals who aspire to quality, objectivity and accuracy. A few researchers do what so many only think they do: force their commercial clients to dance to their tune, rather than the reverse. It would be a disservice to the quest for knowledge if this critique indicted the whole field and all who till it. Statistics have contributed much to our understanding of the world, and they have helped us to grapple with many problems. This book was written with the help of many researchers.

The reader will be interested to see that I sometimes cite studies, surveys and polls to make my own points. I try to use studies that are not fatally flawed; and more important, I do not claim that the studies I cite are more than single small rungs on an infinitely long ladder to truth. Almost without exception, the studies I use do not have sponsors with a financial stake in the outcome. I try to choose studies intelligently—because ultimately that is what we all, as consumers of information, must learn to do. Still, just because I use a study to refute another study does not mean my study is right. It just means I believe it. Caveat emptor.

CHAPTER TWO

The
Truth About
Food

The year: 2173. Two scientists talk about a
man who has just been roused from a 200-year
sleep.

"For breakfast, he requested something called
wheat germ, organic honey and tiger's milk."

"Oh, yes, those were the charmed substances
that some years ago were felt to contain life-
preserving properties."

"You mean there was no deep fat, no steak or
cream pie or hot fudge?"

"Those were thought to be unhealthy, precisely
the opposite of what we now know to be true."

"Incredible."

—Woody Allen, *Sleeper*

If there were two things about food that we knew for sure, it was that milk was good for children and chocolate was bad. Studies found the opposite. Surely wine, cigarettes and paté are harmful to your health. Studies have shown the reverse. For years, whole wheat bread was thought to be better than white. No, says a study. Studies found that oat bran was good for the heart, then not good, then good. Apple a day? A study showed apples can cause cancer. Hundreds of studies have exonerated coffee; hundreds have damned it. People believed so much about food that was not true. Or was. Or may have been.

With each passing year, it seems less likely that research will ever tell the truth about food and human health.

Because we all eat food, food research seems more straightforward and mundane than the miasma of opinion or the exotica of pharmaceuticals. Yet it has become just as suspect as these and for many of the same reasons. While most of the financing for food research comes from the government, private interests with a financial stake in the outcome of the studies are paying a growing share. Researchers may let their egos get caught up in defending a claim they have staked, even when other evidence persuasively contradicts it. "If someone comes out with a finding favorable to what you believe in, you say that's a good piece of work," said Eugene Grossman, a food scientist. "If it doesn't agree, you start nit-picking."

Furthermore, like the human mind, every body is unique, each a tapestry woven with threads from a wide genetic and behavioral palette. In studying human diseases like cancer or arteriosclerosis, it is almost impossible to pull out a single strand and say that this is the one to blame.

However complex and compromised, food research commands an astonishing loyalty from consumers, resulting in alarming shifts of behavior from study to study. A study showing that the paté-consuming French have healthier hearts actually increased sales of the fatty spread in the U.S. While many people would not rush out to take an experimental drug after one small study demonstrated its effectiveness, vast numbers of people will eat or not eat a food based on a single study. That is why studies have become such a big part of the food business.

Research about food has contributed many truths to the world, resulting in longer, healthier lives for those who follow its path. Woody Allen's futuristic fantasy notwithstanding, it is unquestionably true that it is good to eat more fruits and vegetables and less animal fat than Americans typically do. Yet beyond some broad strokes of knowledge, there is little agreement about how coffee, oat bran, margarine, wine and nuts, just to name a few foods, affect human bodies. These uncertainties are exploited by companies and interest groups for their own purposes. That makes it even more difficult to extricate the truly valuable research from the noise.

The old ideal of a steady advance on the truth about food and health has been replaced by many voices coming to many different, often contradictory, conclusions. For a company selling food, that is convenient. More than ever, the giant food companies use studies as marketing tools, a scientific seal of approval for advertising, labeling and public relations. Companies also use positive studies to counter negative studies, and negative studies to counter positive ones. Contradictory research has the added feature of stymieing regulatory action. Meanwhile, the news media, having decided that personal health stories sell, are willing targets. Stories about food research are easy to write and get good play.

There is no truth about food so sacred that it cannot be challenged by research. In fact, the more the study defies common wisdom, the more likely it is to enjoy wide acclaim. Consider these surprises of recent years:

◆ "Milk is the number one health hazard facing young children," wrote a Santa Rosa, California, doctor in support of a new report by the Physicians Committee for Responsible Medicine. The report, released at a widely covered news conference in September 1992, cited a recent study in the *New England Journal of Medicine* about milk contributing to juvenile diabetes. Despite its vaguely neutral name, the committee is actually a pressure group of mostly vegetarians who oppose animal research and support animal welfare groups.

Conflict of
interest?

◆ White bread will not make you gain weight and, when used in a high-fiber diet, is an okay nutritional choice, reported the Cooper Institute for Aerobic Research. Its sponsor for the study: the makers of Wonder Bread. The research: inconclusive, to say the least. The 118 subjects were divided into four groups. One ate their normal diet; one group added four slices of low-calorie bread to their daily diet; one added eight slices of low-calorie bread; and a fourth added eight slices of regular bread. This ended after a mere eight weeks. Predictably, no one in the study had gained or lost significant weight, but the researchers said they *believed* the bread eaters would have lost weight if the study had continued. The study was reported by the Associated Press.

◆ Chocolate may actually inhibit cavities, reported a newsletter from the Princeton Dental Resource Center, citing a study about how the tannins in cocoa inhibit plaque formation. The group also published reports of a study about how sticky snacks like caramel actually dissolve faster in the mouth than starchy foods like potato chips. This research "should dispel myths that foods perceived as 'sticky' or 'chewy' pose the greatest threat of dental decay," said the center, which is financed by M&M/Mars.

The nutrition study is a machine with a thousand knobs. Turning any of them a notch, even well within ethical limits, will dramatically change the outcome of the study. When studies differ, there are many legitimate-sounding—and possibly legitimate—reasons. But the flood of deliberately contradictory studies insures there will be no definitive proof of anything. If a study contradicts another study's position, buyers of research can simply commission more studies. They cannot be absolutely certain the new studies will confirm their position, but they know the researchers whose labs have already produced agreeable results. "Usually associations that sponsor research have a fairly good idea what the outcome will be," said Joseph Hotchkiss of Cornell University. "Or they won't fund it."

◆

OAT BRAN

OATMEAL &
CHOLES-
TEROL

BY THE TIME FRANK SACKS, an assistant professor of medicine at Harvard Medical School, and Janis Swain, a research dietitian at Brigham and Women's Hospital, a Harvard teaching hospital, published their study on the effects of oats on cholesterol, oat bran had become one of the biggest diet fads Americans had ever embraced. The two researchers' simple but extraordinarily controversial conclusion—that oat bran might do almost nothing to forestall heart disease—would make their research one of the most vilified, belittled and challenged studies in modern history.

The oat bran mania began in the mid-1980s, when people were becoming aware of a troubling association between high cholesterol and heart disease. While drugs could lower cholesterol, scientists were also searching for ways to control it with food. One of the first oat bran boosters was Dr. James Anderson of the University of Kentucky Medical College. "I have a very biased opinion on this," said Anderson, who said he typically eats oatmeal for breakfast, oat bran muffins for lunch and bean burritos for dinner. "I was the first guinea pig, and my cholesterol went down 110 points in five weeks. . . . It's clear from our studies that oat bran lowers cholesterol if you carefully control all variables." But Anderson's experiments were done primarily on people in hospitals who had high cholesterol. The next question was whether oat bran could be shown to lower cholesterol in the so-called free-living population.

Select
group

The Quaker Oats Company began doing research on oats and cholesterol in the 1970s. Quaker researchers knew oats formed a gummy mix in the digestive system, and other kinds of gummy soluble fibers were being shown to lower cholesterol. At first, Quaker did its research in-house. Then the company began moving work outside, to Anderson and other researchers. Going outside gave Quaker access to some of the leading researchers in the field, while neutralizing the suspicion that Quaker scientists might not be totally disinterested in the results.

In-house
or
Contract
researcher

In 1986, a study partly funded by Quaker was published with great fanfare in the *Journal of the American Dietetic Association*. The research had been done by a team at Northwestern University, among whose members was Linda Van Horn, an assistant professor. The Van Horn study, as it came to be known, was one of the first studies to test the effects of oats on free-living people.

Two hundred and eight subjects were put on the American Heart Association modified-fat diet for six weeks, and their cholesterol dropped 5.2 percent. Then either oat bran or oatmeal was added to that low-fat diet for six weeks, and their cholesterol dropped 3.3 percent more. The study was widely disseminated by Quaker, and other studies on oat bran by Van Horn and many others followed.

The studies helped transform oat bran from a humble grain to a lifesaver. In late 1987, Quaker stopped selling its cereals simply as traditional wholesome breakfast food and began pitching them as cholesterol-lowering products that could reduce the risk of heart attack. Quaker's advertising cited, though did not name, the Van Horn study, saying that cholesterol had been reduced by "almost 10 percent." It did not note that only 3 percent of that reduction came from the effects of the oats—if that. The 3 percent reduction from eating oats was not statistically different from what happened to a control group, who were solely on the low-fat diet for the whole twelve weeks. That wasn't mentioned either.

Nevertheless, the media seized on the oat bran fad, writing hundreds of stories about the salutary effects of the grain. "Oat Bran May Be the Next Miracle Food," reported one newspaper. "People bent on lowering their blood cholesterol levels should be feeling their oats—or at least eating them," noted the *Dallas Morning News*. Oat bran was a gift from the gods: a prescription for high cholesterol that did not involve giving something up. "[Y]ou may have already eaten your way into a cholesterol problem," declared an ad for Quaker Oats. "[T]he good news, say experts, is you may be able to eat your way back out of it."

Consumers were bombarded with oat bran marketing and oat bran journalism. "Unfortunately, the interests of the press, the researchers and the industry coincide to create a lot more hype than early studies might warrant," said Walter Willett, professor of epidemiology and nutrition at Harvard

University. "Even if some of the first studies are the quick, dirty and cheap ones, if it's a dramatic effect, it gets a lot of attention. . . . It's not that industry creates bad studies, but the positive ones get a lot more attention than they would have if it hadn't been for industry." Or as another researcher put it, "The thinner the data, the thicker the dogma."

That didn't weigh heavily on the many companies that were peddling the health benefits of oat bran. Oat bran was added to more than 300 products, including potato chips, toothpaste, licorice and a beer called Otto's Original Oat Bran Beer, which boasted of containing no cholesterol (as though any beer contains cholesterol). Companies would sprinkle tiny bits of oat bran into a bag of nacho chips and proclaim them health food; a person would have had to eat seventy one-ounce Keystone Oatzels (snack food) a day (at a cost of almost 4,000 calories) to lower their cholesterol by 3 percent. Yet when a food industry newsletter surveyed 160 people about whether they would buy oat bran Coke or oat bran Life Savers, 32 percent said they would. A book about oat bran—*The Eight-Week Cholesterol Cure*—rode the *New York Times* best-seller list for more than a year. Quaker, the industry giant, literally could not keep up with demand. The company, and others selling oat products, flooded newspapers, magazines and television with advertising that cited "recent clinical studies" proving that oat bran lowered cholesterol and reduced the risk of heart attack.

Then, in January 1990, Sacks and Swain delivered their mortal blow. The media, which had fueled the oat bran frenzy with their scientific gullibility, overreacted, declaring the Swain-Sacks study a knockout punch. *Nightline* devoted a show to it. Jay Leno joked about it. As the stock of Quaker Oats dipped, the company's executives attacked the Harvard study. It was too small, it was not representative, it actually showed better results for oat bran than were being reported. One securities executive called the Swain-Sacks study "a piece of sensationalism." Robert Kowalski, who had written the best-selling cholesterol book and had more cholesterol books in the works, was furious. "In one night, they laid waste to everything that had been done in oat bran," he fumed.

The ferocity of the response took Sacks and Swain by surprise. "I knew there was going to be some reaction, but this was beyond what I imagined," said Sacks. The *New England Journal* was inundated by rebuttals and published several of them. "Poorly designed and underpowered trial that draws erroneous conclusions," proclaimed one indignant pair of researchers. Six months after their article appeared, the researchers received subpoenas; as part of a state court battle over allegedly false advertising, Quaker Oats was demanding access to their data, lab notes and oral testimony.

The Sacks & Swain study.

◆

WHEN SWAIN AND SACKS BEGAN their pilot study in the fall of 1985, they said, they had expected a different outcome. Most researchers, especially junior ones, look for a positive result as a way of starting a line of research. "You almost never do a study to disprove a hypothesis," said Sacks, because then you are at a dead end. And scientific journals prefer publishing positive to negative studies—the "file drawer" bias.

Swain and Sacks said they went into the study believing nutrients can lower cholesterol. They wanted to study the mechanism by which that happens. As their nutrient they chose soluble fiber, which is fiber that dissolves in the human gut. Soluble fiber in several different forms had already been shown to lower cholesterol.

The researchers first thought of using pectin, an unpalatable gel that is the basis for jellies, as their source of soluble fiber for their study. But their pharmacist balked at stuffing it into capsules, and pectin in a spoon is so gummy it will pull the fillings out of teeth. Other fibers, like guar gum and psyllium, had their own problems. So Sacks and Swain decided to use oat bran.

Because their study was so small and was done at the hospital where Swain is a senior research dietitian and Sacks is on staff, the two needed little outside financing; what they got came partly from the federal government and partly from the American Heart Association. Quaker Oats says it has financed some fifty studies on oats and health, some done on humans, some on animals.

The Harvard study was, in medical terms, a randomized double-blind crossover trial. Randomized means the subjects were randomly divided into oat bran and non–oat bran groups; double-blind means neither the subjects nor the researchers knew who was in which group; and crossover means the subjects started out with one regimen, then "crossed over" to the other. In this case it worked like this: For one week, the subjects ate their regular diet to establish baseline measurements. Then the subjects were randomly assigned to eat either high-fiber (oat bran) or low-fiber (Cream of Wheat, white flour) supplements for six weeks. The fiber was included in muffins and casseroles that, aside from the fiber content, were supposed to be virtually indistinguishable; the participants were not told which they were eating. But eating close to forty grams of oats a day was no small feat— it meant five big, dense oat bran muffins. Fifteen of the twenty subjects reported suffering the unpleasant gastrointestinal consequences of so much oat bran (raising questions of just how blind the study could be). The subjects took a two-week rest and then for the next six weeks ate the opposite of what they had been eating before. The calorie intake was about the same for both diets.

Most of the early oat bran studies shared at least one shortcoming: They did not control for the so-called substitution effect—what food is being crowded out when someone eats a lot of oats. Swain and Sacks designed their study to measure the effects of the fiber itself instead of the effects of displacing one food, possibly containing more saturated fat, with another. Sacks and Swain used a control group that ate the same muffins, cereals and entrees—but with a low-fiber grain, wheat—instead.

In the end, both the oat bran and the wheat lowered cholesterol by the same amount—about 7 percent. It seemed that the subjects had indeed become so full with muffins or cereal that there was less room for other food. That displacement alone, Swain and Sacks thought, could explain the lowering of cholesterol in both regimens. For Quaker, this was the worst possible news. It meant you could eat any number of foods—pasta, potatoes or rice—and get the same effect as the oat bran Quaker was selling.

Controversial as the results eventually became, to the researchers they were disappointingly negative: considerable effort to produce no effect. The prejudice against negative results is deeply ingrained. Scientists do not make names for themselves by finding nothing. Discouraged, Sacks and Swain sat on their data for more than a year. "I was tired of it, it didn't show much, it was a negative study," said Swain. "But then I figured, well, we had the data, we should do something with it." Added Sacks, "It wasn't until we saw a number of other studies coming out that weren't controlled adequately that we decided we should get our paper out."

The publication of the Swain-Sacks paper in the *New England Journal* guaranteed it would get a great deal of attention. The *New England Journal*, along with the *Journal of the American Medical Association* and the British medical journal *Lancet*, are considered the medical world's most prestigious journals, the ones whose articles most often get noticed by scientists and the media. "Everybody who's doing anything with a clinical component starts at the *New England Journal*, and if they get rejected they go elsewhere," said Bonnie Liebman, director of nutrition at the Center for Science in the Public Interest.

As the storm over the Swain-Sacks study raged, Quaker counterattacked on several fronts. The company, which had just launched several new flavors of oat bran hot cereal, surveyed some cholesterol-conscious consumers to find out what they thought of the Harvard study. Although a company spokesman said respondents were mostly skeptical, Quaker bought full-page newspaper ads listing ten other studies showing that oat bran can indeed lower cholesterol. It issued a news release about the study, and company spokesmen went on television news shows to defend oat bran. Meanwhile, Quaker promised that more positive studies would be forthcoming.

Steven Ink, senior manager of nutrition research and services at Quaker, said the company's oat bran studies are typically initiated by independent outsiders. "We get contacted in most cases by top researchers wondering whether we would be interested in funding their research," Ink said. "We ask for a copy of their research protocol, their proposal.

If we think it has merit, we fund that research with no strings attached. We have no rules on publication. It's as though the government were funding the study. Researchers aren't going to risk their reputations. . . . They're not going to risk their credibility for a small research grant."

In most cases, that is true. Nothing is more damaging to scientists' reputations—and their economic survival—than suspicions of fraud, corruption or dishonesty. But scientists are only human, and in the course of any research project they make choices. Who were the subjects of the study? Young or old, male or female, high cholesterol or low? How were they chosen? How long did the study go on? Was there a control group? Did the subjects cook for themselves or did they get prepared food? How well were other variables—for women, menstrual cycles can wreak havoc with clinical trials—controlled? Since cholesterol levels vary season to season, when did the study begin and when did it end? *[handwritten: MANY VARIABLES]*

In many of the earlier oat bran studies, the subjects had high cholesterol levels. Sacks and Swain instead used mostly young, lean and healthy women, many of whom were also health care workers, dietitians or dietetic interns. The practice of using healthy people near at hand and who because of their profession could be relied on to follow the rules and keep careful notes is common in nutrition research. And it works because most responses to food occur along a continuum. "It's very unusual in nutrition and drug therapy to see a major response in people with high cholesterol and no response in people with low cholesterol," said Sacks.

The researchers' choice of subjects, however, was the target of much criticism. At every opportunity, their critics ridiculed them for testing the very people who least needed to lower their cholesterol. "If you want to test a diet for obesity, you probably wouldn't choose gymnasts, you'd choose sumo wrestlers," said Dr. Anderson, the oat bran believer from the University of Kentucky. Added Joseph Keenan, who also studied oat bran, "He chose the least representative group in society to study." *[handwritten: Attack the Sample Frame]*

That would be a better point if the marketers of oat bran products had been similarly discriminating about who could benefit from their products. But in the eyes of Quaker Oats, every American consumer was equal; each could reduce his or her risk of a heart attack by 20 percent with the help of oat bran. The aggressive promotion of oat bran as a universal health food, featuring the avuncular boy scout Wilford Brimley ("It's the right thing to do"), so irritated some regulators that one, the state attorney general in Texas, sued Quaker for false advertising. "We're in the middle of an oat bran craze in this country that was primarily started and promoted by Quaker in order to sell its products," said the attorney general, Jim Mattox. "Consumers have been duped. Quaker's claims are not true." The complaint accused Quaker of transforming what amounted to a 3.3 percent reduction in cholesterol from oats in the Van Horn study into a 20 percent reduction in the risk of heart disease. Furthermore, the complaint said, studies have shown no effects from oat bran on cholesterol in men, children, teenagers, young adults, the elderly or anyone whose cholesterol was not above average.

Quaker responded by saying that its ads were "truthful and supported by valid, reliable scientific evidence." It is "extremely disheartening," the company continued, "to see the attorney general obstructing . . . the goal of nutrition education."

Van Horn herself said she "wasn't thrilled" with the way her study and others were used by oat purveyors. "My goal was to try to do good science and publish in a peer-reviewed journal and make only those statements justified by the data," she said. "The marketing people have a totally different agenda, and we scientists have no control over what they do with the results. How they manipulate the numbers is disappointing and inappropriate."

Sacks and Swain's study was cited in the Texas complaint against Quaker, and Quaker asked the two for "every single thing in the files," Sacks said. Brigham and Women's Hospital, where Sacks and Swain had done their research, decided to fight. They hired local lawyers and filed a motion to quash the subpoena, which was granted. Quaker appealed the ruling, but a settlement between the Texas attorney general's office and Quaker rendered the subpoena moot. Courts have recognized that "the potential for a chilling effect on research" from the possibility of such subpoenas appears great, wrote the lawyers for Swain and Sacks in their appeals brief. Scrutiny by biased third parties whose interests are arguably antithetical to those of researchers is "both unnerving and discouraging" to researchers, a court had ruled in an earlier suit.

Meanwhile, the oat bran study to end all oat bran studies —financed by Quaker—was completed and ready for release in June 1992. High atop Rockefeller Center, a full media complement—representatives from the three networks, the *New York Times* and some women's magazines—nibbled at pretty plates of pastry while waiting for the news conference to begin. The study to be presented "may very well be the final word" on oats and cholesterol, said the invitation to the news conference, organized for Quaker by a public relations firm.

The "final word" on oat bran was one of a relatively new breed of statistical studies called meta-analyses, or studies of studies. Meta-analyses transform many small, inexpensive and statistically insignificant studies into a large, comprehensive and statistically significant one. If not a final truth, they promise at least "a truth as we know it to this point."

Researchers like meta-analyses, partly because they can bypass the daunting complexities of collecting primary data and partly because they might be able to find an effect too small to be detected by any one study. In meta-analysis, researchers work with everybody else's data, pulling together as much research as they can find on the subject, rejecting the most obviously flawed and consolidating the rest into one big study. Or as Cynthia Ripsin, one of the authors of this oat bran meta-analysis, described it in research jargon, meta-analysis is "the structured and systematic qualitative and quantitative integration of the results of several independent studies." Critics of the method say meta-analyses too often try to equate apples with oranges—"a statistical fruit salad," as one said—and that while doing meta-analysis seems easy, doing it well is difficult.

In the case of oat studies, there were some major differences in the previous oat bran studies that illustrate the difficulties in consolidating studies. Different studies used different kinds of oat preparations—cereals, muffins, breads and entrees. Some studies used oatmeal, some used oat bran.

Some were done exclusively on men, some on a mix of gender and age. Some of the studies were done on people with normal cholesterol, some on people with high cholesterol. Some of the studies lasted eighteen days, some up to three months.

Ripsin, a researcher at the University of Minnesota, conducted the oat bran meta-analysis with some colleagues at the same institution, including Dr. Joseph Keenan, who had already done one positive study about the effects of oat and wheat bran on cholesterol levels. Ripsin and Keenan approached Quaker for financing for their study, which was Ripsin's master's thesis. "They ought to have a vested interest in seeing what's out there," Ripsin remembers figuring. Quaker liked Ripsin's idea and offered a small grant of $13,000 (of an overall budget of more than $50,000, although most of that was soft dollars). The company also came up with a list of studies that might be included in the meta-analysis, including three that had never been published. Of these three, "one was positive, one we considered negative, and the third we never got," said Ripsin.

It has become a fact of life in the world of food and drug research that private industry is expected to pick up a bigger share of the bill. State and federal government financing for colleges and universities to do research and development has flattened in recent years, while the amount of financing from industry has increased dramatically. In 1981, industry contributed $292 million to colleges and universities for research; by 1991, that figure had jumped to more than $1.2 billion. The theory is that if the company may profit from the research, and they often do, the company should pay for it. Increasingly, many food researchers must choose: research funded by an interested party or no research at all.

Of the entire published literature of scientific research on oat bran in the U.S., the lion's share has been at least partly financed by Quaker Oats, the company with the most at stake. And since most of the earlier studies used in Ripsin's meta-analysis of oats and cholesterol had already shown modest benefits, the results announced at the news conference in New York that day were not too surprising: Eating large quantities of oat bran can lower cholesterol by 2 percent to 7 percent, the scientists said.

FINAL FINDING

Ripsin's meta-analysis received widespread publicity: "Oat Bran Does Cut Cholesterol," reported *USA Today*. On the public relations news wire, the headline was even more dramatic: "Landmark Study Published in 'JAMA' Confirms Cholesterol Reduction Benefit of Oat Products in Diet."

Quaker itself credits the study with helping to persuade the federal government that its labels could continue to make health claims. With the government's new labeling regulations, which allowed Quaker to use a muted reference to health benefits on its labels—Quaker Oat Bran hot cereal says, "Can Help Reduce Cholesterol" and then in smaller letters, "when part of a low fat, low cholesterol diet"—the torrent of oat bran research slowed to a trickle. Steven Ink, the nutrition research manager at Quaker, said there may be a few more studies on the subject, but the issue is pretty much settled—in favor of oat bran. As Ink looked back over the past few years, he lamented the loss of some of his company's products—victims of the Swain-Sacks study. "The baby and the bathwater went out together," he said. His one regret was that the company had not been more aggressive in educating doctors on the facts about oats.

As for Sacks and Swain, they still have faith in the results of their study. "Oat bran has little or no effect," said Sacks. "To say something has no effect in science, you have to specify the limits. We specified to see a greater than 3 percent effect, and we didn't see it. That's not worth talking about. It's a real, but trivial, effect. Who cares? It takes a lot of oat bran to lower cholesterol a tiny bit. It's misleading to tell people they could eat oat bran and expect to see any effect."

◆

THERE MAY NEVER BE A definitive answer to the question of whether the agricultural chemical daminozide, known as Alar, causes cancer in humans. But the decision to remove Alar from America's food supply has been made. We will never know if that decision saved lives. It may have. Yet the great Alar alarm of 1989 was a watershed in the history of sponsored research not because the research was right but because it so quickly and effectively changed people's beliefs and behavior about one of their favorite foods: apples. Alar was banned not because of a cool and informed appraisal of the best scientific evidence but because of the coinciding interests of an advocacy group, a celebrity, a public relations company and the media.

Alar had been routinely sprayed on apples to prolong shelf life since the 1960s. But in the early 1980s, a growing body of evidence convinced the federal government that at very high doses Alar caused tumors in laboratory animals; in 1985 the Environmental Protection Agency began to think seriously about a ban. As the process of banning Alar wended its excruciatingly slow way through the EPA bureaucracy, many apple growers stopped using the chemical. By 1989, somewhere between 5 percent and 40 percent—depending on whose figures you believe—of the apples grown in the U.S. were sprayed with Alar. Still there was no government ban.

The slowly declining use of Alar was not good enough for the Natural Resources Defense Council, a nonprofit advocacy group that monitors the environment. The council was pressing for quick action on Alar and other chemicals used on fruits and vegetables. But after years of frustration trying to remove them from the food stream, the NRDC finally found a weapon that ended the bureaucratic foot dragging: a study.

The NRDC's Alar study was a kind of statistical research called a risk assessment or risk analysis, in which researchers plug assumptions into a computer model and try to figure out—with improbable precision—how likely it is that something will occur in the future. Risk assessments are highly imprecise. The National Aeronautics and Space Administration, for example, did a risk assessment of the space shuttle that showed a chance of failure so small it could probably fly every day for 300 years without an accident. Risk assessments are often used in regulatory battles over issues like the environment, where empirical research is impossible. But risk assessments are studies built on studies, and those earlier data are often flawed. In the NRDC's study, a controversial decade-old number was multiplied by a disputed apples-a-day estimate.

The Alar report, whose name, "Intolerable Risk: Pesti-

60 MINUTES
REPORT

cides in Our Children's Food," guaranteed widespread pa-
rental hand wringing, first appeared on *60 Minutes* in
February 1989. The NRDC's public relations man had made
a deal with the television show to keep the report secret until
the *60 Minutes* segment was broadcast. Ed Bradley, who nar-
rated the Alar story, called the NRDC's report "the most
careful study yet" on the subject. The maker of Alar, Uniroyal, would not comment for the show; the only critique of
the study came from a Harvard professor who had reviewed
the study at the NRDC's request; while supporting the principles of the study, he conceded that he might "quibble a
little bit with the calculations."

The study concluded that because children eat so many
more apples and drink so much more apple juice than adults,
even the tiny amounts of Alar still found on the minority of
apples threaten thousands of children's lives. The *60 Minutes*
segment concluded with a Consumers Union doctor saying
that buying apples at a grocery store amounts to "supermarket roulette."

The *60 Minutes* report set off a stampede. Across the
country, Americans accepted the risk assessment contained
in the Alar study. Grocers cleared their shelves of apples,
and schools in New York City, where some students carry
guns and knives, banned apples from their cafeterias. Apples
rotted in their growers' packing houses. At the peak of the
apple scare, terrorized consumers wondered if pouring apple
juice down their drains would poison the ground water.

With the help of an aggressive media campaign,
NRDC's risk assessment put enormous pressure on the government to do something it was not ready to do—yet. Everyone agreed Alar had to be phased out of the food supply
because high doses of it caused tumors in laboratory animals
—the controversial requirement of the Delaney clause. The
question was simply whether it should be phased out immediately or in another eighteen months. NRDC rightly felt that
in environmental matters the U.S. government had not always moved as quickly as it should, and one way to push it
was by arousing public concern. They also knew that many
people had become somewhat skeptical of the government's
desire or ability to protect them.

Study in hand, the NRDC bypassed the government and the scientific journals, where experts might be more challenging, and went directly to the people via a public relations executive named David Fenton. After giving *60 Minutes* its exclusive, Fenton released the report the next day at thirteen simultaneous news conferences around the country. A week later Meryl Streep held a news conference announcing the formation of a new group, "Mothers and Others for Pesticide Limits," and took aim at Alar. "As one of my friends in Connecticut said, this isn't some Hawaiian rain forest," Streep said. "These are your kids."

MEDIA FRENZY

Major newspapers and television news organizations were beside themselves. The story made the covers of *Time* and *Newsweek*, appeared on page one of *USA Today* three times and was reported on *The Today Show, Good Morning America, CBS This Morning, MacNeil/Lehrer* and *Donahue.* Here was a story that had everything: It was better than scary, it was invisible; it involved not only children but also one of America's favorite foods; and it featured a pretty and talented actress and mother. Excerpts from a self-congratulatory memo about the publicity campaign, written by Fenton, were published under the title "How a PR Firm Executed the Alar Scare." Usually, wrote Fenton in the memo, "it takes a significant natural disaster to create this much sustained news attention for an environmental problem."

No amount of counterpropaganda could stop this manmade disaster. The industry hired its own public relations experts, who found scientists to testify to the goodness of apples, took out newspaper ads, distributed video and audio news releases and briefed Congress. Three federal agencies —the Environmental Protection Agency, the Food and Drug Administration and the Agriculture Department—issued a joint statement saying the government believed the Alar levels in apples were safe. But to no avail. Alar was dead. In June 1989, its maker, Uniroyal Chemical, withdrew it from the market.

The National Resources Defense Council's Alar study was far from a perfect study. It contained at least two debatable assumptions. One was its figure for the potency of Alar, an estimate of how many cancers might arise from exposure;

How BAD WAS THE NRDC RESEARCH ??

the other was how much exposure people, especially children, get. No study has ever been done on Alar and human cancer; the results in humans are extrapolated from the results of animal tests. NRDC's potency estimates were based on a study done on the chemical in 1977. That study was later discredited by a scientific advisory panel to the Environmental Protection Agency, which called the data "fundamentally flawed" and "useless for assessing carcinogenic risk from Alar." In the 1977 study, which showed Alar causing cancer in laboratory animals, the animals had been exposed to something like 266,000 times the amount humans would be exposed to—an amount ridiculous even by the exaggerated levels standard in animal research. The other questionable datum at the heart of the NRDC study was the amount of apples and apple juice that children eat and drink. The NRDC used data from a 1985 USDA survey that was small by the standards of food consumption research (2,000 people) and whose response rate of 65 percent was poor. Based on these data, the council estimated that the typical toddler consumes more than thirty-one times as much apple juice relative to his or her weight as the average adult woman. The NRDC study was not formally peer-reviewed; instead it was reviewed by an advisory panel selected by the council itself.

The variables in any risk assessment mean that even at its best it is soft science. Risk assessments, Leslie Roberts wrote in the journal *Science*, "represent a best guess, built on myriad assumptions, some of which are invariably value laden." Another scientist added that "once a risk assessment is done, people tend to forget all the assumptions they made along the way and attach too much certainty to the final number."

The NRDC says it never intended that people stop eating apples—the group says it was actually more concerned with heat-processed apple juice than the fruit itself. "I said that to every reporter I talked to," said Robin Whyatt, one of the study's authors. But many people did stop eating apples, at least temporarily. "When the controversy was at its peak," said Christine Bruhn, consumer food marketing specialist at the University of California, "26 percent of people said they had reduced their consumption of fruits and vegetables because of concern about pesticides. This is the most unhealthy thing a person could do."

And NRDC never intended the study to become known as the Alar study; it was supposed to be a more generic effort attacking not only several pesticides but also the regulatory system itself. But once the study was out, it took on a life of its own: Alar and apples. As a public interest group, the NRDC felt it had a responsibility to alert the public to a possible danger in their food—whatever the means. But as a blueprint for policymaking on science and food, it was one more step on the road away from objective truth. What the council could do, any other company or group in the food industry could do as well.

◆

THE ALAR SCARE REAFFIRMED THAT even in the fateful terrain between life and death there is little consensus among researchers, nor for many questions is there likely to be. Thousands of scientists spend billions of dollars researching the prevention, treatment and cure of heart disease and cancer. Even here, where good scientists have time and money, there is no guarantee of a steadily advancing understanding. As more studies on the same subject accumulate, there sometimes seems to be less consensus than more. Multiple studies create much data to worry about and much to allay those worries.

There is probably no food on earth that has been as widely studied to so little effect as caffeine, the world's most popular drug. Several times a year, a new study about the effects of caffeine, usually studied in the form of coffee, is published to great media excitement. The studies, which are often reported as though they are the first and last word on the subject, are in fact absurdly contradictory and would be funny if the media and consumers did not embrace them so fervently. "Coffee Study Finds Heavy Drinking Boosts Heart Risk," announced the *Wall Street Journal* in March 1990. Six months later, the *Journal* revisited the coffee question. "Coffee Study Finds No Link to Heart Illness," it reported, noting the earlier study and saying "controversy about coffee's effect on health probably will continue."

"When you're looking for small voices within a chorus of many . . . it's unlikely one study could be truly definitive," said Dr. Roy Fried, a former research fellow at Johns Hopkins Medical Institutions who did a study on coffee and cholesterol. "It's a different thing from giving everyone penicillin and suddenly everyone lives instead of dies."

The hundreds, perhaps thousands, of studies on coffee have taught scientists a few things about it. For most people, coffee stimulates the nervous system, makes their muscles more resilient and gives them a heady feeling of concentration and power. But there is much scientists do not know. Despite thousands of studies on coffee's effects on virtually every organ in the body, scientists still cannot completely rule out links to heart disease, cancer, infertility, breast cysts and a dozen other maladies. Dueling studies suggest there may be associations—or there may not.

"You can never prove a negative," said George E. Boecklin, president of the National Coffee Association of the U.S.A., the industry's trade group, which has certainly done its best, financing and publicizing studies that acquit coffee of all serious crimes.

In studying food, researchers have a choice between using animals and humans. As subjects, both are imperfect. Food research on mice or rats is flawed because animals have different physiologies and life expectancies: thirty months versus seventy years. One Food and Drug Administration study showed that when pregnant rats were fed the equivalent of fifty-six to eighty-seven cups of strong coffee at one time, some of the offspring's toes were deformed or missing. Human studies involving some 15,000 women, however, have found no association between caffeine and birth defects.

Humans would be perfect subjects for research on human health, but unlike rats, humans cannot be forced to do what they are supposed to, and then some of them lie about it. Ask a thousand humans what they ate yesterday, and the answers will be inaccurate blends of what they should, could and would have eaten. Even dietitians who have been subjects of nutrition studies say they are tempted to lie about the steak, potato chips or ice cream they ate in private. If researchers in a human study look backward, they face a memory problem; if they look forward, they face the backsliding problem. Studies can be done on hospital patients, who provide better control for the researchers but are hardly typical of the average American, or on so-called free-living people, who are out of sight and out of control most of the time.

To study long-term effects of a food, especially on diseases that can take decades to develop, like cancer, scientists need twenty years. They find coffee addicts reluctant to give up their drug for twenty years. Studies on substances strongly suspected of being killers are even tougher to study. Scientists cannot assign half their subjects to smoke a pack of cigarettes a day.

To further complicate the picture, every human being is different. Some people can smoke a pack of cigarettes a day and live to a hundred. Others have never picked up a cigarette but die of lung cancer at thirty. Sulfite, a food additive used in wine, fruits and vegetables, is perfectly benign to all but a few people; when those few are exposed to it, they die.

Too, coffee is not just caffeine. It is different types and ages of beans roasted at very high temperatures, releasing other chemicals. It is brewed in different ways—boiling, dripping, percolating. It can be caffeinated or not. Like humans, no two pots of coffee are exactly alike. And where does moderate coffee drinking cross into heavy coffee drinking? Four cups a day? Eight? Twelve? For that matter, what is a cup? Five ounces? Six ounces? Eight ounces?

People who drink coffee also tend to have other health habits that may cause the problems blamed on coffee. Picture a person who drinks twelve cups of coffee a day. Now picture what researchers call the "coffee naive"—someone whose lips it does not cross. Aside from the amount of coffee they drink, are the pictures different? Yes. That coffee drinker is also more likely to smoke, to eat pork and potato chips and to exercise less than the coffee naive. For whatever reason, coffee drinking is associated with risk taking, at least where health is concerned. One study even found that heavy coffee drinkers tend to be less likely to wear seat belts. So how can scientists ever know whether the thing that is killing people is the coffee or the doughnuts?

Of course, there are statistical methods for doing just this. Called regression analysis, the technique measures the degree to which variables are related—with more or less success. Because there are statistical associations between things that turn out to have no real-life associations, this kind of analysis can be a dangerous beast. Scientists once believed that people with creased earlobes were prone to heart attacks, a theory now widely ridiculed. On the other hand, it was statistics that first suggested that smoking might be harmful, years before there was persuasive empirical proof.

Regression analysis also involves a great deal of adjustment. "Those adjustments make very strong assumptions," said Persi Diaconis, a professor of mathematics at Harvard University, "like the change from X to Y is linear. Why should that be? If the assumption is wrong, so are all the conclusions."

With so many variables involved in human health and behavior, it is no wonder there is an endless stream of coffee studies, each proving or ruling out ever smaller chunks of the mosaic: "Caffeine, moderate alcohol intake, and risk of fractures of the hip and forearm in middle-aged women" was the title of one 1991 coffee study. In a study on whether coffee affects body temperature, subjects were given the caffeine equivalent of three or four cups of coffee and then, stripped down to shorts and T-shirts, they sat for two hours in a room cooled to 41 degrees. The result: no increase in body temperature.

As each new study arrives, newspapers and airwaves crackle with an excitement usually associated with major news events: "Coffee Not Harmful to Health"; "Coffee's 'Perk-me-up' Effect Confirmed in Study"; "Coffee Each Day Keeps Asthma Away in Italy." Such guileless enthusiasm for each coffee study is one reason scientists love to work on caffeine. So widely consumed is this addictive drug that if even a tiny association between it and disease was established, many lives could be saved and scientific careers made.

The National Coffee Association is an active player in

the caffeine study game. It commissions its own research, and it trumpets other research that supports the business goals of the association's members. When a critical study is published, the association quickly reacts, issuing news releases complete with critical comments from "independent" experts. "The coffee industry is incredibly powerful," said Dr. Robert Superko, who did coffee research at Stanford University. "Once you get on their bad side, they have a very heavy hammer." Superko did one study showing that decaffeinated coffee may be associated with increased cholesterol levels and another showing that healthy men who drank three to six cups of coffee a day could lower their blood pressure by quitting.

Superko believes the industry shapes coffee research by choosing which studies to fund partly based on its hopes, rather than scrutinizing the study design with a cool, objective eye. And industry financing, said Superko, "indeed affects the way you publish the results. The coffee industry puts pressure on you to do it their way."

George Boecklin of the coffee association said that is not true. The only reason the association gets involved in financing research, he continued, is that otherwise it would look as though they had their "head in the sand." The research is done by respected institutions that are given "no strings attached" grants, Boecklin said.

If nothing else, the coffee industry financing assures that its questions are answered. "We go to a high-quality researcher, like the Johns Hopkins Medical School, and say we'd like to support some work in accordance with a study you're doing," Boecklin explained. "Then we keep our hands off. I won't say the author won't let us have first look at his manuscript. But then that study has to be submitted to a journal and peer-reviewed. . . . We can't afford to be not objective; our credibility as an industry would be suspect."

In fact, its credibility as an industry is doubtful, at least insofar as the way it uses research to further its self-interested goals.

During the cholesterol mania of the 1980s, many researchers turned their attention to the subject of coffee and

cholesterol. Some earlier studies had suggested a link between heart disease and coffee, but just what that link was
remained a mystery. Could it be cholesterol? Results of early
studies were, not surprisingly, inconclusive. Some showed
coffee drinking affected cholesterol levels, and some showed
it did not.

After having put out brush fires over cancer, birth defects and heart disease, the coffee association was clearly
worried about this new threat to the already depressed coffee
business. The association invited several experts in the fields
of cholesterol and clinical trials to submit proposals for a
study on the subject. Dr. Roy Fried's proposal won the financing.

Fried, then a research fellow at Johns Hopkins, received
more than $200,000 from the coffee association to do his
study. "They probably figured any negative impact would be
small, but if the study found that it didn't raise cholesterol, it
would be good for them," Fried said.

Fried designed a study of the effects of drinking filtered
coffee (the brewing method most Americans now prefer) on
cholesterol levels. Fried and his fellow researchers first asked
about 100 male subjects to give up coffee for eight weeks to
wash out their systems. Then the men were randomly assigned to one of four groups: Drink four cups (24 ounces) of
regular coffee a day; drink four cups of decaffeinated coffee
a day; drink two cups of regular coffee; and drink no coffee
at all. The results: The cholesterol levels of the men who
drank four cups of regular coffee a day rose. But the silver
lining was that both their "good" and "bad" cholesterol levels
seemed to have risen, canceling out any significantly increased risk of heart disease. "We concluded that, based on
the study, drinking modest amounts of filtered coffee does
raise cholesterol, but that in itself wouldn't increase the risk
of heart disease," Fried said. Fried's study was published
February 12, 1992, in the *Journal of the American Medical
Association.*

Although the only positive result of the study was that
coffee increased cholesterol, both the coffee association and
the media found the negative results more interesting: "Study
Refutes Link Between Coffee, High Cholesterol," said the

Minneapolis Star Tribune. "Coffee is off the hook again," said the *Phoenix Gazette*. Meanwhile, the coffee association's fact sheet said this about coffee and cholesterol: "Most studies involving U.S.-style filter-brewed coffee, including a 1992 study published in the *Journal of the American Medical Association*, have not found an association between . . . coffee and increased risk of cholesterol-related heart disease. Importantly, the *JAMA* study . . . controlled for diet, exercise and smoking, all known contributing factors for heart disease."

"We were very interested in getting that study published," said Boecklin of Fried's work. "It wasn't pure white, he found some slight increases in cholesterol, but we were pleased to see not just the bad stuff, but the good stuff, and no effect from the consumption of decaffeinated coffee. It offset the work by Dr. Superko."

Fried's study was far from conclusive, however. The subjects were all men, and all but seven were white; the experiment lasted only four months (whereas many people drink coffee for most of a lifetime); the study was not double-blinded, which meant the subjects knew what they were drinking; and the maximum amount of coffee anyone drank was four cups a day, while many of the other studies tested more than four cups a day.

The coffee association is fortunate to have as friends several doctors who will make the time to talk about coffee studies. One such expert is Dr. Harvey Wolinsky, a professor of medicine at Mount Sinai Hospital and Medical Center in New York City, who believes that by now any really powerful effects of coffee on humans would have made themselves known. Wolinsky and officials of the coffee association are partial to the Framingham study, which has been tracking heart disease among more than 5,000 adults from Framingham, Massachusetts, since 1948. The Framingham study has failed to show any correlation between coffee drinking and heart disease.

In 1990, when the Kaiser Permanente Medical Center published a study showing a link between coffee and heart attacks, Wolinsky and the coffee association went on the offensive. Too small, Wolinsky complained, and there was also probably some underreporting of smoking. "If you want to get people down on you and hollering at you, write something about coffee," said Dr. Arthur Klatsky, one of the study's co-authors.

Similarly, on the day Stanford's Dr. Superko published a study linking decaffeinated coffee and increased cholesterol, David Wilkes of Canada's coffee industry association released a counterattack calling the study's conclusions "unwarranted" and citing earlier studies showing no correlation between coffee and cholesterol.

It is almost impossible for consumers to sort through studies like these and know what they should be eating and drinking. "No one study will change the world," said Jacqueline Dupont, national program leader for human nutrition at the Agriculture Department's Agricultural Research Service. "Check out where it was done and assume there will be hyperbole. It's reasonable to question, but not automatically assume, that a study is going to be biased on the basis of the sponsorship." Dupont said she herself has questioned the objectivity of some of her fellow scientists. "If you want to show something doesn't have an effect, you do a sloppy study," she said, "and there will be such a wide range of values there will be no statistical significance." Added Bonnie Liebman of the Center for Science in the Public Interest, "If there's no control group, I would just toss it out."

Unfortunately, most Americans would not have ready access to the study itself and would not know how to decipher it if they did. Even relatively lucid scientific studies contain lines like "The final analysis was based on a 'per protocol' basis since the study objective was to test a dose-response relationship of B-glucan on serum lipids." Most members of the media are ill-equipped to judge a technical study. Even if the science hasn't been explained or published in a U.S. journal, the media may jump on a study if it promises entertainment for readers or viewers. And if the media jump, that is good enough for many Americans.

◆

IN THE ANNALS OF RESEARCH on the effects of a substance on human health, nothing better illustrates the way an interested party can harness and exploit research than the Tobacco Industry Research Committee, the industry group representing companies that profit from tobacco. Tenacious, unyielding and well financed, the research committee became a running counterpoint to the accumulating and finally indisputable evidence that smoking is dangerous. The tobacco industry's self-interested research has been a refuge for those who deny one of the few medical certainties of our time: Cigarettes kill.

Between 1954 and 1990, the tobacco research group, renamed the Council for Tobacco Research in 1964, gave more than $165 million to some 800 scientists who have produced 1,200 studies. In the first two decades, some of the committee-sponsored studies concluded that smoking contributes to various kinds of disease—not what the industry group wanted to hear. So in the mid-1970s, it cut its financing for research on smoking and disease and began concentrating on other kinds of research either tangentially related or completely unrelated to tobacco. Meanwhile, it kept up a steady chorus of reassurances to smokers: On a molecular level, we still do not know the mechanism by which cigarettes cause disease (so maybe the scientists are wrong); and not all heavy smokers get lung cancer.

It was only a few decades after tobacco smoking became widespread in this country that doctors and researchers began to believe that smokers were suffering more heart and lung disease than nonsmokers. The first suggestions that smoking might be a deadly habit were made in the 1920s, when medical researchers began to search for the cause of a sudden epidemic of a formerly rare lung disease. Even so, cigarettes steadily gained popularity in the U.S.; by 1953, more than a third of Americans smoked. The cigarette companies promoted the habit as healthful. American women were urged to "Reach for a Lucky instead of a sweet"; another Lucky ad promised the brand would "protect the delicate tissues in your throat."

By the 1950s, however, the accumulating evidence became impossible to ignore. Researchers who had tackled the studies expecting to exonerate smoking—because they themselves were heavy smokers—came away from the statistics shaken by what they found. Although no one could yet say what caused lung cancer, researchers could say without reservation that smokers were more likely than nonsmokers to get it.

As the beating of the warning drums grew louder, the tobacco industry started to become concerned. In 1953, after nineteen consecutive years of sales records, cigarette sales declined. Something had to be done about the damning research. In January 1954, the cigarette industry made its first move in the research wars by forming the Tobacco Industry Research Committee, a consortium of tobacco firms, growers' associations and warehouse groups. Under the title "A Frank Statement to Cigarette Smokers," a widely placed ad for the committee said that "Recent reports on experiments with mice have given wide publicity to a theory that cigarette smoking is in some way linked with lung cancer in human beings . . . we feel it is in the public interest to call attention to the fact that eminent doctors and research scientists have questioned the claimed significance of these experiments."

The committee's first scientific director was Dr. Clarence Cook Little, formerly managing director of the American Cancer Society. In the minutes of a 1954 meeting of the committee, Little is quoted as saying the group's mission would be "to build a foundation of research sufficiently strong to arrest continuing or future attacks" on tobacco. With the help of the public relations firm of Hill & Knowlton, the quest for truth about a public health problem was neatly transformed into a scientific controversy. Time after time, a tobacco council representative would counter a negative study with a response like this, which Little gave in 1963: "There have been and will continue to be speculations and opinions on the causes, but it is a matter of scientific fact that in our present state of knowledge, no one knows the answers."

The tobacco industry is still at it today, only now its research battle is over secondhand smoke. Several studies, including one by the Environmental Protection Agency, have found that every year between 500 and 5,000 Americans who do not themselves smoke but are exposed to other people's smoke get lung cancer. The tobacco companies instantly refuted the studies, saying they were scientifically flawed. In June 1993, they sued the federal government, asking a federal court to nullify the designation of smoke from other people's cigarettes as a carcinogen. Ironically, the plaintiffs accused the EPA of "cherry-picking data"—using only those that satisfied "preconceived and predetermined conclusions."

Outside the tobacco industry, it is almost impossible to find anyone to argue that smoking is not dangerous. But that does not mean the tobacco industry has lost either. Even today, sophisticated and well-educated people can find asylum in the tobacco council's research. When Rozanne Ridgway, an assistant secretary of state in the Reagan administration and herself a smoker, was asked about the ethics of sitting on the board of a tobacco company, she said she had no problem with it. Cancer and cigarettes? she was asked by a *New York Times* reporter.

"I have read the medical facts on both sides," she replied.

◆

MEANWHILE, THE STREAM OF SELF-INTERESTED food studies flows unabated.

◆ Almonds can help the millions of Americans who have high cholesterol or who are eating a high-fiber, low-fat diet to combat heart disease, according to a study touted by the Almond Board of California, an industry association.

◆ Walnuts lower the levels of the fatty substance that clogs arteries, allowing the heart to pump easier, according to a study sponsored by the California Walnut Commission, a trade association.

◆ Rice bran can help lower cholesterol, according to a study disseminated by the Rice Council, a trade group.

◆ Eating citrus can help reduce cholesterol and help reverse a leading cause of heart attacks, according to a study sponsored by the Florida Citrus Commission.

Food research like this has a place in helping people

negotiate the complexities of modern science and nutrition, but it should not take the place of experience and common sense. Studies should contribute to our understanding of our bodies and our health, but they should not be our masters.

CHAPTER THREE

The
Numerical Lies
of Advertising

◆

Pecuniary Truth: Truth is what sells.
Truth is what you want people to
believe. Truth is that which is not
legally false.

—JULES HENRY

So many taste tests litter the American soft-drink land-scape that it should have come as no surprise when in 1988 Diet Pepsi and Diet Coke released taste-test results at exactly the same time. According to Coca-Cola's objective taste tests, Diet Coke was the "winner and still champion." According to Pepsi-Cola's objective taste tests, Diet Pepsi was the "undisputed champion."

The dissonance of the two claims troubled Edgar Dwor-sky, then on the staff of the Massachusetts consumer affairs office. "If both were done scientifically and were based on valid research data, how could the outcomes be opposite?" he wondered. "Something had to be wrong." Dworsky's office asked both companies for substantiating evidence and turned it over to a Northeastern University marketing professor named Frederick Wiseman for analysis.

Wiseman found much to argue with in both Pepsi's and Coke's research. But by the time his conclusions were made public months later, the taste-test advertising had long since run its course. Dworsky's office was criticized for challenging such evanescent claims. "The feeling was, everyone knows that advertising lies, so why waste precious resources on it?"

Everyone knows that advertising lies. That has been an article of faith since the Middle Ages—and a legal doctrine, too. Sixteenth-century English courts began the Age of Ca-veat Emptor by ruling that commercial claims—fraudulent or not—should be sorted out by the buyer, not the legal system. ("If he be tame and have ben rydden upon, then caveat emp-tor.") In a 1615 case, a certain Baily agreed to transport Mer-rell's load of wood, which Merrell claimed weighed 800 pounds. When Baily's two horses collapsed and died, he dis-covered that Merrell's wood actually weighed 2,000 pounds. The court ruled the problem was Baily's for not checking the weight himself; Merrell bore no blame.

The deceptions in advertising that most disturb some people are those that exploit emotions, sensibilities and fan-tasies, persuading people to expect or wish for impossible or unnecessary things. Yet a greater danger may lie in advertis-ing that persuades not with images but with data. Although statistics in advertising arouse widespread suspicion, they nevertheless lend credibility because however vigorously massaged people may suspect the data have been, they still believe some truth underlies numbers. Numbers bring advertising up, but advertising brings numbers down, exploiting— and exposing—their pliability. As doubts about numbers grow, marketers exaggerate more in a sad spiral into chronic distrust. A survey done in the mid-1980s found that on a scale of one (unbelievable) to five (totally believable), claims of being "stronger" or "more effective" got a mean score of 2.32, or somewhat unbelievable. Statistical claims in advertising, such as "three out of four dentists recommend," fared only slightly better, with a mean score of 2.39. A Philadelphia market-research firm found that most consumers thought "new and improved" meant that companies had "found a way to increase the price."

Yet advertising built on surveys, product tests and other statistical information works. It works for cola, soap, cars, political candidates and countless other products and causes. The Pepsi Challenge, a long-running series of taste tests, contributed heavily to the cola maker's robust growth in the late 1970s and, some say, to the New Coke debacle of 1985. Tylenol's claims that more doctors and hospitals preferred its product helped push Tylenol into the forefront of the extremely competitive analgesic market. Volvo's claims that its cars were safe helped to bring the company record U.S. sales.

Advertising is effective, because whatever their doubts, when people go shopping for a specific item, they need information about it. In many cases, advertising is almost the only information they can get, unless the product has been evaluated by one of a dwindling number of independent researchers like Consumers Union. "In polls, people say they're skeptical about advertising," said Ivan Preston, a professor and critic of advertising. "But when they go to buy, they trust. They have to. Who else knows more about the product than the seller? My computer, my stereo, my telephone—I can say I'm suspicious of the companies' claims, but I also concede that they're the experts."

If advertising is information, as its defenders say, it is also information revealed, shaped or withheld based solely on the self-interested motives of one party. Advertisers have no obligation to tell the whole story. They obviously will not concede the superiority of a competitor or their own shortcomings. Until the government insisted, there were no data available in the marketplace on such obvious product attributes as the durability of light bulbs, the octane ratings in gasoline, the tar and nicotine content of cigarettes, the nutrition content of food, gas mileage for cars and care-labeling of clothes.

And if knowledge is power, then deceptive advertising enhances the seller's power and diminishes the buyer's. Only the advertisers and their researchers know what they did to get their results. Advertising exerts a control over the style and substance of our information unlike any vehicle in our society, and its deceptions can be difficult to see. For those who must cope with the consequences of deception, wrote Sissela Bok, "to be given false information about important choices in their lives is to be rendered powerless."

In the marketplace, deceptive advertising can so taint information that people stop considering a product's qualities altogether. "In markets where product claims are viewed with utter suspicion," wrote Robert Pitofsky, formerly head of the Federal Trade Commission's Bureau of Consumer Protection, "high price is adopted as an indication of quality, and price competition and product improvement become economically irrational."

The effects of a steady flow of advertising half-truths and deceptions pouring into our information stream are immeasurable. Each day, America's collective consciousness is exposed to 12 billion display ads, 2.5 million radio commercials and more than 300,000 television commercials. If even a minute fraction contain some kind of disinformation, that is still a massive amount. It cannot help but reinforce people's feeling that there is no such thing as objectivity. Suspicion of deception becomes common, and to deceive seems more ordinary. That tolerance for deceit carries over into realms of information with far graver consequences for the world. "Anything that says falsity is okay and a way of life will contribute to people's feeling that it is," said Preston.

◆

IT IS DIFFICULT TO TAKE advertising claims too seriously at first, because they are based on some of the silliest and most blatantly unscientific research being done today, and that is saying something. When self-interest is not only encouraged but directly rewarded, surveys and studies can border on self-parody. Advertisers use precise statistics to describe qualities with countless immeasurable variables. The makers of the Crest Complete toothbrush announced that their rippled bristles reached 37 percent—not 35? not 40?—deeper between teeth. Continental airlines said its business class offered "up to 38 percent" more leg room—not 35? not 40? "The World's Largest Van for Its Size," boasted an innumerate Volkswagen dealer. Promotional consumer surveys mock and belittle the precision of numbers. A Dixie (cup) survey revealed the "fun and interesting fact" that 45 percent of women would least like to catch a cold from Saddam Hussein —"even if he had won the Gulf War."

The survey is perhaps the most widely used kind of research in advertising and promotion today. The survey offers benefits for everyone. For a company competing in a marketing-driven industry like cola or pain relievers, where the products are almost indistinguishable except for their marketing, winning a survey lifts one above the crowd. Surveys can be incorporated into advertising or, even better, shopped to the media as news. The media themselves have become drunk on surveys of their constituents and the publicity they can generate with awards to advertisers who do "best" in their surveys. And for consumers, a survey pronouncing a car America's most popular offers the comfort of the majority: If more people like it, it must be better.

There seems to be only one rule for doing consumer surveys or other testing designed for advertising, and that is not to take the rules too seriously. There are many ways of creating enthusiastic statistics if standard research methodology is not required, as these studies done for advertising show:

◆ Ninety percent of college students say Levi's 501 jeans are "in" on campus. The students chose from this list: Levi's 501 jeans; T-shirts with graphics; 1960s-inspired clothing; Lycra/spandex clothing; Overalls; Patriotic-themed clothing; Decorated Denim; Printed pull-on beach pants; Long-sleeved hooded T-shirts; and Neon-colored clothing. In other words, there was no way to vote for blue jeans except Levi's 501's. The Levi Strauss & Co. survey became part of a Levi Strauss marketing package called the Levi's 501 Report, "a fall fashion survey conducted annually on 100 U.S. campuses."

◆ Most Americans did not know what a roach disk was, but once it was explained—by Black Flag's research team— 79 percent thought it would be effective. Considering the explanation they got, it's a wonder 100 percent didn't think so: "A roach disk is a type of product that poisons a roach slowly. The dying roach returns to the nest and after it dies is eaten by other roaches. In turn, these roaches become poisoned and die. How effective do you think this type of product would be in killing roaches?" Indeed, with questions like this, advertisers risk producing round numbers like 100 percent, less believable than a figure like 79.

◆ TRIUMPH BEATS MERIT, crowed Lorillard about a taste test pitting its low-tar cigarette against Merit. "An amazing 60 percent said Triumph tastes as good or better than Merit." Here were the real figures on taste: 36 percent had preferred Triumph, 24 percent said the brands were equal, and 40 percent preferred Merit. In other words, MERIT BEAT TRIUMPH. The lesson here is clear, wrote two marketing experts about another Triumph ad claim that was ruled to be misleading: "If you commission a survey in support of a comparative claim, collect only those data that pertain to the claim and are likely to support it."

◆ USAir had the best on-time record of "any of the seven largest airlines," the company's advertising bragged in 1991. USAir conveniently stopped counting at seven; the eighth-largest airline, Pan Am, had the best on-time record of all.

◆ Hospitals recommend "acetaminophen, the aspirin-free pain reliever in Anacin-3, more than any other pain reliever," said an American Home Products ad. In fact, hospitals did recommend pain relievers containing acetaminophen more than other pain relievers. However, acetaminophen is also the active ingredient in Tylenol, and hospitals recommended Tylenol even more than they recommended Anacin-3.

◆ "76% of independent microwave oven technicians surveyed recommended Litton," said an ad for the appliance company. The survey included only Litton-authorized technicians who serviced Litton and at least one other brand. Those who serviced other brands but not Litton's were excluded.

One of the most unbelievable advertising surveys in recent years was Chrysler's "Meet the Americans that beat the Hondas" campaign, which claimed that when 100 California car owners test-drove one of two Chrysler models and either Honda's Accord or Civic, the overwhelming majority preferred the Chrysler to the import. A similar survey a few months later pitted two Chrysler models against Toyota's Camry and Tercel—with similarly one-sided results. Of the 100 consumers in the Toyota Camry comparison, Chrysler said 80 picked its cars. In the Honda comparison, Chrysler said 83 preferred its two models to the Accord. The group that tested the Chrysler cars against the Toyota Tercel Deluxe preferred Chrysler's car 91 to 9, Chrysler said.

It is true that among the 100 people tested—a tiny group—Chrysler came out on top. But whether any other group of 100 people would find the same thing is doubtful. That is because Chrysler's group was not representative of America—not even of California, where all the respondents lived. All were so-called import intenders, defined by Chrysler as domestic-brand car owners "who are thinking about buying an imported car." Not a single one of them owned a foreign car.

A similar survey by New York City area Dodge dealers found that most owners of four models made by other companies—Toyota, Honda, Ford and Chevrolet—actually preferred the Dodge Shadow. Again 100 people were surveyed, all owners of 1988–91 models of one of the other cars. They were given a chance to inspect a 1992 Dodge Shadow and a 1992 version of their own car. But they were only allowed to drive the Dodge. Not surprisingly, more than 70 percent preferred the Dodge to their own cars. Consumers Union looked into the claim because its own research had shown that people were more satisfied with their Hondas and Toyotas than their Dodge Shadows.

These kinds of tests reflect an increasingly common phenomenon in research, surveys that contradict the actual proof of what people prefer: their purchases. In August 1992, J. D. Power & Associates, an Agoura Hills, California, research firm, released results of a survey on what make of replacement tires people preferred for their cars. The survey found Michelin to be the leader. Goodyear, one of the biggest sellers of replacement tires in America, did not even make it into Power's top nine. One hundred and fifty-five million replacement tires are sold every year in the U.S., Goodyear said. So the 31,000 people who responded to the tire survey, representing at most 124,000 tires, constitute less than a tenth of 1 percent of tires sold.

J. D. Power & Associates has become a juggernaut in the world of consumer surveys, rating customer satisfaction of automobiles and computers, among other things. Power's rankings carry enough weight that they are frequently cited in advertising, and companies will pay Power tens of thousands of dollars for the privilege of using them. In 1991, Dell Computer Corporation ranked first in customer satisfaction in Power's first computer survey. Dell paid $72,000 to buy the research and an additional $40,000 to advertise the results. "One has to understand that a survey of this nature will pay for itself in a fairly short order of time," Dell's advertising director told the *Wall Street Journal*.

On a smaller scale, too, data can be used competitively —in supermarket price comparisons, for example, which inevitably find the advertiser's prices lowest. Such studies are usually done with market baskets—a selection of items from one store compared to the same items bought at other stores. If the researchers start in their clients' stores, which they tend to do, no matter how "objective" they try to be, they will choose items displayed at the ends of aisles or in other special displays—items that are being discounted at one store but possibly not at others.

Edgar Dworsky, of the Massachusetts consumer affairs office, remembered a supermarket chain known for high

grocery
Comparison

quality and high prices. "The chain decided to do an advertising campaign along the lines of it costs no more to shop at our store," he said. "They hired one of the Big Eight accounting firms to do a survey. They went to the client's store first and spoke to people after they came through the checkout line, asking if they would help with a survey. They would take the items the consumer had just bought as their market basket.

"That consumer was exposed to the store's merchandising and sale advertising. And of course the competitor doesn't have the same things on sale. So the advertiser will fare very well on the survey."

◆

THE VAST MAJORITY OF BUSINESS research is commissioned for internal use, and the results are both proprietary and confidential. While in marketing, as in most other kinds of research, researchers assert that there is no such thing as truth, firms working for major corporate clients try to get as close as humanly possible. Their clients expect it. In 1987, Beecham Products sued Yankelovich Clancy Shulman, a large market research company, for being overly optimistic in its forecasts for a new cold-water wash detergent. (The suit was settled.) Short of suing, clients can easily take their business elsewhere—there are many good market-research firms. The best firms use rigorous and state-of-the-art methodology and are always searching for new ways to be more accurate. Misreadings of the public mind, like New Coke, can cost hundreds of millions of dollars. Companies with a big idea also want to take the competition by surprise, so the best business-research firms are as secretive and security-conscious as the CIA.

Despite all this gravity, however, an astounding amount of market research produces information that just seems nuts. As the crowded marketplace has exacerbated the difficulty and cost of creating a successful new product, market research has snooped into ever smaller crannies of people's lives and minds: Almost a quarter of Americans don't untie their shoes before they put them on. Most people fold, rather than wrap or bunch, their toilet paper. Thirteen percent of women do not know whether they wear their panty hose under their underwear or the other way around. Six percent of rural men use nail polish or gloss. Some of this information presumably will help marketers sell more toilet paper or shoelaces, and some will be disseminated to the public, either through advertising or journalism. It may offer fleeting entertainment, but it also reinforces a nagging doubt people have about surveys: Why would a rural man tell a stranger that he used nail polish?

One reason there are so many consumer surveys—and so many amenable to their sponsors' desires—lies in the economics of the modern market-research industry. Consumer research, which began in the late nineteenth century, grew steadily in the early years of this century and then, thanks to pent-up consumer demand and the rapid expansion of the economy, took off after World War II. Technology such as early tabulating machinery, ancestral computers, also contributed to the growth of consumer research.

Throughout much of the 1980s, the market-research industry enjoyed real growth averaging 10 percent a year. Myopically expecting such growth to continue forever, many companies overexpanded, investing heavily in sophisticated computer and telephone equipment. But by the end of the decade, industry growth had come to a screeching halt, and many companies were caught with overcapacity. "The demand doesn't even start to keep that huge machine working," said Jack Honomichl, publisher of *Inside Research*, an industry newsletter. "A lot of people thought there was an infinite demand for knowledge. There isn't—far from it. So it's a buyer's market."

◆

IN THE WORLD OF SKEWED advertising research, taste testing is in a class by itself. It has become a widespread form of research for food and even more so for beverages. For some products, especially new ones, taste is everything, and persuading people to taste is the bridge to sales. (Also critical: price and image.) Kraft knew that no one was going to buy its new canned iced coffee on image alone, said Tom Pirko, whose consulting firm does taste tests, among other things. Kraft had to put a lot of "little old ladies" into supermarkets to persuade people to try the drink. Many companies conduct taste tests for their own decision-making, and sometimes they make the mistake of taking the results too seriously. It was, after all, some 190,000 taste tests, at a cost in the millions, that persuaded Coca-Cola to scrap its classic cola formula. Critics said Coke made two mistakes in performing and interpreting those tests. One, the taste testers who voted for the new Coke did not know it would replace, not join, old Coke on the shelves. And second, some of the testing was blind. "Clearly," said Jesse Meyers, publisher of a newsletter called *Beverage Digest*, "shoppers don't buy blind."

America's beverage giants alternate advertising that features taste tests with image campaigns—"It's the Real Thing," "The Pepsi Generation," "Coke Is It." The two types of advertising could not be more different. While image campaigns sell such inherently unsellable qualities as youth, energy and friendship, taste tests appeal to people's rationality. Taste tests bring to the inherently subjective sense of taste the illusion that one beverage can taste quantitatively better than another.

That there is no truth in taste tests is partly the fault of people who taste beverages. Many people—even diehard fans of Coke or Pepsi—do not have taste buds sensitive enough to distinguish between Coke and Pepsi. The blind taste test, which is supposed to eliminate some kinds of bias, can be misleading because people use more than their mouths to "taste" a drink. Without the caramel coloring in Coke and Pepsi, people often confuse them with Sprite or 7UP. When light-colored beer gets a shot of food coloring, people tend to describe it as heartier. "Even though taste is the preeminent criterion of beverages," said Pirko, "it's undefinable, loose and very easy to play with."

The vagaries of taste tests can also be laid at the feet of the research process itself, where there are many variables that can be adjusted. Whichever taste comes first will get some votes just for being first. There are dramatic differences in responses depending on whether a person must choose

BIASES

between just A or B or among A, B and no preference. In forced-choice paired comparison tests of similar products, chance alone suggests that 50 percent, more or less, will choose one product over another; the word "more" can mean very little indeed. But even labeling the beverages A and B, 1 and 2 or even M and Q can affect people's choices. People like A, 1 and M better than B, 2 and Q. Testers sometimes use numbers like 476 and 629.

Temperature and freshness can affect taste, as can the container and the subject's last meal. In one cola taste test, the drinks were first served at 32 degrees Fahrenheit; when another round of drinks was served at 38 degrees, twenty-two of twenty-five people changed their choices. Pepsi is thought to be sweeter than Coke; and sweet, at least temporarily and in small quantities, is almost always preferred in taste tests. Pepsi's drinkers tend to be younger than Coke's, so the age of the testers could be pertinent. Many taste tests use a convenience sample—whoever is walking by at a shopping center, mall, fair or beach—which is not representative of the population.

Pepsi / Coke

"You can't say A weighs more than B *and* B weighs more than A. But in taste tests, the precision of measurement isn't as great as a physical measure," said Bruce Buchanan, an expert in the substantiation of taste claims. "There isn't a universally defined measure. Different researchers using different methodologies can get different results."

After almost two decades of taste-test wars—Pepsi started its Challenge in 1975—Coke and Pepsi must surely realize there is no such thing as truth in taste tests. Yet each company challenges its competitor's results, either with the television networks or with the National Advertising Division of the Better Business Bureau. "I picked Pepsi and I thought I liked Coke" was discontinued because it misstated the survey's design and results. "In tests like these nationwide, more people prefer Pepsi over Coke" was modified because of an invalid taste preference measurement. "Nationwide, more Coca-Cola drinkers prefer Pepsi than Coke" was changed because to qualify as a Coke drinker all people had to say was that among all the soft drinks they consumed, Coke was one. It was changed to "Nationwide, more people prefer Pepsi over Coke." "Coke is lighter than the Challenger" was challenged by Pepsi but substantiated (because it had 5 percent fewer calories). Substantiated, too, was this: "Mello Yello. The taste that beats Mountain Dew."

When Pepsi and Coca-Cola came out with their contradictory taste-test results in 1988, both companies complained to the television networks, which were airing the commercials. To their credit, the networks provide a first line of defense against deception in television commercials. (Cable operators, by contrast, have almost no commercial-clearance requirements.) In a typical year, said Matthew Margo, vice president of program practices at CBS, his office receives some 50,000 submissions, including storyboards for commercials that have not even been made yet. "If someone claims taste superiority, it can't be a quixotic claim or rest on a flimsy foundation of puffery," said Margo. But the standard of proof for network clearance is the relatively generous one of being "reasonable." "It's not a standard of criminality," Margo said. "You don't have to prove it beyond a reasonable doubt."

Even after a network okays a commercial, competitors may formally challenge it. The networks review the challenger's objections, and strongly encourage the two parties to share their research methodologies with each other—anathema to the cola antagonists. Without complete data, neither Coke nor Pepsi could mortally wound the other. "We were stymied because neither side could find a fatal flaw, and we couldn't find it either," said Margo. "We were in the uncomfortable position of running contradictory claims, and that's never good for the credibility of advertising."

(A federal court resolved a similar situation involving contradictory claims of superiority by two hand lotions in much the same way. Procter & Gamble was claiming its Wondra "relieves dry skin better than any other leading lotion," while Chesebrough-Pond's was claiming "no leading lotion beats" its Vaseline Intensive Care. Amazingly, the lotion makers sued each other. Both presented supporting clinical data, and both criticized the other's research. The court found both sets of data of dubious value and no preponderance of evidence on either side to support an argument for false claims. Both assertions continued to run.)

Professor Wiseman of Northeastern, who waded through the data from the Diet Pepsi and Diet Coke taste tests, identified several areas where the two studies fell short. The most blatant was the geographical distribution of the testing points: Coke chose ten "non-random" cities that "virtually ignored the whole western half of the United States," Wiseman found. "And Pepsi only questioned people who were within 100 miles of four of their processing plants." Both used convenience samples.

Other differences: Coke's testers were people who said they drank diet soda; Pepsi's were people who said they drank diet cola. Coke testers rated different attributes of each product before expressing a preference; Pepsi testers expressed their preference first. Coke's product came from the supermarket shelf; Pepsi used specially manufactured brew because the company's reformulated product was not yet available at retail.

Although all three networks allowed the contradictory Coke and Pepsi taste-test results to continue airing, Pepsi did make a slight change in the wording of its spot for ABC. It stopped using the phrase "undisputed champion," since at least one entity—Coke—disputed the claim. The new version of the ad declared Diet Pepsi "the winner and new champion."

To Edgar Dworsky of the Massachusetts consumer affairs office, who has seen his share of misleading advertising claims, the competing Coke and Pepsi taste tests were uniquely disturbing. "If Pampers says its diapers are the most absorbent, I don't have any particular reason to doubt it unless another contradictory fact is known to me," he said. "It's difficult to discern truthful from false advertising unless you have that one additional fact. In this case, the additional fact was the competing claim."

In another case of an additional fact, an acquaintance of Dworsky's had auditioned for an acting part in a "taste-test" commercial. Several months later, Dworsky saw a coffee commercial that sounded like the one his friend had de-

scribed. It portrayed commuters at a New Jersey railroad
station stopping to taste a cup of Sanka and remarking on its
excellence. As Dworsky knew, the commuters were paid per-
formers. This was even less scientific than a taste test—it
was a "dramatization" of a taste test. General Foods eventually agreed to superimpose the word "dramatization" on the
first three seconds of the commercial.

As for ethics, many advertisers see no difficulties. To
them, it would be insane to pay for research intended for
advertising or marketing and not have it turn out right. A few
advertisers demur. "How can two lotions both reduce dryness
better? How can two soft drinks both taste better? How can
two trucks both be gaining new buyers versus each other?"
wondered Thomas Mohl, vice president for market research
at the Kellogg Company. "We need to settle this now . . .
before the reputation of all advertising is irreparably damaged."

◆

DECEPTION, WROTE SISSELA BOK, "is often undertaken by those
who know or assume that they have a more objective view of
the situation than those to whom they speak. . . . [They] sin-
cerely believe that they manipulate the facts in order to convey a 'truer picture.' "

That kind of hubris is frequently seen in research but
nowhere more than in advertising and marketing, where some
people feel they alone will be able to distinguish the truth
from the enveloping murk of prejudice. "I heard one must
not ask biased questions," wrote Alfred Politz, a forefather
of the market-research industry. "But I can't understand
this, because if we are interested in obtaining the truth and it
turns out that a barrage of biased questions can do it better
than unbiased questions, then I would use them."

The degree of truth in advertising fluctuates from time
to time, depending on the moral, political and economic cli-
mate of the times. Since Republican administrations generally embrace the ideal of caveat emptor, conditions through
the 1980s were ideal for flimflam. Encouraging a free-market
approach to information, Ronald Reagan and George Bush

FTC ①

decimated the Federal Trade Commission, advertising's most powerful disciplinarian. The recession of the late 1980s, during which companies could grow only by stealing market share, aggravated the situation. Meanwhile, advertising techniques had become increasingly hard to pin down using traditional legal standards of deception. "Over time, advertisers simply get more subtle, and then the law catches up to them. But there's always a lag time. The law isn't as smart as advertisers are," said Professor Preston.

In that lag time, advertisers swiftly and cynically climb aboard passing trends, exploiting any popular crusade for a sale. When Americans started attending to the deteriorating condition of the earth in the 1980s, marketers quickly began selling their products with environmental half-truths. Mobil Oil claimed its Hefty trash bags were "degradable"; maybe on another planet, but not in the American landfills where they are dumped. Alberto-Culver claimed some of its aerosol products, such as its hair spray, were "ozone friendly"; in fact, they contained ozone-depleting chemicals. Tetra Pak, maker of the environmental scourge called the drink box, said its containers were as recyclable as newspaper; unlikely, since only a handful of pilot projects were even trying to recycle the multilayer container. Long after they had made their claims, these three companies were prohibited from repeating them and made to pay investigative costs. Many others escaped unscathed.

Overseeing advertising claims is a relatively modern phenomenon, another consequence of our increasingly complex world. Until the beginning of the twentieth century, people typically had a "craft knowledge" of most things they bought—they understood how the product was made and how to judge its quality—and advertising rarely outweighed it. But as the number of products and their technological sophistication grew, people could not maintain a craft knowledge of most items they bought—their blender, their lawn mower, even their cake mix. Today a few people retain knowledge of cars or of items used for a hobby, such as fishing or skiing. But most have neither the opportunity nor the expertise to inspect technologically sophisticated goods coming from around the globe.

"decline of Craft Knowledge"

digital
conversa

③

Supply

demand

Around the turn of the century, other changes in the American economy paved the way for modern advertising. The Industrial Revolution transformed the country from a land of overdemand to one of oversupply. No longer did consumers have one choice of bread, sold by the local baker; now they could buy any of a half-dozen kinds sold by large corporations nationally. Commodities splintered into brands, and brand advertising was born. Because many brands were not significantly different from one another, factual information about the product became almost worthless. In the increasingly crowded marketplace, innuendo began to squeeze out the very product information with which consumers might shop smarter.

④ Another, more recent, reason for the deterioration of factual information in advertising was the shortening of television and radio commercials from one minute to thirty seconds to fifteen seconds. "When seconds were the measure, there was little time for reasoned argumentation, comparative analysis, or meaningful product information," wrote Ronald Collins and David Skover.

Some people blame the FTC for the decline of information in advertising. If the FTC was going to challenge every tiny point of fact, companies reasoned, why bother with facts at all? Instead of a quarter-pounder, make it a Whopper. "Ironically," wrote Pridgen and Preston, "the drive for consumer protection through the regulation of false advertising claims may have accelerated the shift away from objective data in advertising, thus lowering the potential value of advertising as a source of hard product information for consumers." A very early example of this can be seen on a label used in 1912 on a patent medicine called Swamp Root. Labels on the bottles sold in England contained twelve falsehoods prohibited in America by the Food and Drug Act of 1906. Labels on the bottles in America made as many claims, but instead of such assertions as "cures Bright's disease," there were less factual claims, such as "Swamp Root makes friends" and "It will be found very beneficial in cases of Debility."

The prevailing feeling about regulation among advertisers is that the free market should take care of deceptive advertising just as it does most other speech and information.

Advertisers love to talk about how smart and sophisticated buyers are—far too smart to be fooled by deception. In fact, some say, since people do not believe advertising claims anyway, they may actually be immune to deception. And precisely because of its acknowledged self-interest, advertising may actually be less deceptive than other vehicles of information, advertising people say. "Advertising is probably the only source of information that very clearly labels its motivation and the source of that motivation," said Tom Dillon, an advertising executive. "In an ad, we know that someone wants us to buy some product or service. In what we read in the newspapers or hear on the air, we do not know what the motivation is." Competitors, too, may be counted on to challenge false claims or to provide a counterpoint to them, argue advertisers opposing regulation.

Finally, as advertisers constantly point out, there are very few outright lies in advertising anymore—at least not from a legal standpoint. It is another kind of deception, called puffing, that is not only widespread but enjoys legal protection. One FTC case described puffery as "exaggerations reasonably to be expected of a seller as to the degree of quality of his product, the truth or falsity of which cannot be precisely determined." Even if an advertiser has no substantiation for his claim, he commits no crime calling his circus, for example, "the greatest show on earth." Or from Coca-Cola: "Coke has brought more people together than any other soft drink." Although neither Ringling Bros. nor Coca-Cola has any objective data on which to base their assertions, they are stated as fact. "All puffs imply facts," wrote Preston, "and the facts which puffs imply are virtually always false."

◆

THE CONSEQUENCES OF USING BAD data or deception to sell products may be less serious than the misuse of research in legislatures, courts or pharmacies, but there are consequences. Maybe the constant repetition of bizarre facts created solely to sell products—48 percent of U.S. travelers suffered from constipation and 47 percent from diarrhea at least once during the last year of travel (Pepto-Bismol/Metamucil); 20 percent of couples ran out of ice during their first dinner party (Krups)—is like dripping water slowly on someone's forehead until he goes crazy. Although probably forgotten quickly, this kind of information adds to people's already formidable overload. And occasionally advertising research promises something more than the thickest catsup or the tastiest soda. In the case of food, advertising sometimes promises good health; of automobiles, safety.

Regulators take a hard line on health and safety claims because the consequences are so grave, and consumers are unlikely to be able to test their veracity for themselves. "If they advertise clear floor wax, and you take it home and it yellows, you don't buy it again," said Stephen Gardner, formerly assistant attorney general of Texas who made a national reputation for himself by aggressively challenging advertising claims. "You can test it easily. If Quaker Oats doesn't lower your cholesterol enough, you die. That's not a good test."

Regulators are also more likely to rush into health, safety and environment issues because false claims can contaminate an otherwise worthy cause. "We were concerned that people would get burnt out on environmental claims," said Gardner. "We didn't want them to give up. Because the fact is, some products are better for the environment than others." Some cars are safer than others, too.

Until the 1960s, most people shopping for a car searched for a good-looking model with high performance. They assumed that cars were safe, because if they weren't, the government would not allow them to be sold. In the 1950s, Ford had tried to capitalize on safety, creating and promoting a car with safety belts, padded dashboard and safety door latches. But the Chevrolet, which emphasized style, sold better. "[Robert] McNamara is selling safety, but Chevrolet is selling cars," complained Henry Ford II about his company's assistant general manager. American car companies got the message: Safety did not sell.

Sell or not, some cars were safer than others. That came to the public's attention in 1965, when Ralph Nader published his best-selling *Unsafe at Any Speed,* about the propensity of Chevrolet Corvairs to go out of control on turns. Several years later, the Pinto was found to have gas tanks that caught fire in rear-end collisions.

In 1979, the National Highway Traffic Safety Administration hired a market researcher named Jack Gillis to find out if safety sells. Gillis found that while people said safety was important to them, they did not seem to act on that when they went to the showroom. Gillis hypothesized that it was because there was little safety information available.

European car companies, meanwhile, especially the Swedish giant Volvo, had been applying themselves to safety since the 1940s. It was Volvo that introduced the first laminated windshield and developed the three-point seat belt. By the mid-1980s, its message of commitment to safety was finally finding willing listeners. Volvo deftly pressed its protect-your-family theme and enjoyed record U.S. sales in 1986.

The American automakers followed Volvo's lead, a reversal from their earlier resistance to safety innovations. A Chrysler commercial showed chairman Lee Iacocca lecturing a board of directors on air bags: "Some things you wait for, some you don't. Minivans with air bags? You don't wait." This was the same man who once said that air bags were so dangerous that a safety engineer had told him they should be used for executions. Meanwhile, an Oldsmobile commercial claimed that General Motors had "pioneered" the air bag. In fact, GM had lobbied against air bags for years, and had a lower percentage of its models equipped with the device than either Ford or Chrysler, according to the Center for Auto Safety. Car advertisements bragged of providing such safety features as side impact protection; in fact, by law all cars must provide it.

Even without the distortions the car companies brought to safety claims, the statistics about car safety are far from straightforward. Most safety claims are based on crash tests performed by the government, in which models are smashed head-on into a barrier at 35 miles an hour. In categories such as the likelihood of head injuries in such a crash, the difference among car models can be more than 100 percent. Unfortunately, the tests measure only one type of crash—head-on—at one speed and without such complications as rolling over, exploding or being rear-ended.

"We tested them at 35, and some of them did very well, some did very poorly," said Gillis, who does annual evaluations of car safety for the *Car Book*. "There was no way anyone could look at those cars and know. Some safety belts work well, and some don't."

Another popular set of safety statistics, those compiled by the Highway Loss Data Institute, are drawn from insurance collision claims and so are somewhat distorted by the abilities of the driver. Although the institute tries to adjust for driver age, big cars still tend to do well partly because they are driven primarily by older drivers; and small two-door imports are at a disadvantage because they are more likely to be driven by youths. "The Chevy Camaro is responsible for more death and injury than any other car," said Gillis. "The car is safe, but it's driven by the most young men."

That is why in 1988, half of the twelve model vehicles rated for personal injury both by the federal government's crash tests and the highway institute got contradictory ratings. The Chevrolet Astro Van finished 60 percent below the acceptable level on the federal government's test, one of the worst in its class of vehicle. But according to the highway institute, the Astro Van had the best record of all vehicles considered. The government said the Pontiac LeMans had one of the best scores among subcompacts; the highway institute ranked it near the bottom.

Except in extreme cases, like the Corvair and Pinto, statistics can rarely conclusively prove or disprove a car as safe. In 1990, the National Highway Traffic Safety Administration closed its investigation of Ford's Bronco II, finding that its rate of involvement in rollover accidents was not significantly higher than that of other similar vehicles. But in the spring of 1992, the Insurance Institute for Highway Safety, an industry group, found that the fatality rate in rollover accidents on one type of Bronco II was the highest of any they had studied. The institute's study did not adjust for road conditions or age of the driver, but those alone probably could not have accounted for the difference, the institute's president said. The institute's study also looked at fatality rather than accident rates, a much smaller data base to work from.

With so much talk about safety in the automobile mar-

ketplace of the late 1980s, it was not surprising that one car
company would finally take its safety claims too far. The fact
that it was Volvo, whose product was, in terms of safety,
genuinely superior, was ironic but not atypical in the world of
advertising claims. As the general level of claims rises, it
becomes difficult to distinguish oneself without resorting to
hyperbole.

In late 1990, Volvo began airing a commercial showing a
monster truck called Bearfoot driving over several cars,
among them a Volvo. Only the Volvo escaped relatively unscathed; only the Volvo had been structurally reinforced with
welded steel rods and wooden planks before the experiment
began. The other cars' roof supports had been cut.

It may come as news to some that using demonstrations
like this in advertising is illegal—after all, shaving cream has
long substituted for whipped cream, mashed potatoes for ice
cream. Certainly the people who were making Volvo's commercial did not seem to think anything was wrong, because
they cut and reinforced the cars in an exposition center where
people were wandering around. An onlooker photographed
the work and contacted the Texas state attorney general's
office, which threatened to sue. Volvo quickly withdrew the
advertising from circulation, but not before the company had
been hit by a hurricane of damaging publicity.

In November 1991, Volvo, with a new advertising
agency, stirred things up again. Volvo's 30-second commercial started with a family considering buying a minivan and
then showed a minivan crash, with an ambulance pulling
away from the wreck. A recent study, said the voice-over,
"found that minivans as a group had an average occupant
death rate twice as high as the car with the lowest death rate,
the Volvo 240 wagon. So if you're considering a minivan instead of a Volvo, maybe you'd like to reconsider."

But the "latest available" data meant accident reports
between 1984 and 1988, before many minivans were equipped
with air bags. Even then, the death rate of the minivans was
a minuscule one in 10,000 accidents.

In the late 1970s and early 1980s, when consumers were
more worried about gas shortages than antilock brakes, car
companies exploited mileage statistics much as they would

later do with safety. The claims, based on internal tests, were generous to say the least. In fact, one company produced a tongue-in-cheek ad for a 200-mile-per-gallon car, which had been driven a long, mainly downhill route at 50 miles an hour. Noting the exaggerated and often unverified claims showing up in car ads, the government changed the rules: Thereafter, car companies could only use EPA mileage statistics.

It is time for a similar standard for safety claims.

◆

TO TRADITIONAL MARKETERS, MUCH OF the research that shows up in advertising is trivial and fatuous—and not worth getting riled up about. It is a tiny part of their $2.5-billion-a-year industry, they say, and anyway there is a bigger problem afoot than silly surveys. To a man—and woman—they point a finger at so-called SUGGERS and FRUGGERS, acronyms for people who sell or fund-raise under the guise of doing surveys. One market researcher even claimed her industry kept America safe from Communism; without surveys, she argued vehemently, no one in the old Soviet Union had had a forum for speaking his mind.

Other market researchers are not so quick to acquit their industry. "I'm upset by what I see," said Solomon Dutka, chief executive of Audits & Surveys, a market-research firm, with passion. "A distortion or adulteration has set in in the market-research business. People used to generate hypotheses; now they generate conclusions." Indeed, in an article of advice in the *Harvard Business Review* about how to do comparative ads without ending up in court, the two authors describe part of the research process: "The marketer decides what the claim will be, guides the researcher in collecting data, and works with agency people to translate the claim into the words and pictures of the advertisement."

Eric Miller, former editor of a newsletter that abstracts and reviews studies and surveys, said, "Fewer studies are being done to get information, and more are being done to substantiate a claim or accomplish a particular promotional goal. The scary part is, people make decisions based on this stuff." Miller considers this an invisible problem, but not a victimless one.

The watchdogs that try to insure a clean flow of commercial information operate on several levels and with mixed success. Several state attorneys general and local consumer affairs agencies actively pursue misleading claims, but their power and budgets are limited. Competitors, who are at least as likely as consumers to be injured by misleading claims, can challenge advertising through an industry group and also through the National Advertising Division of the Better Business Bureau. Under Section 43(a) of the Lanham Trademark Act, competitors can take alleged deceivers to court. And the television networks maintain their advertising standards departments.

At the top of the regulatory heap is the Federal Trade Commission, which requires that advertising be truthful, nondeceptive and substantiated. But the FTC can tackle only a handful of the most egregious claims, usually national in scope. "Do you have the world's largest Ford dealer in your area?" asked a spokesman for the FTC. "Well, I've got the world's largest Ford dealer down here, too. It's not worth it for the commission to challenge a claim like that. It's just not going to stop." Substantiating ads can be an exercise in silliness, too, as evidenced in the FTC's challenge to Wonder Bread's claim to help build strong bodies twelve ways. Both Wonder and the government hired experts to testify that Wonder Bread built strong bodies in precisely twelve ways or that it did not.

In the early 1970s, Robert Pitofsky, then head of the FTC's Bureau of Consumer Protection, tried to describe what kinds of advertising claims would draw regulatory attention and which would not. "If someone says, 'tastes great,' we are not going to ask for substantiation. But if they say, 'Stops three times as fast' or 'costs half as much as all competitors in its class,' we are going to ask what they mean by class." Unfortunately, even that was not possible; the following year, a Senate subcommittee concluded that ad substantiation was neither a useful nor timely response to ad claims. "[N]either individual consumers nor the FTC have the technical capacity to evaluate the validity and relevance of much of the data," the subcommittee said.

In 1983, its staff cut to the bone, the FTC radically weakened its seventy-year-old definition of deceptive advertising. Previously, the standard of proof had been advertising with a "tendency and capacity" to mislead; now the ad would have to be "likely to mislead" to provoke FTC action. Marketers took deregulation as an "imperative to go forth and lie, cheat, and steal at the expense of consumers," wrote Stephen Gardner of Texas.

"I've got to believe that people distrust advertising," said Gardner. "That means to defeat it, you just have to be more deceptive and more clever. Companies say, well, we haven't gotten any complaints about this. Good deception doesn't get complaints because people are deceived.

"When I was a kid," Gardner added, "I really believed that if it wasn't true, the government wouldn't let them say it. When I realized the government couldn't stop them, I decided to become a lawyer."

◆

CONSUMER SURVEYS, WHATEVER THEIR QUALITY, carry enough weight in some industries that they can cause real damage to those who fare badly. That has given rise to mischievous strategies for manipulating them. Surveys done by and for magazines are often managed by their marketing departments, which have close relationships with and can be virtual arms of the industries they cover. Their goal is to name as many winners in as many categories as possible so that the winners will congratulate themselves in advertising. In the personal computing world, which is rife with surveys, *InfoWorld*, a trade publication, gives dozens of awards in categories from best local-area-network circuit board to best programming language for IBM and compatible computers. Magazine surveys often consist of mail ballots, which are necessarily skewed because many people will not take the time to answer questions for which there is no incentive. Whatever kind of people do answer mail surveys, they are almost certainly not representative of the U.S. population.

In the spring of 1991, a magazine called *Corporate Travel* published the results of a consumer survey of the travel industry. In the category of rental cars, the magazine declared Avis the winner of what was to be its first annual Alfred Award, named for Alfred Kahn, former chairman of the Civil Aviation Board. Avis, not surprisingly, quickly launched an advertising campaign touting its standing in the poll.

Joseph Russo, vice president for government and public affairs at Avis's archrival, Hertz, was not amused. He called the magazine's editor and asked if he could see a press release and any other material that might explain the survey's results and methodology. "We've won virtually every other poll that's ever been done," said Russo. (Indeed, surveys like these are popularity contests that tend to favor bigger competitors over smaller ones; and they are almost impossible to duplicate or verify.) "So we wanted to see if we were missing the beat." But Russo said he could not get much information about the survey. "I said, How many people voted in this, was it bigger than a bread basket?"

It turned out that the survey responses had disappeared under mysterious circumstances. The magazine's marketing manager, who had overseen the poll, had left the magazine. "A search of their files has also failed to turn up any statistical tabulation or record of the responses for any category," wrote the president of *Corporate Travel*'s parent to Hertz. Meanwhile, said Russo, "we had corporate accounts saying, I see you guys came in after Avis."

Eventually Hertz filed suit against the publisher of the magazine and Avis, charging false advertising. "We said if we allow this to go on, anyone will be able to do anything on the basis of a survey," Russo said. The parties settled, with Avis agreeing to stop calling itself the car rental company of choice among business travelers.

Although this is a particularly egregious example, transforming magazine surveys into marketing gimmicks has become common. So seriously do some companies take consumer surveys that an official of Vail ski resort in Colorado went to the trouble of having thousands of fake ballots printed for a *Snow Country* magazine survey. Every year the magazine rates ski resorts, a ranking that may affect the spending of leisure dollars. The Vail ski resort in Colorado lost its number-one ranking in 1992; for the 1993 survey the resort decided to fight back, printing its own ballots that could be handed out to its customers. (The real ballots went out by mail.) When a newspaper reporter learned of the plan, the Vail resort canceled its plan to distribute them. Meanwhile, another magazine, called *Ski*, gave Vail its number-one ranking in 1992.

The media not only create their own promotional surveys but also cheerfully purvey others' promotional and frequently nonsensical surveys and statistics. "About 13% Eligible for Sainthood," read a headline in the *Orlando Sentinel*. Another survey, by the International Road Federation, also made headlines in *USA Today:* "Survey: Drive Defensively in Latvia, Turkey."

Kiwi Brands, a shoe-polish company, has found surveys to be an economical way to attract attention. The company commissioned a survey on the correlation between ambition and shiny shoes—"Go Getters Are Going to Get Their Shoes Shined," read the news release—which found, naturally, that 97 percent of self-described ambitious young men believed shiny shoes were important to the way they look on the job.

The shiny shoes survey was just the latest in a series of survey questions Kiwi had asked strictly for promotional purposes. In two earlier surveys, Kiwi had asked people if they were making an extra effort to take care of old shoes in light of difficult times. To Kiwi's delight, the first year 71 percent of people said they were, and the Shoe Care Index was born. The next year, however, only 59 percent said they were fixing up their shoes. Undiscouraged, Kiwi marketed that as good news, putting out a news release proclaiming an economic upturn—fewer people were taking care of their shoes. A Kiwi product manager said that while the Shoe Care Index would "never appear in any leading economics texts, it does survey a more grass roots measure than the GNP or new housing starts."

Marketers are unabashed about using silly data to sell a product. "Obviously these surveys are done with the idea of producing interesting information that will got a lot of play," said John Shiffert, a public relations executive who works with Kiwi. "An earlier survey asked what mistakes people make in terms of grooming, and the No. 1 mistake was not having their shoes shined. That release got pretty good coverage, got on the A.P. [Associated Press] wire as an interesting fact. We got a lot of play out of radio and television. It's a subject people can have some fun with."

Consumers suffer no obvious damage from poor or trivial surveys except a further loss of faith in surveys, and perhaps information itself. The deception leaves no obvious wounds or scars, so it is easy to overlook or to dismiss as a condition of modern life. A few people do not accept that.

"We believe that consumers rely on advertising messages when making buying decisions," said Edgar Dworsky of Massachusetts. "It's not unreasonable to say those messages must be truthful. Is it life or death whether Coke beats Pepsi? No. But today it's a taste claim, and tomorrow it's a health claim. Where's the end?"

CHAPTER FOUR

False

Barometers of

Opinion

When the people have no other tyrant,
then our public opinion becomes one.

—E. G. Bulwer-Lytton

Just before dinnertime one evening in June 1992, about a dozen students and part-time interviewers sat down at desks at the University of New Hampshire Survey Center, a small unmarked office on the school's bosky campus in Durham. At 5:30 P.M., they started dialing.

The center was beginning its quarterly survey of state residents. Because this poll fed the New Hampshire press—a small newspaper consortium underwrote it—the questions were supposed to provide fodder for summer features. What do you think about suntan lotion and American cars? What does the July Fourth holiday commemorate? A question inserted by a psychology professor asked the respondents to rate their mood on a scale of 1 to 100. (Eighty was typical, although one man said, "Now that you've interrupted my dinner for ten minutes, 40.") The interviewers also asked a serious political question: Whom did people believe when Clarence Thomas, Supreme Court nominee, was accused of sexual harassment by Anita Hill? And whom did they believe now?

The interviewers were mostly young women with eager, sweet voices—Jennifer, Tracy and Randy. They would dial computer-generated random numbers; it would eventually take 1,700 numbers to get 500 completed interviews. Each of the interviewers would conduct an average of eight interviews in their four-hour stint. Some would do more, and some would get a long string of business telephones, answering machines —or people who were putting their kids in the tub, could not hear or were not interested in sharing their opinions with a stranger. Although the telephone numbers were distributed to the interviewers randomly, one young poller was dismayed to be rejected by a half-dozen people in the first hour. "I try not to take it personally," she said, near tears.

Researchers love to predict the outcome of their surveys, often placing bets on them, and there was a spirited exchange of opinions on how well Clarence Thomas would fare in this poll. Kelly Myers, associate director of the survey center, predicted Clarence Thomas would get an approval rating well over 50 percent. He thought that because people would have a hard time overcoming their reverence for Supreme Court justices, they wouldn't believe that one of them could have said words like "Long Dong Silver."

But as the survey progressed ("Today, as you look back on what happened, who do you believe was telling the truth —Clarence Thomas or Anita Hill?") it became clear that Anita Hill was at least as believable—if not more so—than Clarence Thomas. By a small (and statistically weak) margin of 34.7 percent to 31.3 percent, Hill was judged more believable. Furthermore, more than a third of the respondents felt Anita Hill had been ill used by the Senate. Subsequent polls on the same topic—by NBC and the *Wall Street Journal, U.S. News & World Report* and Gallup—produced similar results: More people now seemed to believe that Anita Hill had been telling the truth.

To David Moore, then director of the New Hampshire Survey Center, the Anita Hill poll simply proved again how protean public opinion is—if it can be said to exist at all. "Public opinion is a compound of folly, weakness, prejudice, wrong feeling, right feeling, obstinacy and newspaper paragraphs," wrote the English statesman Robert Peel. Peel's recipe is no less true 150 years later, but now modern technology in the form of public opinion polls has given an insistent voice to that inchoate mix.

Public opinion pollers say they are a pillar of American democracy, a direct, nonpartisan line of communication between leaders and the sacrosanct "will of the people." Pollers offer instant feedback on the public's beliefs about social and political topics from sexual harassment to aerial bombing. The grandfather of modern polling, George Gallup, called polls "democracy in action." Polling, said the contemporary Republican poller Richard Wirthlin, "is the purest form of democracy, a much better cross section of the public than those who vote." In 1985, Philippine president Ferdinand Marcos announced that a public opinion survey had shown that most people didn't want an election; because of a poll, there would be no vote.

But polling is not democracy, and it is not truth. Most important, it often is not even public opinion. Public opinion is a great billowing cloud, impossible to capture with a few quick measurements. The doubt inherent in it distinguishes opinion from belief and conviction. Confronted with inconsistent polls around presidential elections, pollers concede they are only taking snapshots—pictures that quickly expire. But while polls capture merely an instant in time, the decisions made by people who rely on them can last for decades.

Unlike accountants, lawyers and doctors, who have some professional rules and regulatory bodies to enforce them, pollers answer only to themselves and their clients. A trade group, the American Association for Public Opinion Research, keeps watch on polling activities, but has no disciplinary power. The polling community excuses itself for its various lapses in accuracy or judgment, saying if there are two systems for measuring a fact as "objective" as air temperature—Fahrenheit and Celsius—what hope can there be for standard measurements of something as elusive as public opinion?

Even so, polls now do more than simply record opinion. Now they also form opinion, as people wait for the polls to see whom or what they should believe. Polls offer the comfort of the majority when people face shocking and complex questions. The polls became a potent weapon for Clarence Thomas's supporters. If Anita Hill was telling the truth, why didn't anybody believe her? "Polls become part of the information process, which can ultimately influence the way people come down on an issue," said Moore.

◆

As ANITA HILL MADE HER televised charges against Clarence Thomas before the Senate Judiciary Committee in October 1991, more than thirty polls gauged public reaction to her. Samples of Americans were asked: Did they believe Hill, naive but ambitious protégée of a powerful mentor, or Clarence Thomas, outraged victim of racial politics gone awry? By significant and consistent majorities, men and women, black and white, all said the same thing. Anita Hill was lying.

It was natural that America's senators would want to hear the voice of the people about Anita Hill. The vote was shaping up to be close (it turned out to be the closest confirmation vote in history), and there was strong opposition to

Thomas for other reasons than his alleged sexual harassment. Polls would be crucial for political defense should the senators vote the "wrong" way. And the people seemed to want the polls, too. The situation was so bizarre and so charged that no one knew quite what to think.

Yet as politicians set off down the 1992 campaign trail early the next year, they quickly realized that something had happened to public opinion. At rallies, the mention of Anita Hill's name brought brisk applause; women opened their pocketbooks to feminist candidates, many citing Anita Hill. The unbeatable Republican Senator Arlen Specter of Pennsylvania, running against a feminist, suddenly wasn't so proud of the prosecutorial role he had taken against Anita Hill. The politicians and the pollers wondered: Just when had Anita Hill become a hero?

The polls had missed a pulse. They had persuaded some senators that a yea vote was politically sound—because the voice of the people had spoken. President George Bush, noting the polls, said he was "very pleased with the way the support all across the country is holding strong for Judge Thomas." But if Bush, the senators and the American people believed they knew public opinion about Anita Hill, they were wrong.

Well before the renaissance of Anita Hill's reputation, there was good reason to suspect the outcomes of the Thomas-Hill polls. Almost all were done in three or fewer days and some even overnight. They were quickie polls, the most likely to be wrong because the questions are hastily drawn and poorly pretested, and it is almost impossible to get a random sample in one night. Without a random sample, the results of the poll cannot be projected onto everyone else; pollers, politicians and the media cannot truthfully claim to know what America is thinking. In quickies, sample sizes dip, and weighting, in which data are adjusted to compensate for the unequal probabilities of selection, soars. Despite their speed, however, the Anita Hill pollers were certain their results were right because the polls all said the same thing.

Less than a year later, they all said the opposite.

◆

Good Points about polls

++

THERE IS NOTHING INHERENTLY WRONG with public opinion polls. In fact, in many ways public opinion polling has become more scientific, and the pollers' statistical techniques have never been better. If polls are done methodically, thoughtfully and without parsimony, they can bring interesting and useful information to decisions. Polls taken over years or even decades can capture shifting sentiments about important issues—as they have for gun control, abortion and health care. Taken as one piece of evidence to consider among many others when making a decision, a poll can be helpful. The best polls will also illuminate the fears and hopes that shape people's opinions.

But as pollers have proliferated, they have ventured into territory far beyond the big picture or the big elections. While there is no official number of pollers in the U.S., the public opinion trade association alone has well over 1,000 members. Some belong to commercial enterprises whose primary business is, or has become, market research, such as Gallup, Roper, Harris; some are media operations—CBS/*New York Times*, ABC/*Washington Post*, NBC/*Wall Street Journal*; some are private pollers who work primarily for political candidates of a specific party; and some are affiliated with academic institutions. Today, any serious political candidate at the national level, many state candidates and even big-city mayors and councilmen commission their own polls. And while the number of polls has risen, so, too, has their frequency. In big political campaigns, polls are now done daily.

With so many pollers constantly polling, there is almost nothing that is not considered a matter of public opinion, no matter how personal or unknowable the subject. *Wall Street Journal* and NBC News pollers paid thousands of dollars so that the public could express an opinion on Hillary Clinton's decision to add Rodham to her name. (Sixty-two percent thought she should not use Rodham; 6 percent said she should; and—gratifyingly—28 percent said it did not matter one way or the other.) The *Washington Post* and ABC News asked people whether Ronald Reagan would get cancer again before he left office. Based on zero information, 33 percent thought yes.

That polls have come to dominate political debates can be seen in the pages of America's newspapers. Between July 1 and November 3, 1992, when Bill Clinton was elected president, the front page of *USA Today* carried fifteen poll-driven stories about the political campaign; the *New York Times* mentioned polls on its front page fifty-three times during that period. In just the eight days before the election, twenty different national polls were conducted, as well as countless statewide ones. Meanwhile, the stock market kept its high-strung finger on the pulse of the polls. "Stocks Gain 15.67 on Report of Poll Finding Bush, Clinton Nearly Even," read one newspaper headline. "Stocks Finish Mixed as Polls Cause Jitters," read another.

Polling looks scientific because of the way the results are expressed—percentage points, cross-tabulations, margins of error, statistical significance. But much of polling—the asking and answering of questions—is a soft science built on the shifting sands of human language and psychology. In hard science, research should be replicable, with identical results. But because public opinion is constantly changing and polls can never be exactly duplicated, there is no way to judge their accuracy. Elections and referenda provide polling's only check, and the report card is decidedly mixed.

Another reason polls are soft information is that people are notoriously unreliable, even as experts on their own opinions. When the people interviewed for New Hampshire's survey were asked whom they had believed a year before, Clarence Thomas or Anita Hill, they now said Anita Hill. Revisionism like that is well known in the polling world. After John Kennedy was assassinated, it was almost impossible to find anyone to admit voting against him, even though he had won by a hair. Similarly, the number of people who remembered voting for Franklin Roosevelt was always greater than the vote he received.

Honest pollers know all this. And although they speak skeptically of the "truth" of polls, the best pollers, especially those who work in big political campaigns, want to get as

close to it as they can. Their sponsors—political parties and
the media—want the best data they can buy, either to peddle
as information or to use in planning strategy. The crimes in
much political polling are more likely to be excessive speed,
cheapness and spin doctoring than deliberately slanting questions or manipulating data.

Pollers have no patience with the widespread feeling
that there are too many polls. The more polls on any subject,
however contradictory, the better, they say. Polls act as
checks on one another, and people are not held hostage to a
polling monopoly. When there were only one or two polls,
contradictions or problems would take months to resolve.
That worked out well for Richard Nixon during the Watergate
crisis. The questions Gallup asked about impeachment were
widely misunderstood. Many people believed that impeach
meant convict, and however troubled they were by Nixon's
behavior, they were not ready to convict. For several months,
Nixon pointed out that the polls supported him. But when
Gallup started asking whether Nixon should be brought to
trial before the Senate, the results changed dramatically.
Today, competing polls would quickly sort this out, pollers
say.

Moreover, the torrent of polls creates a free market,
pollers say—more information and ideas from more directions, with the best triumphing. But like any marketplace,
the marketplace of polls tends to work to the advantage of the
most advanced or powerful producer. The economically and
politically dominant classes who know how to "market" ideas
can also dominate the nation's ideology with polls. "As a
result," wrote Benjamin Ginsberg, a professor of government
at Cornell University, "the lower classes became over time
consumers more than producers of their own opinions, accepting many of the beliefs advanced by the upper classes."

That pollers have the power to shape the national debate
was clear from the questions they asked about Anita Hill and
Clarence Thomas. For the most part, the questions offered
only a stark choice between him or her. Few pollers rose
above that simplistic clash to ask if people would support
taking the time to hear more witnesses or to deliberate longer.
They did not ask people if they wanted to hear from another

woman who claimed she was also harassed by Thomas (and whose testimony was not heard). They did not ask whether people had questioned Thomas's fitness when he said he had never considered the most famous judicial decision of our time, *Roe* v. *Wade*. By the time the polls were finished with the Hill-Thomas controversy, the intricate web of legal and moral issues had been reduced to the level of a vote for dogcatcher.

◆

LIKE PHYSICISTS WHOSE MEASUREMENTS BLUR the subatomic particles they seek to understand, pollers change the people they poll. They do that by forcing them to make an immediate decision. With the exception of the U.S. Senate, no one had to decide for or against Clarence Thomas. As people passionately debated Anita Hill's charges, they may have changed their minds frequently—or never made them up. It was a complicated and emotional matter, and forming an opinion required time, distance, perspective. Perhaps they would never decide who was telling the truth—the New Hampshire survey showed almost a quarter of the respondents still unsure. But the group that was surveyed during the hearings had to decide, and fast. That is what pollers call public opinion.

It is a poller's business to press for an opinion whether people have one or not. "Don't knows" are worthless to pollers, whose product is opinion, not ignorance. That is why so many polls do not even offer a "don't know" alternative. If someone volunteers a "don't know" (and studies have shown many people will guess an answer rather than volunteer their ignorance) the interviewers are often told to push or probe. In choices among candidates, those who say they are undecided might be asked how they "lean." The result is that people seem more decided about issues and candidates than they are.

In real life, decisions on momentous topics are typically made after private thought and conversations with friends, colleagues and families. Far from being the numerical tally of a few hundred people's reactions seconds after learning something, public opinion is a constantly evolving process in which people digest argument and information as well as the opinions, experiences and passions of others. Real public opinion is judgment that comes "out of experience and under the spur of responsibility" as Oliver Wendell Holmes put it. Real public opinion, or at least public opinion that is not as spontaneous, emotional and shallow as mob action, cannot be hurried, and it is virtually never instantaneous.

Yet with the help of sophisticated computers and telephones, the time it takes to do a poll has been steadily shrinking. The morning after the first night's bombing of Iraq, reaction polls found that 40 percent of Americans believed—based on what?—that the war would last only a few weeks. During the 1992 presidential debates, some polls were finished just a half hour after the candidates said goodnight. Pollers talk about speeding the process even further by letting people call in their opinions, using their Touch-Tone phones to enter answers to prerecorded questions. Because of the speed and frequency of these polls, pollers warn that people should expect what might seem to be more volatile public opinion.

Modern public opinion is probably no more or less volatile and no more or less quickly formed than ever. It is simply that the polls can now measure faster than the public's ability to form an opinion worth measuring. The poller Daniel Yankelovich has broken down the process of forming public opinion into seven steps that, on complex questions, can take more than ten years. In the earliest stages, the opinion tends to be vehement but extremely unstable: Anita Hill was lying. It will take several more stages to mature into consistent and coherent opinion. Today's quickie polls are taken in the first stage and declared to be public opinion—until someone does another poll.

Once public opinion stabilizes, polls can come close to reflecting what would happen in a voting booth. That is especially true if there is little new information coming into the public debate. In the case of Anita Hill, however, there was constant new and shocking information: a steady string of persuasive witnesses on both sides, reports of a lie detector test and a raunchy look at sexual harassment in the workplace, not to mention the shock of seeing the members of the Senate Judiciary Committee conducting their business like dissolute, unprincipled Roman emperors. Gauging public opinion then was like drawing a map of a tidal wave.

That didn't stop the pollers. They plowed ahead with their instant polls, using sample sizes that sometimes dipped below 500. In this crucial way, the raw technique of pollers has degenerated over the past generation. Polls in the 1930s and '40s would typically use sample sizes of 2,000 or more to project results onto the country's population; 1,000 has been the modern standard until recently, when, largely because of smaller budgets and tighter schedules, sample sizes have been dropping. The smaller the sample size, the larger the potential error for the sampling. That is especially true if the respondents split relatively evenly. For example, with a sample of 1,000, if a poll shows 60 percent to 40 percent, that would probably be within 3 points either way of the tally if the entire population were polled. But if the sample size was only 100, the margin of error for a 60–40 split would be about 10 points either way, which means the split could conceivably be as wide as 70–30 or as narrow as 50–50. And this is all within a 95-in-100 confidence level, which means that one in twenty times the error will probably be larger than that. In Britain, the big pollers will not ask voters' intentions of fewer than 1,000 people. "Twice as many interviews isn't twice as good, but it's roughly half again better," said the British poller Robert M. Worcester.

Random sampling is defined as everyone in the universe having an equal chance of being chosen. Ideally, every adult in America could be reached at any time by a poller. That is never possible, of course, because some people do not have telephones or are sick or do not speak the language of the interviewer. But the ideal is to eliminate as many of those differences as possible. Once the telephone numbers are randomly generated, it is important to interview someone at that number even if it requires several calls.

Because the Hill-Thomas polls were done so quickly, however, there was little time to call back numbers that yielded an answering machine, a busy signal or someone who could not be bothered at the time. Further skewing any randomness, most of the polls were done on Friday, Saturday or Sunday nights, when a nonrandom group of people can be found at home. The fact that Anita Hill testified during working hours, while Clarence Thomas testified in television prime time, may also have tweaked early opinion.

Nevertheless, the media were awash with the wisdom of the polls. "Thomas Won with the People," declared Everett Carll Ladd, executive director of the Roper Center for Public Opinion Research. "Thomas Support Big, Poll Finds," reported the *Fort Worth Star-Telegram*, citing a *New York Times*/CBS poll with a sample of 501 people. "More Americans Believe Thomas Than Accuser, Poll Indicates," reported the *Washington Post*, whose poll was based on a sample of about 500 people, some 100 of whom could not decide whether he should be confirmed or not even after the hearings. Pollers who were challenged on the speed and anemia of their polls had a ready retort: All the other speedy and anemic polls showed the same thing.

Peter Miller, an associate professor at Northwestern University, pointed out that all five major pollers in Britain predicted a Labour victory in the country's 1992 general election, and all five were wrong. " 'If polls agree, they are all right' is, to me, wrong," Miller said. "Sometimes they are all wrong."

In offices, living rooms, locker rooms and factories, meanwhile, the debate over Anita Hill and Clarence Thomas raged with a personal fury rarely seen in modern political debate. Three-quarters of the 1,264 people surveyed by the *Los Angeles Times* said they had followed the proceedings at least "fairly" closely—40 percent had followed it "very" closely. Newspapers, magazines, radio and television surrendered their columns and airwaves to the debate. Women sounded mad, men defensive, older people confused. But even if people had actually worked out a complex and sophisticated opinion to the problem, they were told to reduce it to baby talk—yes, no or don't know. Despite that, the polls were perceived as more real than what people could see around them. "The turmoil over the allegations of sexual harassment lodged against Judge Clarence Thomas left the nation less divided than the angry rhetoric of recent days would suggest," began one newspaper story about a new poll.

That, said Professor Ginsberg of Cornell, is typical. Whenever poll results differ from other sources of public opinion, the polls are almost always presumed to be correct. Contradiction by polls, he continued, tends to reduce the weight and credibility of other sources of public opinion, which can actually help governments resist the pressure of constituent opinion.

Elmo Roper once wrote that polls "overestimate the amount of information the average citizen has, and underestimate his intelligence." This was certainly true of the Clarence Thomas polls, especially the ones taken early in the confirmation process when most people knew little about him except that he was black and conservative. For overestimating the average citizen's information, take this question from one of *USA Today*'s Anita Hill–Clarence Thomas polls: "How effective do you think Thomas will be as a Supreme Court justice compared with Thurgood Marshall?" Another poll asked, "How good a job will Thomas do at ensuring equal rights for minorities?" A month after Thomas was nominated, 55 percent of respondents in one poll had no opinion of him. Even if they did, who but an omniscient deity could know the answers to such questions?

A little more than a year after the Hill-Thomas hearings, a group of anthropologists from Wayne State University in Detroit presented some findings at the American Anthropological Association about interviews they had done at the time of the controversy. Their sample was tiny, local and not randomly selected, and so their results must be judged only as interesting evidence, not valid statistics. But the interviewers found strong support for Anita Hill. They said they believed their results were different from other polls because they allowed their subjects to express detailed opinions and mixed reactions instead of forcing them to choose simply him or her.

Indeed, James Fishkin, a professor at the University of Texas, has advanced the notion of a new kind of poll that would try to mimic more closely how people form their opinions. Fishkin calls it a "deliberative opinion poll." "[V]olatile, nondeliberative attitudes (and non-attitudes) are reported to us in a stream of findings that purport to establish everything from the public's approval of politicians to its view of competing health care proposals," Fishkin wrote. His deliberative polls, he said, would model what the public would believe if it had more opportunity to consider the questions. For example, in presidential campaigns, Fishkin envisions a representative sample of the population meeting face-to-face with the candidates and subjecting them to extensive questioning. Their views would then be unrepresentative because they would have done something most people could not, Fishkin concedes. But their informed views could be taken as representing, in a sense, what the public would think if they all had a similar opportunity to question the candidates directly.

◆

ONLY A SMALL SLIVER OF the rickety foundation of modern polls is acknowledged by the statistical caveats contained in what some call the nerd box—"About the Poll." Although nerd boxes generally report the number of people interviewed, who interviewed them and when, and the so-called margin of sampling error, they do not begin to address all the problems inherent in any poll. "We [pollers] all know that the most serious sources of error in polls are the things we don't talk about and some we can't begin to estimate—non-response bias, sample design and weighting factors, interviewer bias and error, question wording, question order, screening techniques, etc.," wrote pollers Humphrey Taylor and David Krane.

Nerd Box!

Most Serious error

Margins of error are typically stated only for the full sample, with perhaps a caution that subgroups will have larger, but generally undisclosed, margins of error. But in the main story, the sample is cut into little pieces. Although the caveat box is supposed to inject a note of caution into the report, it actually does the reverse, giving the impression of a scientific seal of approval. At the same time, it shifts the burden of responsibility to the readers to judge whether the polls are valid or not. Whatever their conclusions, they will almost certainly be based on inadequate evidence.

Some researchers will not even state a margin of error because it falsely implies precision. The damage a poor sample can do to a poll may be several points, the poller Burns Roper told a congressional hearing considering polling regulation in 1972. But question error can do far greater damage. "Question error . . . can cause errors of ten, thirty or even more percentage points," he said. It would be impossible, for example, to calculate the magnitude of the question error behind a 1964 *Fact* magazine article, "1,189 Psychiatrists Say Goldwater Psychologically Unfit to Be President." The article was based on a "poll" of psychiatrists who were asked questions like "Can you offer any explanation for his public temper tantrums?" And this gem: "Do you believe that Goldwater is psychologically fit? No or yes?"

To show how much difference poor questions and a non-random sample can make, consider this question posed by Ross Perot. In a mail-in questionnaire published in *TV Guide*, the question was "Should the President have the Line Item Veto to eliminate waste?"; 97 percent said yes. The same question was later asked of a sample that was scientifically selected rather than self-selected, and 71 percent said yes. The question was rewritten in a more neutral way—"Should the President have the Line Item Veto, or not?"—and asked of a scientifically selected sample. This time only 57 percent said yes.

Some caveat boxes offer a hedge for all other variables in their polls, saying, as the *New York Times* does, "In addition to sampling error, the practical difficulties of conducting any survey of public opinion may introduce other sources of error into the poll." There are scores, perhaps hundreds, of such practical difficulties. One small example: Whites respond differently to white interviewers than to black ones. Although it is impossible to know if that affected the Anita Hill polls, with their delicate racial backdrop, it has certainly affected polling on political contests in which a black candidate ran against a white candidate, such as the 1989 races of Mayor David Dinkins of New York City and Governor Douglas Wilder of Virginia—both wrongly predicted as comfortable winners by pollers although both won by a hair. Similar effects may also be found in polls on homosexual rights. Many people want pollers to believe they have no prejudice, but they have no one to impress in the voting booth. Even if they are identified, sources of error like this cannot be quantified.

The Anita Hill pollers were especially interested in the opinions of women and blacks, two potentially powerful voting blocs whose judgment would be a powerful ingredient in the opinion brew. Most of the polls broke down the results for women and men, for blacks and whites, even for black men and white women. Yet because they started with such small samples, breaking the whole into subgroups meant working with quantities in statistical no-man's-land. In one poll about Thomas's nomination, taken before Anita Hill came forward, the entire sample of blacks was 79, so small the margin of error was at least 10 points either way. An ABC/*Washington Post* poll with only about 500 respondents of both sexes found that women believed Thomas over Hill by 49 percent to 41 percent, and stated its margin of error as 5 points. Assuming roughly half the respondents were women, the margin of error for that subset—about 250—is large enough that the truth could well be the reverse.

A few questions show the difficulties of designing a quick survey on a complicated issue without subtly, if unconsciously, shading it. Take this question, for example, from a *New York Times*/CBS News poll: "Some people say Anita Hill's charges should not be taken seriously because she did not make them years ago at the time she said the incidents happened." (So far, so good. That, indeed, was a popular argument against Anita Hill's case.) The question continues: "Other people say the charges should be taken seriously even though they were made for the first time just recently."

This is supposed to be the other side of the coin—the reason Anita Hill should be taken seriously. Instead, it simply restates the negative point—she took a long time to complain. But what would the results have been if the second part of the question had read, "Other people say the charges should be taken seriously because women sometimes have reasons to delay reporting such behavior"?

Here is another one from a *New York Times*/CBS News poll that is slightly off-center. "In the long run, do you think something good will have been accomplished from all the testimony in these hearings, or do you think the hearings were just an embarrassing spectacle that will result in nothing good?" "Embarrassing spectacle" is a colorful piece of negative language; what is its counterpart on the "something good" side of the equation? How about "Do you think these hearings were a useful lesson on sexual harassment from which something good will come . . . ?"

◆

IT IS UPON JUST THESE tiny pinheads the angels of public opinion must dance. That is partly because, although people have been thinking about public opinion for centuries, there is still no agreement about what it is and how to measure it. Despite thousands of books and articles on the subject, modern thinkers are little closer to defining it than Socrates, who believed it to be more obscure than knowledge but clearer than ignorance. A few centuries later, in Europe, the idea that the public had an opinion worth considering, if not obeying, could be found in Shakespeare—"Opinion, that did help me to the crown" *(Henry IV)*—and Machiavelli—"It is not, therefore, necessary for a prince to have all the desirable qualities . . . but it is very necessary to seem to have them." Even so, most monarchs and aristocrats seldom measured public opinion until it boiled over into riot or insurrection.

In America, democracy changed that, as the relationship between citizens and their government changed from adversarial to proprietary. Safety and power came from many people believing the same thing. Empirical knowledge would guide the masses to the obvious solution. In societies of equality, wrote Tocqueville, "men have no faith in one another, by reason of their common resemblance; but this very resemblance gives them almost unbounded confidence in the judgment of the public."

To guide the young American democracy, new systems of measurement were needed. These included "authentic facts," as they were first called, or "statisticks," a term that appeared in an American dictionary for the first time in 1803. Early statistics were mainly used to show progress and growth in geography, population and a few economic activi-

ties. "Statistics signaled America's rising power and glory.
. . . [The statisticians'] choice of statistic facts was informed
by a quantitative notion of achievement: more people, more
trade, more daily newspapers, more gallons of lamp oil. No
opinionated comment was necessary because the choice of
facts already carried the assumption that *more* meant *better*."

Pre-election polling for publication first began during the
1824 contest between Andrew Jackson and John Quincy
Adams, but polls didn't become widespread until the end of
the nineteenth century, when newspapers across the country
began publishing local or regional straw polls. The early straw
polls were geared to publicity more than science: Someone
would take a box to a crowded place—a train station or street
corner—and collect as many ballots as possible. Other straw
polls used coupons that were clipped from newspapers, or
direct mail.

Presidential preference polling finally pushed the small
and fragmented public opinion industry into the modern age
during the 1930s and '40s, when three giants, George Gallup,
Elmo Roper and Archibald Crossley, dominated the field.
Most pollers started in market research, an older discipline,
and then began dabbling in politics—but only at the top level.
Their sponsors were almost exclusively newspapers and magazines; political candidates had neither the money nor the
faith to commission their own polls.

In 1935, George Gallup, America's most famous poller,
founded his American Institute of Public Opinion and began
writing a syndicated column called, grandiosely, "America
Speaks." Gallup boasted some new "scientific" theories of
drawing samples based partly on the way farmers in his na-
tive Iowa tested their crops. And he publicly predicted that
the juggernaut of the polling world—the *Literary Digest* magazine—was headed for a fall.

Literary Digest, a newsweekly, had history on its side:
It had correctly predicted the past three presidential elections. But hubris worked against it. While Gallup was refining
his methods for finding thousands who could speak for millions, the *Literary Digest* was resting on its outmoded laurels.

For its 1936 poll, the magazine confidently sent mail
ballots to some 10 million people, mainly owners of cars and

telephones. These were likely to be members of the middle and upper classes, among whom feeling against Franklin Roosevelt was running high. The *Digest* predicted an overwhelming victory for Republican Alfred Landon. In an arrogant letter to the *New York Times* in September 1936, the *Literary Digest*'s editor, Wilfred J. Funk, derided George Gallup's "so-called 'scientific' poll" as "unseasoned." "That [the *Literary Digest* polls] are a true reflector, a comparison of *Digest* poll returns with official returns in the past will prove," he wrote.

When Franklin Roosevelt won in a landslide, it became clear how fatal was the *Literary Digest*'s underrepresentation of the poor and working classes. The low response rate to the poll—fewer than 25 percent of the ballots were returned— also probably contributed to the disaster. The widely ridiculed *Digest*, which had been struggling before this calamity, declared bankruptcy shortly after. Gallup, who, incidentally, had underestimated Roosevelt's popular vote by more than seven percentage points, prospered.

The pollers learned much about sampling technique from the *Digest* debacle, but they tripped again in the presidential election of 1948, when the three leading pollers— Gallup, Roper and Crossley—all predicted a landslide for Republican Thomas E. Dewey. The pollers mistakenly believed people's minds had been made up weeks before they voted. They were also still using the now discredited system of "quota sampling" to find their responders—interview 500 housewives, 25 farmers, 300 elderly, 100 factory workers. Unfortunately, that system had worked in the two previous elections, giving pollers an unwarranted confidence in it. But the interviewers, typically middle class, tended to approach people like themselves, undermining whatever science there was in the technique.

The 1948 polling debacle led to calls for a congressional investigation and regulation of the industry and jokes about this new pseudoscience called polling. "Everybody believes in public opinion polls," joshed the radio comic Goodman Ace. "Everybody from the man on the street all the way up to President Thomas E. Dewey."

The 1948 election also raised the specter of whether

polls might actually influence the outcome of an election. Burns Roper, whose father, Elmo, started the Roper Organization in 1936, believes the 1948 polls "lulled the Republican supporters into a false sense of confidence and scared the bejesus out of organized labor." The result, he said, is that while the Democrats voted, the Republicans went golfing. Ever since, pollers have been debating whether there are either bandwagon or underdog effects. Results of studies on these effects have been largely inconclusive, and in any case the two may neutralize each other.

The government has taken several stabs at regulating the polling industry, but has largely failed. In 1943, a bill was proposed in the U.S. Senate that would have required pollers to disclose the size of their samples and to preserve their records for two years, but nothing came of it. In 1968, Congressman Lucien Nedzi introduced a truth-in-polling bill under which pollers would have to file details about their polls with the Library of Congress. That, too, went nowhere, but the persistent Nedzi kept reintroducing it and finally got it before a committee.

The hearings brought out the divergent opinions of pollers and politicians but resulted, again, in no legislation. Most pollers opposed any government regulation of their industry, arguing that their methodology amounted to trade secrets and that in any case there was no agreement about proper methodology, so nothing would be gained by revealing it. Also working against the bill: The politicians who would vote on it had won their elections. The ones who had been injured by polls were less likely to be in office.

◆

WHILE THE NUMBER OF PEOPLE willing to participate in polls has been dropping, that has more to do with not wanting to be bothered than with admitting that they don't have opinions. Researchers sometimes wonder what nonrandom characteristic is shared by people who have the time and inclination to tell a stranger their opinions. Polls assume that people will have—even should have—opinions on issues of the day. The sociologist David Riesman had a class theory

about why people share their opinions—knowledgeable or not
—with strangers. Upper- and upper-middle-class people,
Riesman believed, have a "stock of opinions like a well-
furnished wine cellar," but the opinions are more social ac-
couterments than deeply held feelings.

In the lower middle class, many people don't feel they
are consulted about things enough, and they do not want to
be seen as ignoramuses. They also might think it rude—un-
American even—to turn away an interviewer whose job it is
to collect opinions.

In the lower class, there is fear that the interviewer represents the authorities. But if the interviewer establishes rap-
port, the floodgates may open. In few other parts of poor
people's lives are they talked to as respectfully as by an interviewer. So although they may feel powerless in shaping the
world—so powerless they have never voted—they may give
an opinion about it.

Riesman also explored Americans' transition from "con-
science directed" to "other directed," a change with enormous implications for polls and surveys, which feed on
people's obsession with the opinions of others. Riesman believed that like commercial research, the point of polling isn't
to find out what people might want in the ideal world but to
offer them a monopolistically limited range of alternatives.
Pollers ask the questions that have been selected by the buyers of poll data—newspapers, political candidates, govern-
mental agencies, businesses—rather than what may be most
troubling the public. In 1970, for example, there were some
forty major episodes of racial violence in America. Yet only
two of the national Gallup Poll's 162 questions asked about
race relations.

Lately, the trend in poll questioning has been away from
broad and abstract inquiries and toward the narrow and self-
interested. Benjamin R. Barber contrasts these two questions:

Do you want a drug rehabilitation center in your neighborhood?

Do you think that the community needs drug rehabilitation centers, and if so, would you accept one in your neigh-

borhood if you were persuaded that the policy process by which the locations were chosen was participatory and fair?

"Pollsters assume that people can only answer questions of private preference," Barber wrote. ". . . If people are constantly asked to evaluate public policies in terms of their prejudices, they unlearn the arts of civic judgment." Barber suggested calling public opinion polls "private prejudice polls" and prefacing questions with this: "As a private person incapable of public judgment and unwilling to think about the common needs of your fellow citizens, do your undeliberated impulses and private biases make you think it would be in your interest to . . . ?"

Nor can polls measure how intensely respondents feel about the issues, leaching the passion from public debates. Intensity is both subjective and relative; it is even harder to pin down than the opinion itself. Some polls make a stab at assessing intensity—Do you strongly believe that?—but five degrees of intensity is about the limit. Pollers joke about intensity measures—in the "jogger approach" you ask a question and then run away, recording an answer only if the respondent feels strongly enough to run after you. But to Professor Ginsberg of Cornell, the question of intensity is not funny. "The beliefs of those who care relatively little or even hardly at all are as likely to be publicized as the opinions of those who care a great deal. . . ." President Nixon used polls against those who truly had opinions, declaring that a "silent majority" supported him even while the streets teemed with angry demonstrators. If there is any natural or spontaneous form of mass political expression, said Ginsberg, it is the riot.

Producing results regardless of how little respondents care or know about a topic has been endemic to polling since it began. In December 1938, George Gallup produced a poll on the House Committee on Un-American Activities, also known as the Dies Committee, which had been established to investigate "subversive" activities in the U.S. The poll found that 39 percent of the sample had never heard of the committee; of the remaining 61 percent, 22 percent had no opinion on whether the committee should continue its work. Of those who had an opinion, 26 percent wanted it abandoned. So of

100 original responders, 64 either did not like or were non-committal about the committee or had never heard of it.

"Dies Investigation Favored in Survey," said the *New York Times* headline. "Institute of Public Opinion Finds 74% in Favor of Continuing Inquiry." As Lindsay Rogers wrote, a more accurate headline would have been "Public Ignorant of or Indifferent to Dies Investigation. Institute of Public Opinion Finds 36% in Favor; 12% Opposed; 52% Don't Know or Don't Care."

(Rogers, a political scientist and author of a critical book about polling, was the person who coined the term "pollster"; it was intended—pejoratively—to mimic the word "huckster.")

Although polls sometimes capture people's ignorance of a subject, an increasingly popular kind of poll deliberately sets out to prove just how ignorant they are. How ignorant are Americans about the economy? Plenty ignorant, the National Council on Economic Education wants you to know (so you will support the council's cause—economic education). By their very nature these polls prove little, but declaring a "right" answer may exacerbate that. When asked the basic purpose of profits in the market economy, a sizable number of people said it was to "transfer income to the wealthy." The council's pollers counted that answer as wrong. The right answer was to "lead businesses to produce what consumers want." A Los Angeles poll turned up evidence of people's ignorance of the true nature of depression: Almost 50 percent polled described it as "sadness, unhappiness, blue." This was considered evidence of a "lack of understanding" about depression. Depression is, according to the poll's sponsors, the Mental Health Association of Los Angeles County, much more than that.

◆

PRESIDENTS SINCE LYNDON JOHNSON (WHO used to carry his positive poll results around in his pocket) have become expert in poll-spinning, releasing only positive results, leaking results to friendly reporters, inviting pollers into their inner circles and finding out when a poll would be taken, then creating some news. Louis Harris provided the Kennedy, Johnson and Nixon White Houses with prepublication reports of his surveys and offered to discuss them with the presidents. George Bush was the polling president. Early in his term, Bush had planned a trip abroad; when polls told him Americans were worried about domestic affairs, he canceled it. Bush even made the poller Robert Teeter his 1992 reelection campaign chairman. Ross Perot asked his supporters to poll themselves on whether he should re-enter the 1992 presidential campaign; his supporters overwhelmingly thought he should.

The White House switchboard, computers and mailroom —and those of other elected officials—are polltakers of the old-fashioned kind, calculating the popularity of decisions based on calls and letters. As public information, their polls are worthless, unless the results contradict the politician's public position, which seldom happens. After ordering the mining of North Vietnamese ports in May 1972, Richard Nixon reported that calls to the White House were coming in five to one in favor. Here's how it worked: Callers who told the White House operator they were in favor had their vote registered instantaneously; those opposed were put on hold for as long as twenty minutes while someone was found to "record their opinion." Many opponents gave up.

In political campaigns or debates, public opinion polling exaggerates the horse-race factor: Who is ahead? Who is winning? "Score One for Clarence Thomas," shouted one newspaper headline. On the last night of the Republican Party's 1992 convention, a *New York Times*/CBS News poll showed that Bill Clinton's 17-point lead had been reduced to 3 points. The *Times* acknowledged but understated the problem with the poll, saying, "Polls like this one, conducted immediately after a dramatic event, can be fleeting." As Irving Crespi, a veteran poller, said dryly, "Ask someone at an advertising agency about a consumer's intent to buy when they're watching a commercial for the product."

Today the horse race does not stop when a president is elected. It simply becomes an approval rating, an increasingly frequent report card of presidential performance. In Harry Truman's first four years as president, his performance was rated fifteen times. In Bill Clinton's first *four months* as president, he was rated more than thirty-six times; he got his first approval rating a little more than a week after he took office. Thirty-two percent of the people questioned by Gallup for *Newsweek* magazine—plus or minus four percentage points—disapproved of what Clinton had accomplished in his first *nine days* as president.

Horse-race questions are not only simplistic, they are very sensitive to question order. If the preference question comes first—For whom are you going to vote for president? —the poll will elicit one set of responses. But if a series of questions about the condition of the country is asked first and then the preference question, there will probably be a set of different responses. The questions about the state of the country may have brought to mind positive feelings—"Country's doing just fine!"—in which case the incumbent has the edge. Or it may have brought negative feelings—"Country's going to hell"—which usually helps the challenger.

Every horse race has a winner, and although pollers repeatedly warn people their numbers are not crystal balls, they cannot help bragging when their polls come close to the results of the election. Naturally, most of the big polls done just before the election are reasonably accurate: The pollers invest heavily in the final polls, and use sample sizes double or more the size of the early polls. Furthermore, if the poll is done just a few days before the vote, opinion has little time to flip unless there is a major news event.

Because so many people doubt the validity of public opinion polls, politicians can exploit that cynicism when it suits their purposes. Both Bush and Perot believed the polls when the polls pleased them and ridiculed them when they did not. Bush, the polling president, denounced the polls as "nutty" and, demonstrating his ignorance of statistical sampling techniques, tried to prove how unreliable polls were by asking if anyone in the (often bused-in) crowd had ever been polled. In the final weeks of the campaign, Gallup suddenly changed how it filtered respondents for voting intentions and came up with the closest poll of the season—only a 1- to 2-point lead for Clinton. Meanwhile, four other polls were showing the gap to be between 6 and 11 points. Bush suddenly didn't think at least one poll was nutty.

Ross Perot lived and died by the polls, first thriving on people's willingness to support his candidacy even if they did not know much about him, and then dropping out when his poll numbers started to fall in the wake of some gaffes—calling the audience at an NAACP convention "you people," for example. Clinton, by contrast, publicly scorned the polls. "I didn't trust the polls when I had a big lead, and I don't trust them now," he said after Bush's bounce in the polls following the Republican convention.

◆

MODERN TECHNOLOGY HAS PROVEN to be both an enormous boon and a terrible drag on the quality of polls. Now that pollers can do fast polls on anything and get them published almost regardless of their quality, they do. They can make money or attract new customers with call-in or mail-in polls. They can try new interactive polling systems that blur the line between scientific polling and entertainment polling. Polling has become a gimmick, a vaudeville act that undermines whatever integrity remains in measuring public opinion.

In their quest for viewer involvement, television shows also do call-in polls. Call-in polls about anything, whether 800 (free to the caller) or 900 (the caller pays), are worthless. People who pick up the phone and call a number to register their opinion are not random. The *Today* show did one on who shot John F. Kennedy that Bryant Gumbel described as "a totally random survey—it is totally unscientific." *Saturday Night Live* treated call-in polls the way they should be: The show conducted a poll on whether Larry the Lobster should be cooked. In 1980, ABC let viewers choose (for fifty cents a call) whether Jimmy Carter or Ronald Reagan had won a presidential debate. Both Reagan and Carter campaign workers quickly started calling. So many of the Carter forces tried to call from the Atlanta area that they swamped the long-distance lines. Reagan's callers encountered no such trouble and handily won the "poll." When ABC's pollers did their scientific survey, they found a very different outcome. But Reagan's supporters had already proclaimed their candidate's victory.

Perhaps the most infamous call-in poll in recent years was that done by CBS News after President Bush's 1992 State of the Union address. The poll aroused the ire of many in the polling industry, and provoked some uneasy reflection about where their business was headed.

CBS had created a two-headed device to measure public opinion the night of January 28, when Bush addressed a restless nation in the grip of recession. A call-in poll would provide some completely unscientific information while grabbing viewers with the new fad of interactive television; meanwhile, the network's more sober polling unit would conduct a scientific poll of a supposedly nationally representative sample.

There were problems from the start. The network wanted to announce the results of the scientific poll at the same time as the call-in, which meant the scientific one would have to be done in a matter of minutes. Using an earlier poll, the network prepared 2,800 people who had been randomly selected to call CBS on their Touch-Tone phones as soon as Bush was finished speaking. (If they didn't have a Touch-Tone phone, CBS sent them one.) In fact, only 1,241 navigated the technological shoals between them and CBS, a response rate of only 43 percent.

Over on the call-in side, some 24.5 million calls were attempted, as speed-dialers surfed the buttons. Only about 315,000 calls were tallied—an almost laughable rate of less than 2 percent, tilted toward people with fast phones. Furthermore, the questions—such as Are you better or worse off than four years ago or the same?—were preceded on the air by poignant vignettes about problems like unemployment.

On camera, enthusiasm for the polls exceeded their value. An excited Dan Rather said, "We've got a series of questions for you and the means to get your answers . . . right on to the air within seconds. We've never been able to do that before. Nobody else has ever tried it." As Rather, Connie Chung and Charles Kuralt reported the results of the call-in and the real polls, they sometimes lumped them together or compared the call-in with previous scientific polls. Although Rather threw in an occasional caveat, the overall impression was that the call-in and the poll were simply two halves of a whole called public opinion.

In fact, neither was public opinion. The scientific poll was too small, and its responders were different from the general public because they had said they would watch the speech and then call CBS. And to the extent that Americans had an opinion one way or another about the State of the Union address, they probably could not formulate it seconds after the speech was over.

The call-in was no more than a body count of people with high-tech telephones who were aroused enough to stay with it for several minutes. If there was any value in the call-in, it was to give these people an illusion that someone cared about their opinions and perhaps to keep them tuned to CBS.

An even more dramatic illustration of the differences between call-in and scientific polls occurred during a *Nightline* segment when viewers could call a 900 number and, for fifty cents a call, opine on whether the United Nations headquarters should remain in the U.S. Sixty-seven percent of the 186,000 callers wanted the U.N. out. A scientific poll, reported on the same program and based on slightly more than 500 respondents, found that 72 percent wanted the U.N. to remain *in* the U.S.

So-called tracking polls have also become popular. In these, a small sample of perhaps 250 or 500 is polled every day, and the results of two or more days are aggregated to form a moving average. As Robert Worcester pointed out, this allows the media to publish a "new" poll every day, while paying for one every couple of days. While it may be a good gimmick for the media, the opinions are basically always out of date, since the interviews have on average been done two days earlier. A moving average also artificially blunts the real spikiness of public opinion.

A few organizations also experimented with real-time polling, in which people registered their opinions simultaneously with the event they were reacting to—or, in polling parlance, "Continuous On-Line Audience Response." Cable TV's CNN, in conjunction with Gallup, had 480 people punching their minute-by-minute opinions into their Touch-Tone phones as they watched the first and last presidential debates. During the second debate, a group of people at Virginia Commonwealth University recorded their reactions on a box that had a knob and seven settings. Their second-by-second opinions were plotted on a graph, which was superimposed on the television image of the debate, creating a fever line as each candidate spoke.

Defenders of this kind of teledemocracy say it's a welcome break from pundits, the man on the street and spin doctors. Traditionally, as one said, citizens have been "little more than passive recipients of a story line woven by media and campaign experts who never bother to consult them." With real-time polls, no one has to guess what citizens think; they can tell us themselves.

To Albert Gollin, a longtime observer and critic of the public opinion industry, real-time polls are the high-tech equivalent of a reporter sticking a microphone in a stranger's face and saying, "How ya feeling?" "They're mood barometers," he said. "And the task of remembering what to do if you like something or not muffles the emotion. It would take Adolf Hitler appearing on the screen skewering babies to register a minus nine."

Worse, critics wonder whether such polls encourage politicians to market their positions to the latest sentiment, encouraging "oversimplification of complex issues or timidity when forthright moral leadership is needed." They were troubled by the fact that some of the sharpest reactions to the presidential debates came when the candidates resorted to political demagoguery, such as when Bush said, "For thirty-eight years one party has controlled the House of Representatives, and the result—a sorry little post office that can't do anything right and a bank that has more overdrafts than all the Chase Bank and Citibank put together." Instant reactions may also exacerbate the tendency of Americans to mistake majority for truth.

Public opinion polls have also been devalued by the plethora of silly promotional stunts that call themselves polls. As an Emmetsburg, Iowa, radio station names the presidential candidates, listeners are supposed to flush their toilets for their favorite; over at the local sewage treatment plant, the water level is measured to see how many flushes the candidate's name provoked. In the Texas Frijole Poll, customers drop pinto beans into their favorite candidate's jar. In New Hampshire, Dunkin' Donuts customers voted for their favorite candidates by choosing doughnuts. If they bought the Chocolate Frosted, they were supporting Bill Clinton; George Bush was represented by the Glazed Honey Dipped.

Despite their looniness, a few of these indicators enjoy a string of successes, which makes their operators believe they are better than the experts. That's because if sixty-four people flip coins six times, one of them will probably get heads six straight times—and one will probably get all tails. Going into the 1992 presidential election, the *Weekly Reader*, a children's magazine, had correctly predicted every presidential election since 1956. Alas, the '92 ballots—mailed in, just like the *Literary Digest*'s—chose Bush the clear winner. "My publisher wants a report by next week on what happened, and how we can set this thing back on track for 1996," the editor in chief told the *Wall Street Journal*.

◆

IF THE WILL OF THE majority could be ascertained at all times, wrote James Bryce, a late-nineteenth-century British statesman, the democratic ideal would be realized. Voting would be rendered unnecessary. But modern polls do more than record opinions and beliefs. In the case of the Anita Hill–Clarence Thomas hearings, the polls provided a crutch for senators who should have been using their heads and hearts. In political campaigns, polls tell candidates which parts of their strategy appeal to voters, so that regardless of what candidates might really feel about something, they can adjust their positions for maximum popularity. And what good do election polls do for the average voter?

"Isn't it reasonable to suppose that giving the voters accurate information about each other . . . might help, not hurt?" wrote the journalist and author Philip Meyer. Meyer gives an example of how knowing what other people were thinking might enhance a person's vote. Suppose a politically moderate voter is considering the three candidates for president in 1980: Jimmy Carter, Ronald Reagan and moderate Republican John Anderson. The voter might actually prefer Jimmy Carter but hears he is going to lose; instead he or she votes for Anderson to protest the right-wing dominance of the Republican Party.

Meyer believes in the "rational-voter" theory, in which polls are just one more piece of information people use to make a reasoned decision. But without reams of data, which can be very difficult, if not impossible, to get, most people do not have the tools or training to judge poll questions or sampling and interviewing techniques. That is information for which they must trust pollers and the media.

Clarence Thomas thanked the American people for their support. If the polls had revealed a doubting public, he might not have become a justice of the United States Supreme Court. Perhaps the senators should have heeded Harry Truman's feelings about polls before they cast their votes: "I wonder how far Moses would have gone if he'd taken a poll in Egypt," Truman wrote in a memo to himself. "What would Jesus Christ have preached if he'd taken a poll in Israel? . . . It isn't polls or public opinion of the moment that counts. It's right and wrong."

Polls—small, hurried and crude—may have tipped the balance on one of the most important political judgments of our time.

CHAPTER FIVE

False Truth

and the Future

of the World

◆

Out of the air, a voice without a face
Proved by statistics that some cause was just
In tones as dry and level as the place.

—W. H. AUDEN

PUBLIC POLICY

Common sense, common knowledge and the gospels of environmentalism held that disposable diapers were bad for the earth. Yet a study, published to great fanfare in the spring of 1990, found that disposable diapers were actually no worse for the environment than reusable cotton ones.

This was good news for many parents. Cotton diapers may have been ecologically correct, but they were also less efficient and less convenient. Some who bought disposable diapers were guilt-ridden, embarrassed to be seen toting a 26-pack around the neighborhood. Now research exonerated them of a crime against nature. They could love the earth *and* throw away a dozen plastic-and-chemical-gel diapers a day.

The study's sponsor? Procter & Gamble, one of the biggest buyers of research in the United States and, of course, the country's largest maker of disposable diapers. The company controls about half the $3.5-billion-a-year U.S. market with its Pampers and Luvs brands. For several years, it had been fighting a public relations battle against environmentalists and the cloth diaper industry. Although the disposable diaper industry, born in the 1960s, was thriving, the Earth Day mentality had made inroads. Between 1988 and 1990, customers for cloth diapers almost doubled. Even more ominous for the disposable makers, more than a dozen state legislatures were considering various bans, taxes and warning labels on disposable diapers.

A few studies later, the campaign against disposables was all but dead. Researchers paid by the disposable diaper industry had produced a new, improved truth about disposable diapers. Disposables, symbol of the throwaway society, were environmentally correct. In fact, they would no longer even be called disposable; henceforth they would be known as "single-use." The media disseminated the studies' contrarian findings widely. "People Claiming Cloth Diapers Are Clearly Superior May Be All Wet," said the *Louisville* (Kentucky) *Courier-Journal*. "Grass Isn't Greener on Green Side, Environmentally Conscious Choices May Be Doing More Harm," said the *Cincinnati Enquirer*. In statehouses around the country, diaper legislation withered away. By early 1992,

DISPOSABLE → SINGLE USE (!)

Gerber Products, the largest supplier of cloth diapers in the country, said it would close three cloth-weaving operations and lay off 900 workers. "In the past year," Alfred A. Piergallini, Gerber's chairman and chief executive, said at the time, "there was a dramatic change in the cloth diaper market caused by reduced environmental concerns about disposable diapers."

Procter & Gamble's diaper study was a landmark example of the public policy study, a form of research that increasingly shapes people's beliefs and decisions on social, political, economic and environmental questions. Political debates of the 1980s and 1990s on issues from homelessness to garbage to the spotted owl have been driven by research. The industry that generates this research has developed an unspoken but almost inviolable rule: Its numbers will anoint the ideology of whoever commissioned the research. The sponsor is rarely surprised or betrayed.

Studies done for public policy debates rank second only to research done for advertising in their disdain for objectivity and fact. While in other arenas researchers would be embarrassed to admit their study was partisan, in public policy they are not. "Who says it has to be neutral?" challenged an aide to U.S. Representative Fortney H. Stark about a distorted cable television questionnaire his office had sent out. Commenting on the same study, the aide later said, "We're proud that it was biased. Our viewpoint is that cable TV should be re-regulated."

The researchers themselves are not evil. They are devoted to their profession, and they genuinely seek to improve its methods. Yet they have let their ethical habits slip to a level more often seen among lobbyists and public relations executives. A Washington economist, who asked not to be named because his former employer is still a member of the House of Representatives, described two studies he did on a hydroelectric dam project planned for the home district. "My boss says, 'Write me the best justification for this project that you can.' So I did this cost-benefit analysis that made the project look like a gold mine. About a month later, he calls me in and says, 'Give me the most objective, independent, comprehensive analysis of this project you can.' I came back to him and said, 'This project is a dog.' He knew how to use me and that's fine. Researchers are for hire."

Exaggeration, hyperbole, creative projections, wild assumptions and hand-waving are the building blocks of public policy research, where people fight for the ear of the people and the good of the world. Anything goes. Most public policy wars are fought on huge plains, where people are counted in the millions, economic impacts in the billions and the very survival of mankind and the earth may be at stake—the very places it is most tempting to justify means with ends. Public policy studies are seldom challenged by either the press or public because they address mammoth and complex questions about which most people have little if any personal experience or knowledge. Nor has the press, by and large, learned to accord research studies the routine skepticism that reporters bring to more obviously self-serving news releases.

The creative manipulation of public policy studies crosses all political, gender, racial, religious and age lines. Whatever your beliefs and politics, your team does it. Organizations from Procter & Gamble, the country's largest advertiser, to the smallest and poorest social action groups sponsor advocacy research. No result is too absurd or self-evident to be peddled to the press.

◆ "Rental Housing for Poor Still a Problem, Study Says," announced a newspaper headline about a study sponsored by two nonprofit advocacy groups for the poor.

◆ "Americans Want to Live to 100 Years, Survey Says; Fear Nursing Homes, Losing Independence," reported the nonprofit Alliance for Aging Research, which advocates more investment in scientific research about aging.

◆ "Life on Streets Dangerous for Homeless Youth," concluded a study sponsored by the Chicago Coalition for the Homeless.

Public interest groups are masters of the tactical study. Their motives for their creative numbers are less commercial than industry's, but they can be just as self-centered. Public interest groups thrive on attention from the press because that is how they recruit new members. While business may understate hazards, public interest groups tend to exaggerate them. "Each group convinces itself that its worthy goals justify oversimplification to an 'ignorant' public," wrote Daniel E. Koshland, Jr.

Among life-and-death issues, researchers are not quite so fastidious about creating perfectly neutral questions for their surveys. A mail survey for the environmental guerrilla group Greenpeace asked people's attitudes on several issues. Among the leading questions was this: "Depletion of Earth's protective ozone layer leads to skin cancers and numerous other health and environmental problems. Do you support Greenpeace's demand that DuPont, the world's largest producer of ozone-destroying chemicals, stop making unneeded ozone-destroying chemicals immediately?" *loaded*

But from industry: "Do you favor setting up an additional Consumer Protection Agency over all the others, or do you favor doing what is necessary to make the agencies we now have more effective in protecting the consumer's interests?" asked a survey commissioned by the Business Roundtable, which was opposing the creation of a federal consumer protection agency. Seventy-five percent of those surveyed said they opposed creating such an agency. The survey was released during the height of congressional debate on the subject. *leading*

And from a Connecticut representative to Congress, a body that has become addicted to questionnaires: Would you support universal health care if it would mean the loss of thousands of jobs, particularly in Connecticut?

Legislators know most studies prepared for policy debates are sponsored by a self-interested industry or lobby. What they may not realize is that such research nevertheless influences the course of events. Occasionally a piece of research has a decisive influence on the outcome of the debate —Procter & Gamble's diaper study, for example. But more often, contradictory studies simply paralyze the decision-making process, shelving the resolution of immediate problems. "Someone will produce a study that statistically demonstrates X or Y," said Ray Sentes, a Canadian political science professor who has studied the effects of asbestos on human health. "So the workers have to rush out and get an epidemiologist to do a study for them. And so it goes. For ten years we flash studies at each other. If the practical outcome of a scientific study ends up being delay of any activity, shouldn't the scientist say, 'You don't need this study'?" For issues like the health effects of asbestos, Sentes noted, it would take several studies of thousands of people over dozens of years to come up with meaningful results. "They don't have the time or the money or the data," he said. "So they do these slash-and-burn studies that get plonked into the middle of the public policy process."

Strategic research has dominated modern debates over abortion, gun control, family leave, recycling, school choice and the speed limit, just to name a few. Each issue has its dueling polls. The timber industry has its polls showing most people wouldn't sacrifice a single job to protect an endangered species; and nature groups have their poll showing that most people support the Endangered Species Act. Proponents of school choice have surveys showing that people want it, and opponents have their surveys showing people do not. Gun control activists have surveys showing that many people want increased regulation of guns; the National Rifle Association has surveys showing the opposite.

The battle over abortion rights has produced hundreds of surveys showing contrary results. In June 1991, the abortion warriors—Planned Parenthood and the National Right to Life Committee—each produced survey results showing people's opinions of a recent Supreme Court ruling that the government could prohibit the discussion of abortion in family planning clinics that received federal funding. Planned Parenthood's survey asked this question: "Do you favor or oppose that Supreme Court decision preventing clinic doctors and medical personnel from discussing abortion . . .?" Sixty-five percent said they opposed the ruling.

The other survey first asked people if they favored or opposed the Supreme Court ruling. The survey described the ruling as "the federal government is not required to use taxpayer funds for family planning programs to perform, counsel or refer for abortion as a method of family planning." The Supreme Court, of course, had said no such thing: the question was whether the government should be permitted, not required, to finance family planning programs where abortion was discussed. No one was talking about abortion as a method of family planning. And the Supreme Court was ruling on whether such clinics could discuss, not perform, abortions. Even so, only 48 percent said they favored the court's decision. Then the survey asked, "If you knew that any government funds not used for family-planning programs that provide abortion will be given to other family-planning programs that provide contraception and other preventive methods of family-planning, would you then favor or oppose the Supreme Court's ruling?" Here the group got the mandate it was seeking, the one they pitched to the press: 69 percent said they favored the decision. In hearings before the House of Representatives, which was considering an amendment that would prevent the regulation from being enforced, the National Right to Life poll was cited. The amendment was defeated.

Since bigger numbers almost always mean bigger allocations or more attention, most of the numbers flying around policy debates exaggerate on the high side. The National Association for Perinatal Addiction Research and Education says as many as 375,000 babies who may have been affected by drugs are born every year; that is, 375,000 babies whose mothers ingested either alcohol or a drug at one point in their pregnancy. In the late 1970s, the American Cancer Society predicted that cancer would claim the lives of at least 8.5 million Americans in the 1980s. In fact, between 1980 and 1990, 4.5 million Americans died of cancer. And while it costs only $3,205 to provide disposable cups, forks, plates, etc., for one school for one year, it costs a staggering $12,413 for reusable material—or so argued a Tennessee school district fighting the mandated use of reusable materials. The disposable figure included the price of buying the materials, the labor of handling them and their waste disposal; the figure for reusables included the cost of the materials, the labor to wash them, the cost of the washing equipment and the water. It not did compare the cost of making the reusables and disposables, nor did it take into account environmental costs. Furthermore, if it is so economical to use disposables, why have they not replaced glass, china and stainless steel in every home in America?

"Even if congressmen discount for biases in the material they are given," wrote James Payne, "this does not solve the problem. When you cut a 50-fold exaggeration in half, you are still left believing a 25-fold exaggeration."

The size of the homeless population has been the subject of several studies whose estimates range from 230,000 to 3 million. Homeless advocates have estimated 2 million to 3 million people have been homeless at some time during the previous year. (On any particular night, advocates say, the number of homeless may be closer to half a million to one million.) The advocates' number was derived from estimating the percentage of the population that was homeless—1 percent—and building in a huge margin of error. Martha Burt of the Urban Institute said that the last time 1 percent of the population was homeless was in the heart of the Depression. "Nineteen thirty-three is what 1 percent homeless looks like," she said.

In 1984, the Department of Housing and Urban Development estimated there were between 250,000 and 300,000 homeless. That figure was developed from sixty local experts estimating how many homeless they had in their cities. Their answers were added together and then projected to the nation. In 1987, the Urban Institute estimated 500,000 to 600,000 homeless. That number was derived from sampling homeless shelters and soup kitchens in cities with populations of more than 100,000 and then doing elaborate weightings and adjustments.

In March 1990, the Census Bureau sent 15,000 census takers out one night—S night, it was called, for streets and shelters—to count the homeless. They found 230,000. Homeless advocates quickly disputed the figure, saying that with a few exceptions the census takers did not go to any city with a population of less than 50,000; they did not count any homeless people they saw in alleyways or streets; and they, like other homeless researchers, had no way of counting the people sleeping on the couch or floor of someone's house who might be looking for shelter the following night. Research built on shelter data is inherently skewed because a huge part of the homeless population—single people who are highly impaired and chronically homeless—tend not to use shelters.

In November 1993, another count of the homeless in two big cities—New York and Philadelphia—was released. This study counted the homeless using computer records of Social Security numbers at city shelters. The study found that 3.3 percent of New York's population had stayed in a shelter sometime over the past five years. The stay could be as short as one day. Should one one-day stay sometime in the past five years define a person as homeless?

It is not possible to count the homeless population precisely; they are transient, wary of authority and sometimes mentally ill or addicted to drugs. Sadly, the issue of counting the homeless long ago overwhelmed the moral debate on what to do about people living in the street, as though without agreeing on the numbers there could be no agreement that homelessness is a problem. A decade after the plight of the homeless appeared on the national agenda, there is still a sizable homeless population. Statistical formulas do not solve our problems any faster or better, and they cannot eliminate politics, as the political scientist Kenneth Prewitt points out. They simply push politics back one step, to disputes about methods: "Arguments about numerical quotas, availability pools and demographic imbalance become a substitute for democratic discussion of the principles of equity and justice."

In public policy debates and deliberations, words like decency, right and wrong, peace, fairness, trust and hope have lost their force. Numbers, which can offer so much illumination and guidance if used professionally and ethically, have become the tools of advocacy. Even if their cause is worthy, people who massage data undermine the power and purity of statistics that may be crucial to future decisions. There are numbers we will never know, and we should admit it. It is essential to understand the homeless before making policy about them. But in this case, as in so many others in public policy, understanding is not the same as counting.

◆

THE COMPLEXITY OF THE RESEARCH done for modern public policy research is overwhelming. Until the 1950s, social science research—in economics, sociology, anthropology—was generally done in the field, where people would directly observe other people. In recent years, that kind of research has been overwhelmed by computer models, and social, economic and political decisions are now more likely to be based on elaborate projections and assumptions than empirical evidence. Computer models can tackle bigger problems faster, but they can also be easily finagled. There are so many large numbers, and an almost infinite number of interlocking variables, that the slightest changes in either can cause tremendous repercussions. In *The Triumph of Politics*, David Stockman wrote of debates among President Reagan's economic advisors on what numbers to plug into an economic model to make the economy come out looking right. The forecasters represented different schools of economic thought—monetarists, supply siders—which guided their assumptions. "The forecasting sessions, which formerly had been crucibles of intellectual and ideological formulations, degenerated into sheer numbers manipulation," Stockman wrote. "The supply siders yielded a tenth of a percentage point toward lower real growth; the monetarists yielded a tenth of a percentage point toward higher money GNP. The supply siders yielded another tenth; the monetarists yielded another tenth. Round after round it went.

" 'We've got to get Murray his inflation back,' I exhorted them, which shows I had truly gone haywire." ("Nobody," Murray Weidenbaum of the Council of Economic Advisors had said, "is going to predict a two percent inflation rate on *my* watch. We'll be the laughingstock of the world.")

Yet more and more policy research depends on computer models, which offer a definitive look into the inherently unknowable future. These snapshots of possible outcomes can be useful information when society weighs finite resources against a multitude of problems; the fact that a tool can be misused does not make it a useless tool. But the intricacies of human decision-making often cannot be reduced to mathematical formulas, and the more complex the decision-making, the less accurate the model will generally be. Furthermore, the models are notoriously friendly to their sponsors' interests. A computer model found that if airlines could not hire replacement workers during a strike, fares would rise so high that only the rich could fly, and some airlines would go bankrupt; the study was prepared for the Air Transport Association, an industry group. A computer model showed that if advertising was taxed in Minnesota, the industry as well as the state's entire economy would be damaged; the study was sponsored by the Communications Industry Coalition, an industry group. And it was a computer model that found that a cut in the capital gains tax would create 750,000 new jobs and decrease the federal budget deficit by $61 billion over ten years. The study was released by the office of Senator Robert Kasten, Republican of Wisconsin, a strong supporter of a capital gains tax cut.

Computers now even figure the value of a human life not just in dollars but in *tax* dollars. The late Aaron Wildavsky, a political theorist at the University of California at Berkeley, theorized that any regulation can maim or kill by slowing economic growth, thus depressing the standard of living and the health of the population. For every $1.9 million to $7.5 million in regulatory costs (in the form of taxes), economists have estimated, one person will die.

A study by the National Center for Policy Analysis, a Dallas public policy research institute, found that forcing office buildings to keep their air clean may be one of these regulatory killers. Despite some missing links, the institute's study tries to follow the complicated chain between regulation costs and death. "Although we do not fully understand the causal mechanism, studies . . . conclude that higher incomes lead to longer life expectancies and vice versa," the institute's study said. For example, in the United States there is a strong negative relationship between income and automobile accidents, the study says, and poverty is one of the most important correlates of cancer. (The poor also smoke more than the affluent, and get worse health care—two problems whose solutions would save many more lives than that of indoor air.) The study looks at mortality rates of different income groups, estimates what the indoor air regulations will cost in taxes, and predicts how much that additional tax will push people into lower-income, higher-mortality categories. So, the study concluded: "With $10 billion in regulatory costs, a male earning close to the minimum wage would have an increased probability of dying that is 10 times the increase for a male earning $33,000 and 218 times the increase for one earning $66,000."

Tactical research done for policy debates is not necessarily wrong; but it is very difficult to know whether a particular piece of research is right or wrong. An assumption here, a variable there—it is simple to manage data without stepping outside ethical or professional boundaries. And since studies like the ones done for the diaper debate are complex webs of British thermal units, waste water effluents and pounds of atmospheric emissions, it is very difficult for the average person to read them critically. It is foolish, even dishonest, to make a decision based upon any one study. Lifecycle analysis, which dominated the diaper debate, is not only a malleable science, it is a primitive one, lacking rigor, precision and, for the most part, critical scrutiny.

Four studies largely controlled the diaper debate of the late 1980s. One was Procter & Gamble's 1990 analysis of the environmental impacts of disposable and cloth diapers, produced by the consulting firm of Arthur D. Little Inc. and smoothly delivered into the hands of state legislators and the media.

The others were:

◆ A 1988 study appraising disposable diapers as garbage, sponsored by the cloth diaper industry. This study had been very effective ammunition for opponents of disposables until Procter & Gamble's study neutralized it.

◆ A 1990 study sponsored by the diaper arm of the American Paper Institute and produced by a research company called Franklin Associates, which showed—again—that disposables and reusables were, environmentally speaking, equivalent.

◆ A 1991 study, sponsored by the cloth diaper industry, assessing the total environmental impact of cloth and disposable diapers. It found cloth diapers environmentally superior.

Three of these studies were variations of lifecycle analysis, a computer model that calculates the "cradle-to-grave" effects on the environment of making, using and disposing of a product. (Franklin's study had all the hallmarks of lifecycle analysis, but the firm called it a "resource and environmental profile analysis"; Little called its study "Health, Environmental and Economic Comparisons.") Lifecycle analysis began in the 1960s as an internal tool to measure the efficiency of companies' manufacturing processes, and even today most such studies are proprietary and confidential. But in recent years, the marketing potential of these studies—proving a product's environmental friendliness—has been widely exploited. Unfortunately, there is no standard method for conducting analyses like these, no certifying agency and rarely any peer review except that solicited by the research firm itself. No one but the researcher says when the cradle starts or when the grave ends. "Spin controllers' favorite joystick," wrote one reporter about this kind of research.

Ideally, lifecycle analysis would give us information useful for making intelligent choices about the products we use. It is helpful to know that while fluorescent light bulbs require less power and so contribute less to pollution, they also contain toxic mercury; even so, their environmental advantage is widely believed to outweigh that drawback. But in most cases, it is an apples and oranges problem: How much carbon monoxide equals a gallon of dirty water? How do you balance the manufacture of sodium silicate (for cloth diapers) against the manufacture of sodium hydroxide (for disposables)?

Like all computer modelers, lifecycle researchers have wide latitude in making assumptions about things that are essentially unknown facts. Whatever their motives, researchers' assumptions will necessarily guide the research in some direction. In the case of diapers, the important question of how many diapers babies use a day or week will heavily influence the outcome. Obviously, the more diapers babies use—of either kind—the worse for the environment. The two studies commissioned by the disposable diaper industry assumed that each cloth diaper change required not one but 1.9 or 1.79 diapers (some parents do double up cloth diapers for greater efficiency). The cloth diaper study assumed 1.72 cloth diapers per change. Another question that required assumptions based on few hard statistics: How long does a cloth diaper last? The disposable diaper studies assumed 90 and 92.5 uses per life. The cloth diaper study assumed 167 uses per life.

Cost or

or Benefit?

There are also differences in the way the same activity may be accounted for. One disposable study counted co-generation, the burning of manufacturing wastes for energy, as a benefit; the cloth diaper study did not, because co-generation has other environmental impacts, including air pollution. The studies sponsored by the disposable industry projected the effects of composting or recycling some paper diapers; in fact, there are very few composting facilities operating in the United States today, and the prospects for more are dim. The Arthur D. Little study found that the labor (at six dollars an hour) of throwing dirty diapers in the washing machine is a significant cost, ignoring the fact that washing clothes is a cost of daily life that every member of the household pays. Does it therefore make environmental and economic sense for everyone's clothes to be disposable?

But those questions are easy compared with other assumptions that can be built into these analyses. How do you depreciate the washing machine used to clean cloth diapers when it is also being used for other household laundry? What value do you put on the water that fed the cotton for the cloth diapers or the trees for the disposable ones? How do you account for the pesticides used in cotton fields? The Franklin study even included the energy impact of exporting cotton to China, where many cloth diapers are made.

The answer to any of these questions is whatever number a researcher can defend.

Carl Lehrburger, then a developer of recycling programs for an Albany, New York, waste management firm, performed the lifecycle analysis of cloth and disposable diapers commissioned by the cloth diaper industry. Lehrburger, thoughtful and forthright on the subject of industry-sponsored research, said that while he stood behind his study's conclusions, sponsored research is inherently subjective. "You can't have an industry study done by that industry be 100 percent objective," he said. "There are too many judgment calls, too many meetings between the sponsor and the organization doing the study. So it's more or less objective." There are undoubtedly lifecycle analyses that show a sponsor's product in a poor light, he said, but since most of this research is proprietary, those studies simply will not be released.

There is no one single truth about diapers, Lehrburger said, because people and diapers are still evolving. Disposable diapers, for example, are much thinner and lighter than a decade ago. The truth about diapers is "three-dimensional," Lehrburger continued, because it involves not only scientific processes and calculations but also consumers. "A city in California with strict water rationing might have a different truth than a city in the Northeast with a solid waste crisis," he said.

Nevertheless, industries and companies that have sponsored lifecycle analyses and liked the outcome have used them in national advertising and marketing. This practice attracted the attention of a group of nine state attorneys general, an informal consortium of environmental watchdogs. In 1990, the group met with businesses, consumer groups and government officials to produce a set of guidelines, called the "Green Report," on appropriate environmental claims for marketing and advertising. The following year, in its second report, the task force concluded that although product life assessments, as they called lifecycle analyses, may someday be useful for assessing environmental effects, there was still no consensus on the methodology. "Moreover, the few product life assessments that have been conducted by the business community have come out in favor of the manufacturer who paid for the assessment and against that manufacturer's 'target' competitor," the report said.

Lifecycle analysis was "one of the most unfortunate types of studies ever introduced into public debates," said Elizabeth Collaton, director of the solid waste project at the Environmental Action Foundation, an environmental advocacy group. "The political and scientific reality doesn't offer either side very defensible data. There are things that can never be quantified, like the social value of a clean lake. And then there are things that lifecycle analyses don't look at, like the effects on the economy of jobs created by smaller, decentralized operations versus national conglomerates." Furthermore, lifecycle analyses are expensive to produce (comprehensive ones can run in the tens of thousands of dollars) and market, so "he with the deep pocket wins," said Ann Beaudry, a consultant to the National Association of Diaper Services.

Procter & Gamble acknowledged that its search for environmental truth about diapers was a response to competitive forces. "There was a political and competitive battle going on with cloth diapers," said Scott Stewart, a Procter & Gamble spokesman. "The Lehrburger report [released in late 1988] came to the conclusion that cloth is best, and disposables are killing the earth. We found it not in our interest to be directly critical of the Lehrburger report but to go beyond them and say, 'Let's try to get some people with a track record in lifecycle analysis to take a look at this.'. . . Now we've inventoried our environmental effects, and there are some pros and some cons. As Paul Harvey would say, 'We're not doing nothing about it.' "

◆

NOT DOING NOTHING ABOUT IT is becoming a common reason for commissioning research about public policy issues. If there is trouble, it is better for insiders with a stake in the outcome to investigate than a skeptical outsider. So when a public outcry about inaccurate information coming from credit bureaus broke out in 1991, the national trade association for the credit bureau industry announced that it would fund a study to determine the impact of bad credit information on consumers. (The study found that a minuscule two-tenths of 1 percent of all consumers who had been denied credit should have received it; consumer groups use the figure 20 percent to 30 percent.) Similarly, the accusation that using cellular telephones might cause brain cancer—and the subsequent plunge in cellular phone stock—prompted the cellular phone industry to announce that it would spend more than a million dollars commissioning new research on the safety of cellular phones. Five months later, the industry announced that initial studies on the subject "do not suggest a linkage" between cellular phones and cancer.

But far more common is the study done to prompt action, to raise voters' or legislators' awareness of a problem that deserves the nation's attention. Amassing data to advance a social agenda—"moral statistics"—dates back to the early nineteenth century in the United States, when moral reform was associated with scientific knowledge. In 1816, the Philadelphia Society for Alleviating the Miseries of Public Prisons prepared a statistical report on the country's prisons. For the most part it was presented simply as objective numerical evidence; the facts showing a growing prison population would surely speak for themselves. At around the same time, temperance groups jumped into the statistical stew. Based on extremely primitive methodology, the temperance movement asserted that half of all sin was caused by intemperance. Poverty and religious groups quickly embraced the new tool of persuasion by statistics. "It is hard to say whether reformism led to statistics or statistics to reform," wrote Paul Starr.

Despite the growing amounts and sophistication of data, it was not until the twentieth century that science surpassed deeply held beliefs about right and wrong as the primary determinant of most public policy—faith in intelligence. The new scientific optimists believed that policy arguments would come out of the darkness of received doctrine and prejudice into the light of scientifically produced fact. The policy rationalist believes that "if the risks are 'acceptable,' and the benefits are greater than 'costs,' what person can argue that . . . the proposed policy is 'wrong,' 'immoral,' 'unjust' and 'a waste of time and effort'? These arguments are 'unscientific' and 'value-laden' with the citizen's personal, irrational prejudice."

By the late twentieth century, *statistics*—in the sense of facts about the state, numerical or not—had become not only a requirement for policy jockeys of whatever stripe but also the only sure way to put a cause on the national political agenda. "To be measured is to be politically noticed, and to be noticed is to have a claim on the nation's resources," wrote Kenneth Prewitt. The physically handicapped in New York initially resisted being counted, for fear of stigmatization, but they reversed their position when they realized that statistical visibility brought political visibility. Similarly, when a new survey in 1993 showed America's homosexual population to be only 1 percent, compared with the Kinsey-generated figure of 10 percent, homosexual rights organizations denounced the lower number as inaccurate.

Because of a decline in some kinds of government regulation, retrenched federal budgets and the Paperwork Reduction Act, the government itself produces fewer statistics now than it did in earlier decades. At the Bureau of Labor Statistics, for example, "we eliminated quite a number of series," said Janet Norwood, formerly the bureau's commissioner. That creates a vacuum private interests are happy to fill. "The private sector is expanding its production of data," she said. "Some of the data collected by the private sector is very good, but some of it is very poor. Unfortunately, the data of poor quality isn't usually so labeled."

In public policy, even more than elsewhere in research, it is critical to disguise one's partisan views behind the apparent objectivity of an "independent" researcher. Academics, especially those from well-known universities, are best because they also bring prestige. Ed Starr, an economist with the Small Business Administration, describes the game: " 'I'll see your UCLA and raise you two MITs.' 'Yeah, well I'll see your MITs and raise you a Chicago and a Harvard.' Public policy research is a canceling-out kind of phenomenon."

Whatever their affiliation, academics can be susceptible to sponsors' pressures. Without any words being spoken, academic researchers know what outcome would most likely result in another research contract. "A funder will never come to an academic and say, 'I want you to produce finding X and here's a million dollars to do it,' " said Paul Light, of the Hubert Humphrey Institute at the University of Minnesota. "But it's a subtle influence. It looks like if you produce finding X, you might have another study in your future. And once you're on that treadmill, it's hard to get off." That the understanding is implicit is one of the most dangerous aspects of sponsored research. "It's not the client dictating the results, it's the researcher self-censoring, unconsciously finagling the results to please the client, to get a grant renewed," said the historian and author David Noble. "It's institutionalized, which makes it all the more difficult to monitor."

Co-opting experts without their knowing they have been co-opted is important, wrote the authors Bruce Owen and Ronald Braeutigam in *The Regulation Game*. Hiring researchers as consultants or giving them research grants "requires a modicum of finesse; it must not be too blatant, for the experts themselves must not recognize that they have lost their objectivity and freedom of action."

Hundreds of private firms also do research for hire. Whatever their predilections—or financing—researchers often affix adjectives like "independent" and "nonprofit" to their neutral names. The Health Effects Institute/Asbestos Research, which describes itself as a private nonprofit Cambridge-based research organization, is partly funded by the federal government and the rest by real estate developers and other industry groups with a financial stake in the outcome of the institute's research. The nonprofit Epilepsy Institute received generous funding from the makers of three epilepsy drugs.

"When someone says Arthur D. Little, I think *Procter & Gamble*," said Ann Beaudry, the cloth diaper industry consultant. "Other people think *Cambridge-based, independent think tank*."

◆

MOST POLICY DEBATES NOW FEATURE two or more sets of numbers, so now multiple studies are often required from each side before a victor emerges. In addition to its lifecycle analyses, the paper diaper industry also commissioned other research projects proving subsets of the disposables-are-better argument. A study in large part funded by Procter & Gamble found that cloth diapers may increase the risk of diarrhea outbreaks in day-care centers, which neatly countered environmentalist pressure on state legislatures to allow cloth diapers there. (The study found significantly fewer fecal coliform bacteria on the toy balls, changing pads and chairs in rooms where disposable diapers were used than in rooms where cloth with plastic overpants were used.) Critics of the study say more important variables are how often the caretakers change the infants and how often they wash their hands.

The American Paper Institute's diaper group commissioned the Gallup Organization to survey mothers with children age three and under and found they would be unhappy if paper diapers were taxed or banned. Here is one question from the study: "It is estimated that disposable diapers account for less than 2 percent of the trash in today's landfills. In contrast, beverage containers, third-class mail and yard waste are estimated to account for about 21 percent of the trash in landfills. Given this, in your opinion, would it be fair to tax or ban disposable diapers?" This produced predictable results: 73 percent said it would not be fair to tax diapers, and 84 percent said it would not be fair to ban them.

The same question could be rephrased and it would certainly produce a different outcome: "Disposable diapers, a single product used by a small fraction of the population at any one time, are estimated to account for about 2 percent of the trash in today's landfills. Two percent translates into about 18 billion dirty diapers a year—a mound of material that didn't exist a few decades ago, is used for a few hours and will not degrade for centuries to come. Given this, in your opinion, would it be fair to tax or ban disposable diapers?"

The move to regulate disposable diapers began in Nebraska, where the corn growers' association had succeeded in pushing through the legislature a bill requiring all disposable diapers to be biodegradable. (A key ingredient in biodegradable plastic is corn starch.) Maine passed a bill concerning diapers, and Wisconsin considered, but defeated, a bill to tax disposables. But the most important legislation was that considered by California's legislature in 1990. That bill included several pieces, but its most controversial provision was a requirement that packages of disposable diapers carry a warning about the environmental problems associated with disposables. Lobbyists for Procter & Gamble argued that with all the water and power used to wash cloth diapers and the gas guzzled by the diaper service delivery trucks, the two types of diapers were environmentally equal. The Senate agreed and gutted the bill, leaving only one small part intact.

Here, as elsewhere in public policy research, the study

served a function as important as persuasion—justifying a decision the politicians may have made for other reasons. "No one wants to say, 'I opposed this thing because I'm not interested in offending the disposable diaper industry,' " said Craig Reynolds, chief of staff for the state senator who introduced the diaper bill. "No, they say, 'I agree with you that the environment is important and I have this study showing that cloth diapers could increase pollution. I'm such a good friend of the environment, I just couldn't get myself to support this bill.' "

In September 1990, the one part of the California bill—requiring day-care centers to accept children wearing cloth diapers—that survived the legislature was vetoed by the governor. He, too, cited the Procter & Gamble–sponsored life-cycle analysis.

The final surrender in the war against disposables may have been that of Patricia Poore, editor of an environmental magazine called *Garbage*. In an article in the magazine, Poore conceded that she had stopped using cloth diapers on her own baby, and furthermore that research showed disposables were neither a major garbage problem nor a plague on the environment. Ironically, Poore blamed the cloth diaper industry for having brainwashed her into thinking that disposables were somehow ecologically deleterious. "I did not like the tactics of the anti–disposable diaper crowd," she wrote. "There is only one word for their methods: propaganda."

Meanwhile, Procter & Gamble, one of the biggest users of packaging in the U.S., was busily mining the marketing gold in environmental concern. In advertising both in the United States and abroad, Procter & Gamble exploited two themes: Studies showed their diapers were no worse for the environment than cloth, and the landfill problem would be taken care of as soon as the company figured out how to turn soiled diapers made of plastic, virgin paper and a chemical gel into a "rich soil conditioner." "Ninety days ago, this was a disposable diaper," read a Procter & Gamble ad picturing compost.

Governments here and abroad took exception to some of Procter & Gamble's assertions. In Britain, the Advertising Standards Authority, acting on a complaint by a women's

environmental group, concluded that Procter & Gamble's advertising mentioning its lifecycle analyses was misleading.
Procter & Gamble pulled it. In New York City, officials
charged that the composting ad was misleading because most
New Yorkers didn't have access to composting facilities.
Nine state attorneys general also challenged the compost ads,
and Procter & Gamble paid $50,000 in "investigation costs"
and agreed to modify future ads. The "Green Report" now
recommends that composting claims be well qualified and
that they include such material facts as people should not try
composting their dirty disposables in their backyard bins.

◆

MUCH OF THE NUMBER CRUNCHING for policy debates is not
fraud; it is more like well-meaning prophesizing. "It's that
scientists don't continually tell people you can't really use
this to predict the economy," said Jack Douglas, professor
emeritus of sociology at the University of California at San
Diego. "If they were really honest, they would say, this is just
a hypothetical model. But they allow it to pass as if it has a
reliable, practical application for society."

Risk assessments and cost-benefit analyses are two popular computer models that can provide valuable help in out-
lining in broad terms the arguments for and against a certain
course of action. Risk assessment, frequently used by industry or government to show how many lives will be saved or
lost because of a disease, regulation or substance, can prove
the ultimate value of some pesticides while showing that others should not be used at any cost. Risk assessment already
guides the spending of some $150 billion a year on health,
safety and environmental rules. Researchers use risk analysis
to calculate what are empirically incalculable odds. Using
risk analysis, astronomers seeking funding for a telescope
calculated the chance that the earth would be hit by asteroids
at two million to one.

It was risk assessment, too, along with cost-benefit analysis that resulted in the swine flu debacle of 1976. This case
illustrates how much we sometimes depend on computer
models to make momentous policy decisions that may affect

every citizen of the country. Furthermore, the case of the swine flu vaccine proves that many people do not understand how to use risk assessments to sort out acceptable from unacceptable risks.

The first signs of a new outbreak of the ferocious swine flu virus broke out in Fort Dix, New Jersey, in the early months of 1976. Since the last major swine flu outbreak, in 1918, had killed half a million Americans, government officials were understandably worried. They were immediately confronted by two unanswerable questions: Would 1976 be another 1918, and, if so, should every American be inoculated against the virus?

Expert opinion in this case consisted of many different kinds of experts guessing the answers to those questions. In several instances, experts estimated that the probability of a 1918 reprise was "greater than zero." All real-world events have a probability greater than zero; but even a 2 percent probability would still be 50-to-1 against. To policymakers, however, "greater than zero" represented an unacceptable risk.

There was risk, too, in inoculating the whole country because the swine flu vaccine had potentially dangerous side effects. Furthermore, there was the question of how much a flu epidemic would "cost" the country compared with what an inoculation program would "cost." Here, the projections and assumptions became so intricate that the terms "cost" and "benefit" were rendered almost meaningless. For example, noted Robert Formaini in *The Myth of Scientific Public Policy,* if everyone stayed healthy, the productivity of the massive health care sector of the economy would fall to zero. And to pick the kind of weird and abstract nit common in this research, would a mass health program that spared a future Hitler or Stalin ever show net benefits? Formaini wondered. But eventually a cost-benefit analysis would show that while the cost of inoculating every American would be about $135 million, the cost of not inoculating them would be almost $6 billion.

Armed with those dramatic numbers, scientists and policymakers convinced Congress and then-President Gerald Ford that it would be irresponsible not to initiate a mass inoculation program. Vaccination began in October 1976 and continued until December, when reality answered the two questions the experts had estimated. There would be no return of the 1918 flu epidemic, and the vaccine itself would kill more people than it saved.

◆

ALTHOUGH MOST PUBLIC POLICY STUDIES are ultimately aimed at decision-makers—the holders of the purse strings—they are far more powerful if they hook the media and public, too. That is why researchers and their sponsors spend so much time speaking at press conferences, issuing news releases and whispering in sympathetic reporters' ears. There are some topics so appealing to the media, however, that simply releasing a report on the subject guarantees publicity. One of those topics is children.

In the spring of 1991, the Food Research and Action Center, an advocacy group, issued a news release about a study of the eating habits of low-income families with young children. The release began with a shocking statistic: "Millions of kids are hungry in America."

That night, the CBS Evening News began this way: "A startling number of American children in danger of starving. Dan Rather reporting. Good evening. One out of eight American children under the age of twelve is going hungry tonight. That is the finding of a new two-year study." Stories about the study also appeared in the *New York Times*, the *Washington Post*, the *Boston Globe*, *Newsweek* and many other places.

The study had the worthy goal of ending childhood hunger. But it was deeply compromised not only by its methodology but by the way it was disseminated to the press and public. Eliminating hunger in children is such an obviously moral decision that it is sad to see it become a victim of a statistical war. But that is what happened.

There were several problems with the hunger study, ranging from small mathematical errors (62 percent white plus 34 percent black plus 19 percent Hispanic equals 115 percent) to questionable methodology.

◆ The survey was a composite of seven local studies,

which had been administered by seven different state or local advocacy groups, such as the Alabama Coalition Against Hunger and Michigan's Hunger Action Coalition. As advocates, they may not have been completely indifferent to the results.

◆ Sample sizes for each of the smaller studies were anemic—from 257 to 434—and even taken together the group was not statistically representative of the whole nation.

◆ The survey did not attempt to ascertain actual food intake but asked only subjective questions about hunger. A yes to only one of eight questions about hunger put a person in the category of "at risk" for hunger. One question was, "Did you ever rely on a limited number of foods to feed your children because you were running out of money to buy food for a meal?" Is this really hunger? A yes to five questions—another example: "Did you or adult members of your household ever cut the size of meals or skip meals because there was not enough money for food?"—classified the family as hungry.

Finally, the study was contradicted by the federal government's regular food consumption surveys, which measure actual food intake. That research suggests that many people with low incomes in America are more likely to be overweight than underweight, although that says little about the nutritional content of their food.

The media blew up the results still further. Dan Rather's opening, for example, misread the research in several ways. The study did not say starving; it said hungry. The study said one in eight was hungry at least once in the past year; Rather said one of eight was hungry tonight. And almost no one—*ABC Nightly News* being a notable exception—bothered to distinguish between hunger and what the report called chronic mild undernutrition.

Most of the study's financing came in the form of a grant from the Kraft General Foods Foundation—whose corporate parent is a major beneficiary of government food subsidies. The research did its advocacy job well. At least half a dozen members of Congress issued statements supporting the study. Leon E. Panetta, then a California representative, had earlier introduced legislation to increase funding for food stamps. "[Panetta's] efforts got a boost March 26, with the release of a FRAC study of childhood hunger that drew national attention," reported the *Congressional Quarterly*.

Within a few weeks, the study, called the "Community Childhood Hunger Identification Project," or CCHIP, received a second wave of publicity from people critical of its methodology. The backlash was led by the Heritage Foundation, whose own conservative agenda opposes giving taxpayers' money to the poor. The foundation issued a highly critical backgrounder and published a critical article in its magazine. Two researchers from Virginia Commonwealth University wrote a paper attacking it.

Whether or not the study was accurate was irrelevant to many of its supporters. When Richard Lesher, president of the U.S. Chamber of Commerce, wrote a newspaper column complaining that the "Great Washington Phony Fact Factory" had produced the hunger study, he was assailed by people saying the correctness of the data was less important than the study's worthy goals. "Whether the numbers are 1 out of 8 or 1 out of 16, childhood hunger is a long-term competitiveness problem for our country," wrote Kraft General Foods chairman to Lesher. Senator Robert Dole, hiding behind statistical ignorance, also took Lesher to task: "As I'm no statistician, I can't render an expert opinion on the validity of [the] study," Dole wrote. "I do know that we don't have a really good handle on the extent of hunger in America. . . ."

The project director of the CCHIP study acknowledged that it was not perfect. "In most of our policy debates, we don't have perfect information," said Cheryl Wehler, who does not consider her work advocacy. "That doesn't mean we throw it away. If we let every public policy issue go until we have perfect data, we won't be able to address these problems."

Wehler said the study was based on classic research methodology and was rigorously overseen by researchers from several academic institutions. The questionnaire went through two large pretests, where it was determined that the low-income subjects would be more likely to give information to interviewers like themselves. Response rates were high, she said, and editors reviewed every interview. But when the report is done, the researcher no longer controls it, she said.

"There are times when advocates take over and use data in ways I wish they wouldn't," Wehler continued. "If you don't have the money to do a nationwide survey, you have to do some projections. They don't always note that they're projections. I also have no control over the media. Dan Rather's statement was absolutely incorrect. We oversimplify information, and we partly do that to advocate our positions and partly to sell our newspapers."

◆

IT IS RARE THAT A public policy study contradicts the beliefs of its sponsor. Contradictory studies suggest data so compelling that the researcher is essentially forced to shoot him- or herself in the foot by displeasing whoever is paying the bills. The sponsor usually fights back, trying to neutralize the research by disavowing it. When a survey commissioned by an alcohol industry group found that most Americans do not believe the alcohol industry is responsible, honest or ethical, the president of the group said the survey reflected perceptions rather than reality and that the industry "is more credible than the public perceives it to be." In 1986, two (Republican) political appointees to the United States Department of Agriculture deleted several chapters of a study showing that a government supplemental food program seemed to be improving fetal health. The appointees then wrote their own summary of the findings showing far less conclusive results.

In the spring of 1991, the Women's Legal Defense Fund, a women's rights advocacy group, called a news conference to announce the results of another study on the economic impact of forcing employers to offer unpaid leave for illness or parenthood. The study had been sponsored by the Small Business Administration, which opposed mandated federal leave.

In the eight years since Congress began considering family-leave legislation, the subject had become a well-tilled field of research.

◆ A Chamber of Commerce report put the cost of family leave to business in the billions.

◆ A General Accounting Office study estimated it would cost employers $330 million to offer family leave.

◆ A 1990 study by the Institute for Women's Policy Research found that the *absence* of family-leave policies cost taxpayers $4.3 billion in welfare, food stamps and other support for people who had been fired rather than given leave.

◆ A 1991 Gallup survey, sponsored by the National Federation of Independent Businesses, a trade group opposing family-leave legislation, found that women of childbearing age might actually be hurt, not helped, by family-leave legislation.

◆ A 1993 study of state family-leave laws by the Families and Work Institute (family-leave supporters) found that 91 percent of employers found family leave was not hard to implement.

It was numbers stew. Each study bit off a different piece of the huge and complex picture. So, for example, while the early studies concentrated on the cost to business of mandated family leave, the Institute for Women's Policy Research turned the question upside down, calculating the cost to workers of *not* having family leave. "The research changed the frame of reference," said Heidi Hartmann, director of the institute. "The intellectual claim was more important than whether the figure was five dollars or ten dollars."

As Congress considered family leave in succeeding sessions, a steady stream of new, improved numbers flowed into their offices. "Each study added to the mass of facts and figures to gain support," said Donna Lenhoff, general counsel of the Women's Legal Defense Fund. "It was part of our strategy each Congress to have researchers look at new aspects of the cost-benefit analysis. We sent the studies to all the members of Congress and alerted those who were lobbying for the legislation to use the studies to say, 'Here's new information.' We sent the studies to editorial boards to give a hook for new editorials. Each study created a rash of those and built support."

(Despite increasing support in Congress, family leave fought a losing battle against the executive branch. George

Bush vetoed a family-leave bill in 1990, and among his final political misjudgments of 1992 was a second veto of a leave bill. A family-leave bill passed soon after Clinton's inauguration and was quickly signed into law.)

The Small Business Administration, a quasi-independent government agency representing small business owners, had long opposed mandated family leave, reflecting the feeling of the White House. The SBA argued that family leave would be a financial hardship for small businesses and that most businesses accommodated their employees anyway. In 1987, the SBA's office of advocacy, which monitors executive and legislative developments that might have an impact on small business, issued a request for proposals for a study on family and medical leaves. A panel of outside experts chose the proposal by Eileen Trzcinski of Cornell University and William Alpert of the University of Connecticut, who planned a national survey of businesses.

The two economists sent questionnaires to some 10,000 business owners asking whether they offered employees leaves and what benefits employees on leave continued to get. They also asked a question that, to the best of their knowledge, no one had asked before: If they had granted someone a leave, how did they cover for the missing employee and how much did it cost? Trzcinski and Alpert's 1,730 usable responses provided an answer their sponsor was not necessarily going to want to hear: It seemed to be cheaper to grant someone a leave than to fire and rehire.

Although the SBA can consign the research it commissions to the file drawer for a year (unless a Freedom of Information Act request is filed), the SBA publicly released the report. A week later, with SBA approval, Trzcinski appeared at a news conference arranged by the Women's Legal Defense Fund. A report of the conference went out on the Associated Press wire, and scores of newspapers and television and radio stations picked it up.

The report aroused so much attention that the SBA tried belatedly to discredit it. The SBA first suspended distribution of the study, citing technical errors and the absence of a research summary accompanying it. Then the SBA created and sent to Congress its own research summary, which contained some different interpretations of the report's findings. For example, while Trzcinski and Alpert had projected family leave's cost to employers to be about $600 million, an SBA extrapolation of the same survey data found the cost would actually be at least $1.2 billion.

But what, in the end, did it matter what yet another study found family leave would cost? "I think family and medical leave would be a good thing even if it cost $5 billion," said Trzcinski. "But some people might think it was worthwhile only if it wasn't too costly. I would prefer to talk about the ideology rather than the numbers and sort it out on that level. But to have those numbers gives your ideological position more legitimacy in a public policy debate."

◆

ALTHOUGH THERE WAS MUCH to argue with in Procter & Gamble's version of the truth about diapers, the company's research persuaded many policymakers and ordinary people. "It went from being one of the most obvious examples of a choice where one was clearly right and one was wrong to this completely muddled argument," said Jeffrey Tryens of the Center for Policy Alternatives. "The environmentalists got hammered for painting everything in black and white."

Procter & Gamble's "truth" also echoed loudly through the halls of the federal government. In the fall of 1990, the Environmental Protection Agency issued a booklet called the *Environmental Consumer's Handbook* advising people to use reusable products rather than disposable ones and, among other things, picturing a mother holding an infant wearing a cloth diaper. Among the recommendations was that "while disposable products for your baby may be necessary sometimes . . . consider using cotton or terry cloth diapers." Shortly after it was issued, the EPA withdrew its booklet, saying there were errors in it. Two years later, it issued a new version. It no longer pictured the infant wearing a cloth diaper, and the advice about cotton diapers had been deleted.

The Environmental Action Foundation filed a Freedom of Information Act request to get the memos and documents the EPA received in response to the booklet. Sure enough,

Procter & Gamble cited the Arthur D. Little study as a reason why cloth diapers were not necessarily superior to disposables.

Although the National Association of Diaper Services has contemplated another study, John Shiffert, its executive director, is discouraged by the prospect of an unbroken string of contradictory studies. "It has pretty much boiled down to what your guy says versus what my guy says," Shiffert said. Even so, Shiffert retains his belief in an objective reality.

"I'm sure it's possible to come up with the absolute truth," he said. "Whether anyone would believe you is another matter."

CHAPTER SIX

Drugs

and

Money

◆

*The only ethical principle which has
made science possible is that the truth
shall be told at all times.*

—C. P. SNOW

In the summer of 1986, two studies arrived in the offices of the *New England Journal of Medicine*, the biomedical community's most influential journal. Both concerned the effectiveness of an antibiotic called amoxicillin on middle-ear infections in children, and both papers were based on the same set of data. One found the drug effective; the other did not. The positive one was written by a doctor whose laboratory had over the past five years collected $1.6 million in research grants from pharmaceutical companies. The other was written by a bioengineer who had cut himself off from all pharmaceutical industry money.

Perhaps no case of biomedical research more starkly illustrates the dangerous ground that lies between researchers and the wealthy drug companies that pay them. It is rare —practically unheard of—in biomedical research for contradictory papers to emerge from the same data collected by co-investigators on a study. Dissent is supposed to be handled collegially and internally before the paper is published. That one of the researchers on this study was a purist, the other a pragmatist, guaranteed a long and bloody battle over the conflict of interest inherent in much biomedical research.

Six years earlier, Dr. Charles Bluestone had set up the Otitis Media Research Center at Children's Hospital in Pittsburgh. He named Erdem Cantekin, a young biomedical engineer with whom he had worked in Boston, research director of the center. Cantekin had earlier joined the Department of Otolaryngology at the University of Pittsburgh Medical School, and he was steadily promoted, from assistant professor to tenured full professor. Beginning in 1980, Cantekin and Bluestone began working together on a federally funded study of treatment options for otitis media, or middle-ear infection, a condition that costs America's parents more than $500 million a year. The center also began to do privately financed research on ear infections for drug companies.

In 1983, Cantekin approached his department chairman and told him that he was troubled by the ethics of mixing public and private financing in studies to determine the effectiveness of drugs. "I . . . informed him that I had grave doubts about the scientific validity of research commissioned and funded by pharmaceutical companies seeking to prove

BLUESTONE - drugs work
CANTEKIN - drugs don't work

the effectiveness of their products," Cantekin said. "He answered that I was free as a matter of personal choice to disassociate myself from industry-sponsored work, but that he could not require a primary investigator of the center to refuse industry funding." Cantekin decided not to participate any further in privately financed clinical trials. But he continued his work on the federal project.

*The federal study was a double-blind placebo-controlled randomized clinical trial to test the effectiveness of amoxicillin, an antibiotic, with or without decongestant/antihistamine, on persistent secretory otitis media in infants and children. There were to be 1,040 subjects enrolled. Halfway through the study—after 518 subjects—Bluestone stopped the project, claiming efficacy had been proven. He began it again with a slightly different protocol; instead of studying just the antibiotic amoxicillin, the center would study the effects of two other drugs, Ceclor and Pediazole, on ear infections. For that, Bluestone's laboratory would receive more than $160,000 in research funds from two pharmaceutical companies. Because of what he later described as an "oversight," Bluestone did not tell the government that he was now also receiving private funds for the federally funded study.

More $$: While Bluestone continued his research on antibiotics and ear infections for several years, he personally received more than $50,000 a year in honoraria from three pharmaceutical companies that make antibiotics—most of it in the form of speaking fees. The drug companies gave Bluestone another $25,000 a year in travel expenses.

By 1986, Cantekin and Bluestone had produced a set of data. But while Bluestone looked at these data and concluded that amoxicillin was effective, Cantekin looked at them and concluded that the drug was not. Both submitted their studies for publication. Dr. Arnold S. Relman, then editor in chief of the *New England Journal of Medicine*, told the University of Pittsburgh and the Children's Hospital that only one manuscript could be considered, since "there could be only one responsible investigator or team of investigators officially recognized by the sponsoring institutions." Which, Relman asked, was the official version? Both institutions said Bluestone's paper was the "authorized" version. The *New En-*

gland Journal returned Cantekin's paper without so much as a single peer review. Bluestone's paper was peer-reviewed and its positive results published in 1987. While the paper concluded that amoxicillin was twice as likely as a placebo to cure middle-ear infections, it also showed that only 30 percent of the patients on amoxicillin were successfully treated.

In June 1987, Cantekin submitted his paper to the *Journal of the American Medical Association*, which requested some revisions. Cantekin submitted them, and *JAMA* agreed to publish the paper. Before it could do so, however, Cantekin's department chair notified the journal that Cantekin had been charged with "breach of research integrity" and, ironically, acting with reckless disregard for the truth. The academic bureaucracy at the University of Pittsburgh, whose Otitis Media Research Center received more than $3.5 million in grants from pharmaceutical companies between 1983 and 1988, had begun what would become a long process of disciplining and demoting Cantekin. Because Cantekin was tenured, the university could not fire him. But he was removed as director of the research center, stripped of his academic responsibilities, and his office was forcibly moved from Children's Hospital to the attic of a Giant Eagle supermarket. His computer tape of the data from the study was taken away while he was on vacation.

Cantekin and Bluestone had two major differences, and many minor ones, in interpreting the data. The researchers wanted to use different instruments to assess fluid buildup in the ear. Bluestone chose to use otoscopic measurements, in which an observer looks into the ear through an instrument and assesses the amount of fluid. Cantekin argued that the more objective measure of tympanometry should be used. Tympanometry works like sonar, sending acoustic waves into the ear and recording the feedback. The Bluestone group argues that since the study was double-blinded, the subjectivity of the otoscope would not matter. Cantekin argues that he has statistical proof showing the otoscopic measurements were biased.

Cantekin and Bluestone also disagreed about what period of time to consider as the primary endpoint, when the researchers would conclude that the drug could be con-

sidered effective. The study tested the drug every four weeks
for three months, but Bluestone chose to concentrate on a
four-week endpoint. Cantekin argued that because ear infections so often recur, the endpoint should be eight weeks. And
finally there was the important question of hearing loss. Bluestone did not address it; Cantekin did.

In each case, Bluestone's choices had the effect of making the drug appear more effective. Using tympanometry, the
drug did not seem to be effective; using otoscopic measurements, it did. After eight weeks, there were as many cures in
the placebo group as in the drug group. And the drug had no
effect on hearing loss, the biggest threat of repeated ear infections.

The National Institutes of Health, which took a baf-
flingly tolerant stance toward Bluestone's double funding, reviewed fifty studies done by Bluestone with private financing.
Of the twenty-seven that could have been categorized as positive, negative or neutral, twelve were positive, ten were negative and five were neutral. On this basis, the NIH concluded
that there was no apparent conflict of interest, because the
numbers of positive and negative studies were roughly the
same. The NIH analysis did acknowledge that "in a few of
the marginally positive studies . . . there appeared to be a
tendency to be optimistic and recommend further testing." A
later NIH analysis of a small number of these studies found
that Bluestone and his colleagues tended not to evaluate the
"biological significance of their data," resulting in reports
that were "less than objective."

A report from the Office of Scientific Integrity, while
finding no actual wrongdoing on Bluestone's part, quibbled
with his methodology and his objectivity. "[T]he coincidence
of the large pharmaceutical company honoraria to Dr. Bluestone and the less than objective reporting of the efficacy of
pharmacological treatments present the appearance of conflict of interest," the OSI said.

Five years after Cantekin had first submitted his paper
for publication, it finally appeared in the *Journal of the American Medical Association*, accompanied by an editorial, "The
Cantekin Affair." In it, the writer Dr. Drummond Rennie
raised two questions with enormous implications for biomed-

ical research. Who owns the data produced by federally funded studies? And what outlets are there in science for whistle-blowers like Erdem Cantekin?

In March 1990, an international group of researchers published the results of a study of more than 3,600 children with ear infections; its findings were consistent with Cantekin's and directly contradicted Bluestone's. The study found that antibiotics were not effective for treatment, and that rates of recovery were *higher* for patients who did not receive antibiotics. Although this did not prove Cantekin's research correct, it certainly gave it weight. Had Cantekin's research been published earlier, doctors would have had the benefit of this point of view. As it is, more antibiotics are prescribed for children's ear infections—and for longer periods of time—in the United States than anywhere else.

Bluestone remains director of Pittsburgh's ear research center. Because of ongoing litigation, he would not comment on Cantekin's charges. Earlier Bluestone had told the *Washington Post*, "[The Otitis Media Research Center has] contracts with several drug companies. . . . So the proof that there is no conflict of interest is that we don't have an allegiance to any one pharmaceutical company."

Dr. Relman, editor in chief of the *New England Journal* when the two studies were submitted, defends his decision to publish Bluestone's paper and reject Cantekin's. "The journal can't act as policemen for all scientific research," he said. "We can't send a truth squad to Pittsburgh. That's not our business. The university said Cantekin is not being accurate with the facts. I don't know for a fact whether Cantekin is right or Bluestone is right. But these are not just different interpretations. If you read both papers carefully you would have to conclude that either Cantekin is a liar or the first guys are liars."

Cantekin himself is even more convinced that there should be few, if any, associations between academic researchers and private funding. "I did research for drug companies for many years," he said. "You try your best to be objective, but you know if you don't come out with the results the drug companies expected, there will be no more funding. Things which are actually equivocal are called unequivocal.

"The ultimate goal of the pharmaceutical industry is to make money," he continued. "The goal of medicine is curing people. One is self-interest, one is altruism. It's an intersection of two different social systems."

◆

WHILE MOST BIOMEDICAL RESEARCH MONEY comes from government and foundations, private companies' share has been growing. For all expenditures on research at colleges and universities—much of it biomedical—the federal government contributed $10.2 billion in 1991; industry's share was $1.2 billion. But while the federal contribution has doubled over the past ten years, industry's has quadrupled. A 1990 survey by the American Federation for Clinical Research found that 34 percent of its members received corporate research grants; the average grant was about $30,000 a year. (To some doctors, the number seems higher. "If everyone in medicine quit just because they took money from a pharmaceutical company, there wouldn't be anyone left," said one obstetrician and gynecologist.)

As commercial interests have insinuated themselves into biomedical research, the amount of information Americans get—and seem to want—about disease and its cures has increased dramatically. Newspapers and magazines feature regular health stories, which have also become standard features of television and radio shows. Twenty-five years ago, it was rare for a biomedical study to break out of the boundaries of the medical community; now such studies regularly command the attention of millions.

Doctors, whose first allegiance is supposed to be to their patients, have traditionally stood between the self-interested drug companies and trusting consumers. Today it is no longer so clear where doctors' allegiances lie. The $63-billion-a-year pharmaceutical industry holds a formidable purse, which it is willing to share with doctors who do drug research. Federal research funds have been squeezed as more researchers compete for lab support. Doctors and universities sign multi-million-dollar, multiyear contracts with pharmaceutical companies that will prosper if their products are found effective by university researchers. Until thousands of people have used a drug over several years, the industry's self-interested research is the only information consumers have about a drug. "Take a new drug when it first comes out, while it's still safe and effective," goes a medical industry joke.

Unless there is evidence of misconduct (the deliberate misrepresentation of something as fact by someone who knows it is not), it is very difficult to discover and virtually impossible to prove that a piece of biomedical research has been tainted by conflict of interest. No study is perfect, and problems can arise in the labs of even the most conscientious and honest researchers. Biology is enormously complicated anyway, and like all research, biomedical studies begin with choices. Although biomedical research incorporates rigorous scientific rules and is often critically scrutinized by peers, the information can nevertheless be warped—by ending a study because the results are disappointing; changing rules—the protocol or analytic tools—mid-study; not trying to publish negative results; publicizing preliminary results even with final and less positive results in hand; skimming over or even not acknowledging drawbacks; and, especially, casting the results in the best light or, as scientists say, buffing them.

"People who do drug research are good scientists," said Elizabeth Heitman, a medical ethicist at the University of Texas–Houston Health Science Center. "But there may be a tendency to want to keep your sponsor happy because of the possibility of future funding. It's not overt, but it's the kind of thing where you might be tempted to put a more glowing cast on a medium-successful outcome because if the results are good, you might be invited to go to a meeting in San Francisco next year to give a presentation."

Bias is a subtle and complicated influence, hard to detect in someone else, even harder in oneself. Good intentions do not eliminate bias, which is why science has developed methodologies to deal with it. Without those methods, and sometimes even with them, bias is a fact of life in research. Bias, wrote T. C. Chalmers, is the "unconscious distortion in the selection of patients, collection of data, determination of endpoints, and final analysis." It can happen at any point in the process, but most often occurs in the data collection.

In 1983, Chalmers did an experiment on bias in which he analyzed 145 clinical trials involving treatments for heart attacks. He divided the trials into three groups. One group consisted of trials that were highly controlled for bias, meaning they were both randomized (subjects were chosen randomly) and blinded (patients did not know which treatment they were getting). Another group was partly controlled for bias (it was randomized but not blinded). The third group was not controlled for bias; it was neither randomized nor blinded. Studies in the group with the most bias control proved a therapy to be effective only 9 percent of the time. Studies that were partly controlled for bias showed the therapy to be effective 24 percent of the time. And studies with no bias controls at all showed the therapy was effective 58 percent of the time.

An example of how bias can creep into research was a study, recalled by Roger Porter, of a new epilepsy drug. The study was not blinded. During the evaluation period, a patient had a seizure at home that was atypical and not witnessed by the investigator. The investigator had to decide whether to classify the attack as a seizure or not, giving him or her a way to influence the trial. By calling the event a nonseizure if the patient was on the new drug, or calling it a seizure if on the placebo, the study could be biased for the drug.

On any day of any month, the morning newspaper will carry a report of new medical results that may be plausible or interesting—and were sponsored by a company with a direct interest in the outcome. The news account may name the sponsor, or it may not. A selection of studies reported in the media:

◆ A new product called Ricelyte, used to treat infant dehydration caused by diarrhea, proved superior to an older drug for the same condition. Mead Johnson Nutritionals, which makes Ricelyte, gave financial support for the study.

◆ Bald men are three times likelier to have a heart attack than hairy-topped men, found a study sponsored by the Upjohn Company. Upjohn makes minoxidil, a hair growth agent that had been suspected of increasing risk of heart attack. By finding that baldness was associated with heart attacks, the study exonerated the sponsor's product.

◆ The drug AZT prolongs survival for minorities as well as whites, rebutting an earlier study that found differences in the two groups' responses to the drug, according to a study by Johns Hopkins University and the Maryland Department of Health. The study was funded by grants from the federal government and from the Burroughs Wellcome Company, the maker of AZT.

◆ A change in diet may not significantly reduce mildly elevated cholesterol levels, according to a study sponsored by Merck & Company. Merck makes lovostatin, a cholesterol-lowering drug.

◆ Prescription drug prices are falling, reported the Boston Consulting Group in March 1993, just weeks after the Clinton administration had criticized high drug prices. The study was sponsored by Pfizer Inc.

The consistency of research support for the sponsor's desired outcome intrigued Richard Davidson, a general internist and associate professor of medicine at the University of Florida. "It struck me that every time I read an article about a drug company study, it never found the company's drug inferior to what it was being compared to," Davidson says. He decided to test that impression by reviewing 107 published studies comparing a new drug against a traditional therapy. Davidson confirmed what he had suspected—studies of new drugs sponsored by drug companies were more likely to favor those drugs than studies supported by noncommercial entities. In not a single case was a drug or treatment manufactured by the sponsoring company found inferior to another company's product.

The Food and Drug Administration, which must approve a drug before it can be marketed in the United States, offers the best protection against tainted biomedical information. Pharmaceutical companies work closely with the FDA to design and report their studies, and the FDA demands rigorously conducted animal studies and clinical trials. The tremendous expense of marketing a new drug and the threat of liability suits also encourage drug companies to seek the truth about their drugs' efficacy and side effects. Yet even inside the companies, some bias is almost inevitable. Researchers may become too attached to a product, either because they may have "wasted" years on it or because it feels good to be on a winning team.

Tainted biomedical information has two disturbing consequences. It raises the cost of pharmaceuticals as drug makers prove to doctors and consumers that their new me-too drug is better than an older, cheaper brand. And because of the way it is presented, it warps our notion of how science works, portraying a tedious, disciplined and often disappointing search as an unbroken string of life-extending miracles.

Conflicts of interest in biomedical research are not simply a matter of direct financial ties between researchers and drug companies. Science has its share of ambitious professionals whose conflicts may be subtler than money. It is a coup to make a scientific discovery, and it is difficult for young scientists to "climb the standard ladders of academia" if their experiments "don't work." That also helps to explain why the bias is almost always in the direction of the new drug rather than the placebo. "All physicians who are conducting a clinical trial of a new drug (or other therapy) are hoping that the new drug will be effective, . . ." wrote Roger J. Porter. "Even worse, from the standpoint of study bias, everyone else associated with the trial also wants the new drug to work": the physicians, the nurses, the nurse's aides, the technicians, the patients, the patients' relatives. "Everyone wants . . . to be associated with the discovery of something new and useful for the alleviation of human disease."

Many doctor-researchers have developed elaborate rationales for accepting money from interested sources. They believe they are too clever, sophisticated and well trained to be swayed by financial inducements. They say pharmaceutical money allows them to do worthy research no one else would care to finance, research that might treat or even cure disease. They say the peer-review system insures that good science will survive, wherever the money came from, and bad science will not. A 1990 report by two American Medical Association councils explicitly permitted doctors to profit from their research, saying that researchers "may ethically share in the economic rewards" of their efforts. The profits must be "commensurate with the value of his or her actual efforts," the report said, leaving it to the researchers to judge the value of their own efforts. While academic researchers argue they must be allowed to use private industry to compensate for their modest salaries, they say the money is too little to tempt them to risk their reputation. It is all they have, they say. If they lose their reputation, they become worthless.

But the staggering amounts of money that can be made from a new drug or medical procedure have raised the stakes in this already extremely lucrative corner of research. Under current law, drug companies are granted monopolies to sell new drugs—at any price—for five to ten years, according to the Office of Technology Assessment. Prices for new biotechnology drugs range up to several thousand dollars a dose. With the recent explosion of biotechnology companies has come yet another troubling marriage of commerce and medicine: Wall Street's rampant speculation on the outcome of drug research, in which the greedy gamble on the future of drugs before they have been proven effective—or even safe.

◆

AMID THIS LANDSCAPE, THERE IS an occasional anomaly: a study showing that an expensive new drug is actually less effective than an older, cheaper one. That study almost certainly will not have been sponsored by the drug maker.

In 1991, a group of researchers at Indiana University School of Medicine found that inexpensive over-the-counter painkillers were just as effective in treating arthritis of the knee as a prescription anti-inflammatory drug. The study involved 184 patients with osteoarthritis, who took one of two over-the-counter pain relievers, acetaminophen or ibuprofen, or a prescription drug of high-dose ibuprofen. After four weeks, about 40 percent of the patients in each group had less pain and more motility in their knees.

The reason most doctors do not realize that cheaper existing drugs might be as good as new expensive ones is partly because the drug companies do not always test their drugs against other drugs. Often, drug makers test new drugs against placebos, where any effect at all is noteworthy. (Me-too drugs—variations on popular existing drugs—are often tested on competitors so the drug maker can tell doctors, "Ours is as good as theirs but with fewer side effects.")

The Indiana study was financed by the National Institute of Arthritis and Musculo-skeletal and Skin Diseases in Bethesda, Maryland. The center has a small budget to support clinical studies that drug companies would not be interested in financing. For example, the institute financed a study on the effects of fluoride on osteoporosis, which, since there was no patentable product, would not have interested drug companies.

"Ordinarily, drug companies aren't too interested in testing their product against someone else's product," said Dr. Michael Lockshin of the center. ". . . You don't necessarily trust the drug companies to test every question. They're not in the business altruistically."

Until recently, academic doctors looked contemptuously on pharmaceutical companies and their research; when Max Gottlieb, the fictional doctor in Sinclair Lewis's novel *Arrowsmith*, left academia to join a drug company, his colleagues proclaimed, "Max Gottlieb falling for those crooks . . . I wish he hadn't gone wrong!" The American Medical Association's code of ethics, adopted in 1847, said, "Equally derogatory to professional character is it, for a physician to hold a patent for any surgical instrument, or medicine."

But gradually, academic researchers and pharmaceutical companies have made peace with each other, becoming increasingly intertwined in the 1970s and early 1980s as inflation ate into the research dollar, and drug companies faced more competition from abroad. The companies hired academic researchers either as consultants or by giving their labs contracts for specific kinds of research. In 1974, Harvard Medical School began a twelve-year agreement with Monsanto; in return for licenses on any patents that arose from the research, Monsanto would give Harvard $24 million for cancer research. Other big universities quickly followed the money trail of what are known as "technology transfers."

Today, researchers and even university endowments may also have an equity stake in a drug company and much to win or lose if the treatment is proven effective or not. "Let me be the first to admit that if I owned 50,000 shares of United Pharmamentarium Limited, it would weigh heavily on my mind as I thought about what to write in my report concerning the efficacy and safety of the company's newest gadget or nostrum," wrote Arthur Caplan, director of the Center for Biomedical Ethics at the University of Minnesota. "I don't expect the average researcher to be any less immune to the siren song of making a fast fortune. . . . If you can't bring yourself to part with your stock or fat consulting fee, then you shouldn't expect anyone to trust what you have to say about the effectiveness of a drug, device or medical product."

The interlocking interest of science and business also means the loss of an important voice in scientific debates, the one with no commercial motives—the one that seemed most trustworthy. "In the past, pure scientists took a snobbish view of business," wrote Michael Crichton in *Jurassic Park*, where genetic research ran amok. "They saw the pursuit of money as intellectually uninteresting, suited only to shop-keepers. And to do research for industry, even at the prestigious Bell or IBM labs, was only for those who couldn't get a university appointment." This antagonism "kept university scientists free of contaminating industry ties, and whenever debate arose about technological matters, disinterested scientists were available to discuss the issues at the highest levels.

"But that is no longer true," Crichton continued. "There are very few molecular biologists and very few research institutions without commercial affiliations. The old days are gone. Genetic research continues, at a more furious pace than ever. But it is done in secret, and in haste, and for profit."

◆

UNTIL THE PAST TWO DECADES, consumers didn't know the names of many prescription drugs and rarely presumed to tell their doctor what to prescribe. They assumed the doctor would make an educated choice based on knowledge and experience. That changed in 1977 with the introduction of a

*Regulation in
Drug Advertising*

drug called Tagamet, an ulcer treatment that made the nightly news before it became commercially available. People came to their doctors demanding the drug.

Drug companies got the picture. They did not have to filter their drug research through doctors and medical journals. They did not have to wait for FDA approval. They could market their drugs directly to the consumer by way of the news media.

The drug studies most often reported in the media are clinical trials, where drugs or treatments are tried on humans. It is here that society is most vulnerable to biomedical research because it is the final step before a drug goes into widespread use. Late in 1993, the dangers of drug testing became more tragically clear than ever. In a test of a drug to treat hepatitis B, five of fifteen patients who took the drug for four weeks or more died. Two others required liver transplants. When the Food and Drug Administration reviewed earlier tests on the drug, the agency found that five other patients may have died from taking the drug. The researchers, who knew of the deaths, attributed them to causes other than the drugs. "Optimism," said Dr. David Kessler of the FDA.

Clinical studies are expensive, time-consuming and virtually impossible to replicate, making untruth harder to uncover. But they can be enormously powerful. A single, unduplicated clinical study, effectively published, can reach virtually everyone in the country.

The drug Retin-A had been used to treat acne vulgaris for almost two decades when in 1988 it was suddenly transformed into a miracle drug for a much more common affliction—wrinkles. A study published in the *Journal of the American Medical Association* found that Retin-A, a potent vitamin A derivative, could actually reverse wrinkling caused by the sun. The article featured pictures of patients taken before and after they had rubbed Retin-A on their faces and arms for four months, showing improvement. An editorial accompanying the article was topped with a headline containing an exclamation point—unusual punctuation in medical journals: "At Last! A Medical Treatment for Skin Aging." The study was widely and enthusiastically reported by the

*Retin
A—
for
Wrinkles*

media. All three network news shows reported the study. Retin-A was a "facelift out of a tube," declared *U.S. News & World Report*. "A cream that turns back the clock," announced *Business Week*. The month after the study was published, sales of the twenty-dollar tubes quintupled over the year-earlier period.

The Retin-A study was far from perfect, and it was far from conclusive. The study itself was based on a tiny sample of thirty people, all white, in one hospital over just four months, and it was compromised by several methodological problems. Improvements in wrinkles were partly judged subjectively—by looking at them—and even the claimed improvements were less than dramatic. The side effects of using such a powerful drug daily were unpleasant.

The study was partly sponsored by the Ortho Pharmaceutical Corporation, the maker of Retin-A. The lead researcher on the study, John J. Voorhees, professor of dermatology at the University of Michigan Medical Center, had received more than a quarter of a million dollars in research grants from Johnson & Johnson, which owns Ortho Pharmaceutical.

Four years later, the same research laboratory produced another study, this one showing that Retin-A lightened or even obliterated liver spots. The study was a little longer (ten months) and a little bigger (fifty-eight patients) than the wrinkle study. But like the wrinkle study, it was partly funded by Ortho Pharmaceutical and written by, among others, John Voorhees. Once again the media took notice. "Johnson & Johnson's Retin-A Can Ease Problem of Liver Spots, Researchers Say," reported the *Wall Street Journal*. "Study Finds Cream Clears Age Spots," declared the *New York Times*.

Once a drug is approved for one use, as Retin-A was for acne in 1971, doctors have wide latitude in prescribing it for other uses. If doctors believed Retin-A could diminish wrinkles, they could prescribe it. But companies cannot *market* the drug for other uses, either to doctors or consumers. Despite the positive findings in its pilot study, it would be years —if ever—before Johnson & Johnson got FDA approval to sell Retin-A as a wrinkle treatment.

In an aging culture increasingly anxious about wrinkles, that was too long to wait. Ortho Pharmaceutical hired a public relations firm to arrange a news conference at the Rainbow Room in New York City's Rockefeller Center. The well-attended conference was held the day before Voorhees's article was published. Voorhees announced the results of his preliminary research, saying, "Obviously, the implications are pretty big." In a news release, the American Medical Association announced the upcoming study of Retin-A and wrinkling. It also commissioned a 90-second video release for television. (The journal routinely announces its upcoming articles, said Dr. George D. Lundberg, the journal's editor. "The science was sound then, and I think it's still sound. How broadly applicable it is is still a question.")

But the study was compromised by several problems:

◆ Of the original forty patients involved in the study, three dropped out because of severe skin irritation and seven others dropped out for unspecified reasons, leaving a small sample of thirty. Only fifteen of those used Retin-A on their faces; the others used a placebo.

◆ Eleven of the subjects had such severe side effects from the drug that they had to use potent steroid creams to counteract them.

◆ The lighting, camera angles and possibly the facial expressions in the before-and-after pictures of Retin-A users were different.

◆ Although the study was called double-blind, which means neither the doctors nor the patients were supposed to know who was getting the drug and who the placebo, in fact it was obvious from the redness, scaling and other side effects of Retin-A who was getting what. ("There is probably some bias," Voorhees told reporters Leslie N. Vreeland and Mary Granfield, who investigated the Retin-A study for *Money* magazine, "but it's certainly not all biased.")

◆ In almost all placebo-controlled studies, some of the placebo group will show improvements. In an August 1993 study of placebos, researchers found that two-thirds of patients receiving medically worthless treatments improved, even if temporarily.

◆ The study ended after four months, so there was no

way to know whether any improvement could be sustained. Even Barbara Gilchrest, a Boston University dermatology professor who wrote the accompanying editorial (at last!), conceded that "the average improvement was quite subtle and hence may not satisfy the expectations of a demanding public for long."

The kinds of problems that afflicted the Retin-A research do not necessarily mean the outcome of the study is wrong. But the consistent pattern of outcomes *always* supporting the sponsors cannot be a coincidence. In this case, in addition to the $253,120 in research grants Voorhees had received from Johnson & Johnson before the Retin-A news conference, he received another $689,750 the following year. Voorhees was also a paid consultant to the company in 1988 and 1989, and, in addition, he received thirteen honoraria payments in 1988, including one for the Retin-A news conference. Barbara Gilchrest, the editorialist who was described in news reports as a "researcher not involved in the new study," had received $3,600 in honoraria from Johnson & Johnson before the editorial. The following year the company paid her $9,000 for four activities. Her department at Boston University had received $393,380 in Johnson & Johnson research grants in the two years before the editorial and four grants totaling $185,406 in 1988–89.

If nothing else, Retin-A's abrasiveness may make wrinkles and liver spots look better, irritating the skin and causing it to puff and smooth out. But what many consumers embraced as truth was still far from it. Five years later, the FDA had still not approved Retin-A for treating wrinkles. An FDA advisory committee that recommended such approval was tepid in its appraisal, requesting additional data on Retin-A as a possible carcinogen.

◆

DESPITE THE MANY TEMPTATIONS MODERN scientists face, they still believe their discipline is self-correcting because it is open, verifiable and subject to close review by scientific peers. In American medicine, however, all three of these pillars are deteriorating.

The studies that appear in the best scientific journals are subject to peer review, the process by which scientists evaluate one another's work to decide what gets published. Under peer review, research papers are sent to two or three other scientists for criticism and comment. Especially in this age of increasing specialization, the peer-review system is the only way generalist editors can "edit" or weed out poor research. But the peer review system is stretched thin. The sheer volume of biomedical journals—some 15,000 journals publish about 250,000 articles a month—puts insupportable demands on the system. Peer reviewers are unpaid volunteers, and they can't take the time to scrutinize the raw data, let alone replicate the research. The specialization of medicine means the pool of people capable of doing any particular review is diminishing. Whatever the outcome of the peer review, the editor of the journal may decide to accept or reject the article for editorial or personal reasons. Scientists say that peer reviews are increasingly done by graduate students or postdoctoral fellows who do not have enough breadth of experience and that peer reviewers compete with the authors for research money, possibly biasing their opinions. Critics also say peer review is biased in favor of well-known professors from prestigious schools—the so-called halo effect—and those who use "current fashionable approaches." And what scientist wants to break the news to another scientist that he or she has just wasted years on a poorly designed piece of research?

Even regular contributors to journals decry the state of the peer-review system. "Despite this system, anyone who reads journals widely and critically is forced to realize that there are scarcely any bars to eventual publication," wrote Drummond Rennie, professor of medicine at the University of California at San Francisco. "There seems to be no study too fragmented, no hypothesis too trivial, no literature too biased or too egotistical, no design too warped, no methodology too bungled, no presentation of results too inaccurate, too obscure and too contradictory, no analysis too self-serving, no argument too circular, no conclusions too trifling or too unjustified, and no grammar and syntax too offensive for a paper to end up in print.

"The function of peer review, then, may be to help decide not whether but where papers are published."

The similarities between legitimate medical journals and drug-company newsletters designed to look like legitimate medical journals has also muddied the pool of biomedical information. Although the sponsorship of these newsletters, supplements and journals is generally noted on the publications, it is not always. In 1991, the FDA took action against Bristol-Myers Squibb for printing a newsletter called *Oncology Commentary '90* that was designed to look like a medical journal but discussed only Bristol-Myers drugs. The company's name appeared nowhere on the publication.

The openness of the scientific process is also disappearing. Sponsors of private biomedical research, racing to market with competitive drugs, often forbid their researchers from sharing their findings with other scientists. A 1986 survey by a group at the Kennedy School of Government at Harvard University, which queried more than 1,200 faculty members in biotechnology departments, found that a quarter of the faculty working with industry support would not be allowed to publish without the sponsor's permission. Only 5 percent of faculty receiving funds from nonindustrial sponsors said they were similarly restricted.

Verifiability is also no longer an effective deterrent to fraud or poor science, because the modern biomedical research system is structured to prevent replication, not to insure it. Duplicating another scientist's research is prohibitively expensive and time-consuming. Once a drug is proven effective, there is no incentive for the drug company to sponsor more research; and who else would sponsor research on, for example, Retin-A? Nor does the government want, for the most part, to finance studies that are largely duplicative. In addition, academic credit tends to be given only for new findings.

The new model of sponsored science could be seen in the contract signed in December 1992 by the Scripps Research Institute in La Jolla, California, the largest private research institution in the United States, and Sandoz Pharmaceutical Corporation. In exchange for $300 million over ten years, Sandoz would have first rights to any discoveries made at Scripps, which specializes in immunity and cardiovascular diseases. The contract gave Sandoz the right to keep other researchers off the Scripps campus, to take work a Scripps scientist is doing and move it back to Switzerland and to restrict associations of Scripps scientists with other scientists or companies. Agreements like that "come perilously close to making a research institution's scientists indentured scholars to a single corporate entity," Dr. Sheldon Krimsky of Tufts University told a House subcommittee. Under pressure from the federal government, Scripps later modified the agreement, giving Sandoz less power to direct Scripps research projects not directly funded by the company.

The growing number of possible conflicts of interest in biomedical research has been the subject of other government concern. In September 1989, two agencies of the Public Health Service issued a set of proposed guidelines that would have strictly regulated potential conflicts of interest, prohibiting, for example, researchers from holding equity interests in companies affected by the outcome of their research, or from accepting honoraria from sponsoring companies. Three months later, bowing to strong pressure from both scientific groups and the biotechnology industry, the Secretary of Health and Human Services discarded the guidelines as "regulatory burdens which may be unnecessary or counterproductive." The Public Health Service has since been working on a new set of conflict-of-interest rules. Meanwhile, in June 1993, the Food and Drug Administration announced that it was planning to require drug companies to disclose significant financial ties to doctors testing drugs and some medical devices as part of the drug application process.

Many scientists blame the apparent bias of drug studies on publishers, not researchers. Medical journals prefer exciting positive results to boring negative ones. Drug companies have neither incentive nor obligation to publish research showing their drug was not effective. Under contract research, scientists typically do not have the option of publishing negative results about a sponsor's drug. Sheer volume of studies can also create an impression that the product is more important than it is. Because of statistical variability, a few studies will automatically show a greater effect than others, and those often get the attention of the medical journals.

In May 1993, a new study, sponsored by the drug maker, showed that a drug called TPA saved just 1 percent more lives than a drug that cost a tenth as much. Earlier studies had shown TPA to be no better than the other drug. Nevertheless, researchers involved in the latest study hailed it as definitive research proving TPA's effectiveness.

The media further taint biomedical information by hailing the arrival of each new miracle drug based on one clinical trial. Writing in the journal *Science, Technology, and Human Values*, Leon Trachtman observed that some 90 percent of the new drugs touted in newspaper reports never reached the market or were driven from it because they were ineffective, too toxic or both.

The media also favor the most positive studies of all, even—or maybe especially—when a positive result is scary. In 1991, the *Journal of the American Medical Association* published two articles about rates of cancer associated with exposure to nuclear radiation. One article was "positive"—it found that white male employees at the Oak Ridge National Laboratory were more likely than average to get leukemia. The other was "negative"—it found that people who lived near nuclear facilities had no increased risk of cancer. The two articles were published in the same issue; each was six pages long; was accompanied by editorial comment; and was given equal space in a journal news release.

Two Canadian researchers analyzed the subsequent newspaper coverage of the two studies. Nine newspaper stories were dedicated solely to the positive study; ten covered both studies; and not a single newspaper covered only the negative story. In stories covering both studies, the positive one was given significantly more space than the negative one.

Reporters face deadline and competitive pressures, and their editors want a major story simple enough for anyone to understand. If reporters equivocate about the study's conclusions, they handicap the story's chances for page one. To their credit, reporters and editors increasingly note the sponsorship of studies, but then suggest either explicitly or by implication that it was irrelevant. "Vesnarinone is made by Otsuka America Pharmaceutical, which paid for the study," reported the *New York Times* about research showing that a new drug might treat congestive heart failure, "but scientists at the medical centers carried it out independently of the company."

Nowhere can the changing ethics in biomedical research be seen more clearly than in biotechnology research, where the stakes are enormous, the investors avaricious and impatient and the competitive pressures crushing. The drug Centoxin, a proposed treatment for often-fatal bacterial infections, or septic shock, in hospital patients, was a textbook case of how commercial interests can threaten to overwhelm scientific rigor in judging a new drug.

Centoxin was an especially difficult drug to test because septic shock can be caused by either gram-positive or gram-negative bacteria. Centoxin would be effective only on the gram-negative variety, but because septic shock kills so quickly, the drug had to be administered before the type of infection had been determined.

Under FDA rules, the designers of a clinical drug trial must state precisely how the study will be conducted and analyzed and which patients the drug is intended to help. Centocor, the manufacturer, set its initial endpoint for the study at fourteen days and began testing the drug on some 500 patients. After fourteen days, there was no statistically significant difference in death rates between the patients who received Centoxin and those who received a dummy drug. (In a subgroup of 200 patients, who were later found to have gram-negative infections, the drug did show significant benefits.)

After twenty-eight days, however, there was a marginal improvement in survival among all the patients. Centocor filed a revised protocol with the FDA, changing its endpoint from fourteen to twenty-eight days.

Researchers are permitted to change their protocols, but in this case, the FDA knew a company official had looked at the data before the protocol was revised. The FDA said it was concerned that the results may have been biased. Centocor would have to "submit data from an additional well-controlled trial" before its drug could be approved, the FDA ruled.

Until this ruling, Centoxin, which was being produced and tested by Centocor, a young, aggressive biotechnology company, had looked like a hot prospect for patients and investors. The clinical trials seemed promising, the FDA's advisory committee had recommended the drug's approval, and the stock of a company that hadn't started selling its most important product had risen as high as fifty-nine dollars a share. Centocor had already hired a huge sales staff and built two manufacturing plants for Centoxin. The company had begun holding medical symposia to introduce Centoxin to doctors. It had even set the price—more than $3,500 a dose. And if it worked, it would save thousands of lives a year.

Centocor quickly launched another clinical trial. But after only a few months, the truth about Centoxin emerged. Interim data showed that for patients with the gram-positive infection, more would die from Centoxin treatment than from a placebo. In January 1993, the company stopped the trial. For all practical purposes, Centoxin was dead. All the investors on Wall Street could not make Centoxin work.

"The wild oscillations in [biotech] stocks are a pathetic indication of the gullibility of intelligent people who know a great deal about their business but also nothing about science," said Professor Drummond Rennie of the University of California.

◆

INFORMATION GENERATED BY DRUG COMPANIES comes to doctors and consumers not only through published research studies but also through advertising and marketing. The pharmaceutical companies are master marketers. Here is how Drummond Rennie described symposia, a popular drug marketing strategy: "I'm the advertising guy for the drug. I tell a journal I will give them $100,000 to have a special issue on that drug. Plus I'll give the journal so much per reprint, and I'll order a lot of reprints. I'll select the editor and all the authors. I phone everyone who has written good things about that drug.

I say, 'I'll fly you and your wife first class to New Orleans for a symposium. I'll put your paper in the special issue of the journal, and you'll have an extra publication for your c.v. Then I'll put a reprint of that symposium on some doctor's desk and say, 'Look at this marvelous drug.' "

Unlike most advertisers, drug companies are held to strict FDA standards about the style and content of their ads. Because drug advertising must educate people about the drugs, the FDA says drug ads must "present true statements relating to side effects, contraindications, and effectiveness." That is partly why prescription drug advertising is so rarely seen on television; 30 seconds is not long enough to provide much meaningful information.

Even so, the industry's advertising should be scrutinized very carefully. Unlike the editorial content of medical journals, drug advertising gets little, if any, screening. In 1992, three doctors from the University of California at Los Angeles School of Medicine tested whether drug advertising lived up to the FDA's relatively modest standards. The researchers first selected more than 100 advertisements to test. Then they went looking for doctors who would review and comment on the ads. As a safeguard, the researchers at first planned to exclude any physicians who had accepted consulting fees, honoraria or research funds of more than $300 from the pharmaceutical industry in the past two years. "Careful screening revealed an insufficient number of physicians who met this criterion," the researchers wrote matter-of-factly.

The results of the study, financed by government and foundation grants, were that advertisements were frequently misleading, had little or no educational value, and the quality of a substantial minority was poor or unacceptable in several areas. The reviewers said 62 percent of the ads they saw should have been either rejected or significantly revised before publication. The article provoked a storm of controversy among doctors, many of whom claimed that they were not so naive as to get their information about drugs from advertisements.

Yet it seems certain that doctors, even if unconsciously, succumb to the siren song of drug advertising. In 1982, Dr. Jerry Avorn of Harvard compared the persuasive powers of scientific and commercial information. He asked eighty-five doctors their opinions of two drugs, both of which had been found in controlled studies to have minimal effects or effects little different from over-the-counter medications. Both drugs were heavily advertised as being effective. Nearly half the doctors said one of the drugs, an analgesic called propoxyphene, was more potent than aspirin even though scientific evidence had shown its pain-killing properties to be "at best equivalent to aspirin," Avorn reported. The results for the other drug, a cerebral vasodilator, were similar. More distressing than the doctors' choice of heavily marketed but unproven drugs was the doctors' unconsciousness of their own gullibility. Sixty-eight percent said drug ads have "minimal importance" in their prescription writing.

◆

DRUGS HAVE TRADITIONALLY BEEN HELD to two standards, safety and efficiency. But with the increasing criticism of rising drug prices, pharmaceutical companies had to devise a new way to show their drugs were cost effective: the pharmo-economic study.

Cost-benefit and other kinds of economic research on drugs started in the late 1970s, and grew rapidly in the late 1980s. As people became more concerned about the escalating prices of drugs, the drug companies had to prove two points. One was that the enormous investment they make in producing new products justifies high prices. So, for example, estimates for the cost of bringing a new drug to market range from $231 million to $500 million, depending on whose numbers are used. Included in some of these figures are not only the costs of development, but also a soft number called "opportunity cost"—the return on the money invested in drug development had it been invested elsewhere.

Drug companies also had to prove that however expensive their product, it was still cheaper than alternative treatments, like surgery.

With the rise of managed care health plans, these economic analyses, sometimes called prospective randomized economic trials, have become important factors in the way drugs are chosen. Unlike clinical trials, however, which are overseen by both company scientists and the federal government, cost studies are paid for by marketing departments, which then use the favorable results to promote sales. The FDA does not look over the companies' shoulders, and there is no peer review unless the analysis is published in a journal. Unlike clinical studies, too, economic studies generally use data and analytic methods that vary in precision and power and are completely unstandardized. It is very difficult to detect and prevent bias in these studies.

As with other kinds of computer modeling, cost analyses of drugs can be controlled in many ways that fall short of scientific wrongdoing. Writing in the *New England Journal of Medicine*, Alan Hillman and others noted some of those ways. "Pharmaceutical companies . . . fund projects with a high likelihood of producing favorable results. . . . [T]hey exclude products that may compare favorably with the sponsor's own. Sometimes, only favorable clinical data are released to investigators. Pilot studies are commonly performed to assess the likelihood of favorable results. . . . Some projects are funded in steps, so that losses can be cut if the initial results are not favorable. . . . Investigators may be threatened with the withdrawal of current or future funding unless specific changes in methods, presentation, or results are made."

Hillman and his colleagues proposed a set of eight recommendations to help insulate researchers from potential bias. They urge, among other things, that research grants be given to institutions rather than individuals; that researchers should publish valid findings whatever the results; that comparisons be based on relevance, not the likelihood of producing favorable results; and that investigators use conservative assumptions (biased against the results desired by the funding company).

Many companies have also begun using so-called quality-of-life studies to distinguish a drug that is essentially identical to a competitor's product. Such was the case with two brands of blood pressure medicine, both of which have been shown to be effective and to have similar side effects. But in an April 1993 study, one of the two drugs was found to make people feel more sluggish, blue and in generally poor health.

The other seemed to improve people's feelings of vitality and general good health. The maker of the one that made people feel better is Bristol-Myers Squibb. The sponsor of the study (for $2 million): Bristol-Myers Squibb.

Pharmaceutical companies also use studies to protect their image, which has suffered from a growing perception that they profit too well from illness. In 1991, a study by the Batelle Medical Technology Assessment and Policy Research Center concluded that because of medical science and lifestyle changes, 11 million fewer people would die of heart disease in the next twenty-five years than would die if there were no such changes. Forty percent of that reduction would come from drugs that have not even been invented yet. The study was sponsored by Schering-Plough Corporation, which issued a news release about it. Batelle issued its own release.

"Their press release emphasized the continued development of medicine," said a Batelle spokeswoman. "Ours emphasized that in some cases medicine didn't make any difference. They were looking at the sections of the research that bore out their hypothesis. When people are selling their houses, they don't say it has termites, they say it has wall-to-wall carpeting."

◆

THAT WE TRUST OUR HEALTH, perhaps our lives, to self-interested researchers is clear from the story of silicone breast implants, which were widely known to be completely safe until thousands of women began suffering a host of inexplicable diseases.

Fistfuls of silicone were first implanted in American women's breasts in the 1960s, long before Congress began requiring FDA approval for medical devices. Because the implant was grandfathered out of the eventual requirement, for more than a decade breast implant makers were not required to prove their products were safe. Finally, however, the FDA would classify every medical device on the market according to its potential risk. In 1978, an FDA advisory committee recommended that breast implants be considered a Class 2 device, requiring a lesser standard of safety evidence than

Class 3. Then-FDA commissioner Donald Kennedy overruled the committee over the vigorous protests of the manufacturers and, appallingly, plastic surgeons, to whom breast implants were bringing a brisk business. For more than a decade, the classification of breast implants would be argued at a plodding pace. Meanwhile, the makers of breast implants would not prove that their implants were safe. There would be no widespread long-term monitoring of what happened to women with implants.

Self-interest sometimes dictates no research at all, especially in the face of anecdotal reports of problems. Dow Corning Wright, whose $600-million-a-year implant business represented about a third of the market, had long used silicone safely in other medical devices. For its breast implants, the company said it did some 329 studies and found no harmful effects.

A study could be as small as one in 1973—the subjects were four dogs. According to a published article about the study by two Dow Corning scientists, the dogs remained in normal health. In fact, as later emerged, one dog had died and another had developed a large tumor. In a 1985 memo, a Dow Corning official said most of the company's safety claims had been based on this dog study. The study lasted only two years; women get their breast implants for life. In another study on rabbits, silicone had migrated in some, causing inflammatory reactions. In one internal memo, a salesman said Dow Corning's decision to sell one "questionable" batch of implants "has to rank up there with the Pinto gas tank." The company's only research on breast implants' effects on women did not ask specifically about autoimmune disease. "[Women are] serving as guinea pigs in a vast, uncontrolled clinical trial," the late Representative Ted Weiss of New York wrote in a letter to the FDA.

In 1988, the FDA finally ordered implant manufacturers to provide the agency with safety and efficacy data. Bristol-Myers, whose implants were already in the bodies of thousands of women, withdrew its product from the market, saying it would need more time to do safety research. Three other companies whose implants were already in wide use submitted research that the FDA rejected as too poor even to review. Four other manufacturers began the review process, including Dow Corning, which released 30,000 pages of safety studies to the FDA. In late 1991, the FDA said it had found Dow Corning's safety data inadequate, and in January 1992, it announced a moratorium on breast implant sales until somebody did some decent research. While it tested whether implants were safe, Dow Corning argued, breast implants should continue to be available to women.

Nervy!

Throughout the two years of controversy over breast implants, Dow Corning fought the government not with data proving its implants safe but with a cynical and expensive public relations campaign. The company underwrote personal appearances by more than a dozen women who had breast implants. The women flew around the country at Dow Corning's expense, telling the public that they had never had any trouble with their implants. Meanwhile, the company complained that the news media had "reported only the sensationalistic, anecdotal side of the breast implant story."

PR Not DATA

Correctly perceiving that Washington would blow with the wind on this sensitive women's issue, Dow Corning commissioned a poll that showed that 90 percent of women did not want the government to interfere with a woman's right to choose implants. The survey results were released the day before an FDA advisory panel began hearings on implants.

Poll

The survey's question about a woman's "right to choose" included the phrase "as long as they are fully informed by their surgeons." Such a thing would be impossible because rigorous safety tests had not been done, and because most plastic surgeons did not think the company should be forced to do more safety tests. If that had been noted, surely the results would have been different. Dow Corning, which was testing its product on unknowing subjects, raised the feminist flag, invoking a "woman's right to make her own medical decisions." Furthermore, a Dow Corning statement continued, no convincing scientific evidence existed showing a connection between silicone implants and cancer or disease of the immune system.

Neither did any convincing scientific evidence showing the reverse.

(Just four months later, a Gallup Poll found quite different results from Dow Corning's poll. Thirty-one percent of the people questioned said silicone implants should be banned entirely, and 29 percent said implants should be available only on a limited basis.)

So insistent was Dow Corning of its implants' safety that the FDA finally forced the company to disclose some unfavorable safety studies, even though such studies are often considered confidential commercial information. The FDA also complained that the company's Implant Information Center hot line was misleading callers about risks.

Meanwhile, the American Society of Plastic and Reconstructive Surgeons assessed each of its members $350 a year over three years to assemble a $4 million treasury. The society used it to hire lobbyists and public relations experts and to launch a mail and telephone campaign to persuade legislators that silicone implants should not be removed from the market. The society flew 400 women with implants to Washington to lobby on Capitol Hill. It was plastic surgeons, after all, who in the early 1980s began describing "micromastia," or small breasts, as a treatable "disease."

For all their efforts, however, the manufacturers and the doctors could not reverse the tide of public opinion. A growing number of independent researchers were producing evidence that implants were causing health problems. With its reputation and stock price falling and its legal bills mounting, Dow Corning hired former U.S. Attorney General Griffin Bell to evaluate and report on the safety of breast implants. Citing attorney-client privilege, the company refused to release the details of Bell's report.

Nevertheless, parts of it became public, including the fact that Dow Corning workers had over a period of years falsified records about the manufacture of its breast implants. The falsifications concerned the temperature at which the silicone was heated. The heating process makes the silicone less liquid and less likely to migrate into other parts of the body. It is migrating silicone, or gel bleed, that some doctors believe instigates the autoimmune disease seen in some women with breast implants. The company became aware of the heating problem in 1987, but did not tell their customers, the doctors or the FDA.

In studies conducted during the 1970s, a University of Texas researcher named John Paul Heggers found that the human immune system created antibodies against the silicone in breast implants. He took his findings to Dow Corning, where executives "just weren't interested," Heggers said.

"That he couldn't get us interested is a pretty accurate statement," a Dow Corning executive told the *New York Times*. "We prefer to do our own immunological work here." Twenty years later, in March 1993, Dow Corning reported that its own studies on laboratory rats showed the silicone gel used in implants was a strong irritant of the immune system.

Meanwhile, both breast implant manufacturers and doctors were, for the most part, advising women with implants not to have them removed. The surgery carries its own risks, and the studies are not yet conclusive. "My advice to those patients who are simply anxious," a plastic surgeon said, "is to wait for the next three to five years and see what trickles out of the research tube."

Until a large-scale epidemiological survey of breast implants is completed, women will have no definitive answers about the silicone in their bodies. Such a study is under way. It is being financed by Dow Corning.

CHAPTER SEVEN

Research

in the

Courtroom

*One man's justice is
another's injustice.*

—RALPH WALDO EMERSON

In the spring of 1991, the *New York Times* reported at the top of its front page that a "new scientific study" "directly contradicts" the well-established view that the Dalkon Shield contraceptive device had mangled—even killed—many women. Intrauterine devices, this study found, do not increase the risk of pelvic infections.

It was an amazing reversal. The medical and legal worlds had definitively recognized the danger of this birth control device named for a policeman's badge. The manufacturer, the A. H. Robins Company, had withdrawn it from the market. Robins was in bankruptcy because so many victims had filed and won lawsuits, in what was then the largest product-liability litigation of the twentieth century. Now came a study saying the whole imbroglio was based on bad information.

It was oddly fitting that another study should appear in the final hours of the shield debacle, just when many women were starting to receive compensation for their injuries. Studies had appeared at every turn the device took as it carved its cruel path through the nation's social history. Now this report —partly financed by the shield's maker—would loom over the last chapter, a ready weapon against women who challenged the amount they were offered. Once again, a study would maneuver the legal system toward justice—or at least toward one party's version of it.

The ideal of seeking truth through advocacy is tested most often in America's courts of law. At the heart of the legal system is the belief that truth lies among the self-interested claims of competing parties. The ethics of research are quite different. Self-interest, though acknowledged to be inevitable, is seen as something to be staunchly resisted. Although scientists and social scientists who appear in court insist their work meets their profession's highest standards, in fact their work *always* supports their clients' positions, or else it and they are simply dropped from the action.

The bald self-interest at the heart of litigation research is only one of the many ways it differs from the academic search for truth. A court constructs its view of the truth from the materials before it. If a witness says black is white, and no one contradicts it, then for purposes of the court, black is

2) white. Legal adversaries stake out extreme positions, making consensus unlikely. In research, however, as in many other parts of life, consensus is an indicator—though an imperfect one—of truth.

3) The methods by which the two disciplines seek truth also differ. In uncorrupted research, the ideal is to search for an unknown, probably hypothesized, truth; in law, it is to assemble facts to support a predetermined position. Or as the cynical lawyer in Frederick Busch's courtroom novel *Closing Arguments* said, "When we figure out what truth we're telling, then we'll work on how to tell someone that particular truth."

4) In law, if something happens once, it is a piece of evidence; in research, one piece of evidence is barely a start. While the law knowingly excludes evidence, its standard to establish a truth—a preponderance of the evidence, or probability greater than 50 percent—is less rigorous than ideal research. Full disclosure is built into the ethics of research; true science gives other researchers the chance to challenge a study by trying to replicate it. In law, lawyers have the right not to disclose adverse factual evidence.

Uses in law

Research and law make tense bedfellows, and the truth they produce is a deformed and troubling creature. Yet self-interested research plays a growing role in legal battles. Survey research has become a standard weapon in trademark, unfair competition, environmental damage assessment, obscenity and change-of-venue proceedings. Other kinds of research—medical, epidemiological, statistical—are common in product liability, discrimination and "toxic tort" actions.

◆

IT IS IN RESEARCH PREPARED for the courtroom that it is easiest to see the subtleties of creating a subjective study that looks objective. Although studies prepared for litigation are clothed in scientific garb, they are conceived, designed and executed with self-interested motives. The question before judges and juries has increasingly become which self-interested data are —or seem—least undermined by self-interest.

In the 1970s, a squabble over rights to the name Domino

—between the pizza company (Domino's) and the sugar company—erupted in federal court in Atlanta. In the course of the protracted litigation, <u>each side commissioned a survey</u>. The sugar company, which wanted the new pizza company to stop using the name Domino, needed to show that people were confused about whether the pizza pies were somehow related to the sugar company. The pizza company needed to show that people felt no confusion about the origins of the pizza pies. The two surveys easily produced the requisite, incompatible truths.

It was simple. The pizza company simply conducted its survey exclusively in Domino's Pizza outlets, where chances were excellent that people would know the pizza from the sugar. The sugar company, conversely, did its survey in ten cities, eight of which did not have Domino's Pizza outlets, and interviewed only women who were at home during the day—likely sugar buyers.

Lawyers assume—depend on—a certain subjectivity in their paid researchers, which they assess partly by studying the researcher's previous publications or testimony. Lawyers are unabashed about expecting their researchers to be biased, just as they know they should never ask a question whose answer they do not know. "I would go into a lawsuit with an objective, uncommitted, independent expert about as willingly as I would occupy a foxhole with a couple of noncombatant soldiers," a former president of the American Bar Association said. Yet unless it pretends to be unbiased, scientific and objective, the study will carry little or no weight.

The kind of scientific research that belongs in the courtroom has been the subject of heated debate for decades. In 1923, a federal appellate court, disallowing lie-detector results, ruled that only science widely accepted by scientists should be allowed as evidence. "Just when a scientific principle or doctrine crosses the line between the experimental and demonstrable stages is difficult to define," declared the court in *Frye* v. *United States*. But the court's doctrine, which came to be known as the "Frye rule," said the science must be "sufficiently established to have gained general acceptance."

For fifty years, the Frye rule held sway in federal and state courts. But by the 1970s, scientists and lawyers had recognized that the effects of some new technologies—environmental, chemical, pharmaceutical—were overtaking the science of proof. It would take years, perhaps decades, to prove that asbestos caused lung cancer, or that the hormone diethylstilbestrol (DES) caused cancer in daughters of women who had taken it. Should isolated cases, which might eventually form a pattern, be dismissed because science had not caught up with reality? At the same time, the growing complexity of many kinds of legal actions—antitrust and discrimination, for example—required courts to look outside for expert advice. In 1975, the Frye rule lost most of its teeth when new federal rules of evidence allowed into courtrooms science not widely accepted by other scientists. The test became not acceptance but whether "scientific, technical or other specialized knowledge will assist the trier of fact to determine a fact in issue" and whether the witness "is qualified as an expert by knowledge, training or education."

The result, some legal critics complain, has been the invasion of courts by junk science and fringe scientists purveying whatever theory will result in the largest payoff for their sponsor. An oft-cited example is the doctor who testified that a soothsayer had lost her psychic powers because of the dye she was given before a CAT scan, resulting in a huge jury award. The business of providing scientific testimony is booming, with pages of classified advertising in lawyers' journals offering scientific consulting for any side of any issue. A Maryland expert broker promised that "If the first doctor we refer doesn't agree with your legal theory, we will provide you the name of a second."

Proponents of the "let it all in" doctrine say wide acceptance is neither an assurance nor an essence of truth. Indeed, unless scientific claims can be verified by some kind of technological display—building a machine that flies or does not— it is very difficult to prove many scientific beliefs. "Junk versus non-junk is a social judgment," said Sheila Jasanoff, professor of science, policy and law at Cornell University. With the growing corporate sponsorship of research, others say junk science is more a business than a social or legal judgment. "Junk science is any science that industry doesn't condone," said one researcher.

In 1993, the U.S. Supreme Court, which had already made known its feelings about quantitative information—"statistics are not irrefutable. They come in infinite variety and, like any other kind of evidence, they may be rebutted"—considered the question of scientific research in the court-room. The high court reviewed a personal injury suit against the maker of a morning sickness drug, Bendectin, sold from 1957 to 1983 by the company now called Merrell Dow Pharmaceuticals. A federal district court, like others before it, had dismissed the suit after barring expert testimony that the drug caused birth defects. That court ruled that because the plaintiffs' scientific claims had been neither published nor peer-reviewed, they were not admissible. An appeals court affirmed the decision. The plaintiffs appealed again. In a legal brief, a bitter Merrell said it was being victimized by "scientific shamans who . . . are willing to testify to virtually any conclusion to meet the needs of the litigant with resources sufficient to pay their retainer."

In ruling that the more liberal federal rules of evidence superseded the stringent Frye rule, the Supreme Court reaffirmed the responsibility of federal judges to decide whether the scientific testimony was credible enough to assist the jury. "We are confident that Federal judges possess the capacity to undertake this review," the majority ruled. A minority of two disagreed, saying the ruling would turn judges into "amateur scientists."

1943 S.C. Decision

◆

As THE ROLE OF SCIENCE in the law evolved, so, too, did the role of survey research. Surveys, the descriptive measure of what people think and how they behave, had gained acceptance in commerce and politics in the 1930s, but courts did not admit survey results until 1954. Before then, judges looked on surveys as hearsay—someone speaking for another—impractical to cross-examine and thus useless for legal purposes. In the early days of survey research, the 1930s and '40s, surveys were also seen as technologically unsophisti-

1954

Survey in Court

cated, little better than educated guesses. When a prosecuting attorney once criticized Elmo Roper's research director for testifying about the same research methods that had failed so miserably in the 1948 presidential election, courtroom observers applauded. But slowly, courts became more hospitable to survey research, allowing it to speak, if not for the truth of the matter, at least as an expression of a state of mind. Surveys became a standard weapon in many kinds of litigation.

A presumption of bias taints any research done specifically for the courtroom, and judges cast an exacting eye on methodology. As early as 1962, a district court judge, commenting on a case testing whether the word "thermos" had become generic for vacuum bottle, said, "The method of poll taking adopted by each of the parties . . . was designed to elicit the kind of evidence each wished to bring out."

Perhaps because judges must evaluate so much conflicting research, they do not easily surrender their common sense to surveys. Dismissing two surveys proving that when most people heard the word "cola," they thought it meant Coca-Cola, a Delaware court noted that the existence of cola beverages is a well-recognized fact: "We see no reason why the court should pretend ignorance of that with which the general public is familiar." Another judge, rendering an opinion at odds with research results, said, "The conclusions of market researchers and other expert witnesses are [not] binding on the court. . . . [T]he court must . . . rely on its own experience and understanding of human nature."

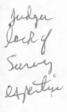

Sophisticated as some judges are about survey methodology, others are not, challenging such basic techniques as sampling—allowing a few parts to speak for the whole. When a Sears, Roebuck store claimed it had overpaid local sales taxes to a California city, it used statistical sampling to estimate how much it was owed. Based on a random sampling of 33 of 826 sales days, the store claimed $27,000. But the court objected to a "guess" when there were "facts" available, and ordered the store to do an audit of every one of the 826 sales days at a cost of $3,500. The total, which the city paid to Sears: $26,750.22.

For researchers, preparing studies for the legal system

Risks of Survey in court

is so risky that many simply will not do it. In court, researchers know, they and their work will be subjected to a level of scrutiny they rarely face from the public or even from their paying clients. (John Henry Wigmore, the dean of legal evidence, called the witness stand "the slaughterhouse of reputations.") Any flaws in a study will be pounced on and magnified. The other side probably has its own survey, prepared by another expert with excellent credentials and finding exactly the reverse. Once a survey is introduced, it will become a central issue in the case, and might draw attention away from other strong elements. Researchers are under oath and on the record, and they risk embarrassing inconsistencies—or even perjury charges—if they change their stories dramatically from testimony to testimony. They cannot have too close a relationship with the lawyers who retained them, but it must be close enough to know they are answering the questions unique to each legal action.

The ethical standards of research have slipped, by stages, so that now there are different rules for survey research done for the court. In surveys for litigation, researchers put less in writing, because opposing lawyers will second-guess every choice. They streamline their studies, making them as simple, narrow and direct as possible, and omit factors that might soften or cast doubt on their central point. In survey research for the courtroom, many researchers say every question must be pretested, and interviews must be validated (checked by a supervisor) at a higher rate than usual. Some researchers, however, do not pretest their surveys, or do so less than usual. "It's very easy to be accused of changing a question simply because it did not produce the desired response," said Harry O'Neill, vice chairman of the Roper Organization.

"Rules" for Court Survey

Since it has become standard procedure for many kinds of cases to produce two sets of competing data, judges and juries often fall back on the more subjective judgment of credibility: which expert had better credentials, was more articulate or held up better under cross-examination. Some legal scholars believe the courts could end the prostituting of opinions and the ping-pong of courtroom research by having the court commission independent experts to do neutral studies. Such court-appointed experts would cost less than partisan experts, contended R. J. Gerber, an Arizona superior court judge, and experts would be more available to the poor, who are at a disadvantage in research wars. The 1985 *Manual for Complex Litigation* recommends another alternative to the current system: Competing attorneys would jointly sponsor a survey, whose results would be binding.

An alternative But as Fred W. Morgan, a marketing professor, pointed out, "because each opponent would be interested in developing a survey that's likely to yield results supportive of its position, negotiating a mutually acceptable research design would be very difficult." As to a neutral court-appointed expert, others say that would only transfer the battle from the choice of the data to the choice of the expert. The person who has risen to the most preeminent position within the field is not necessarily the smartest or the wisest.

◆

IN COMPLEX CASES INVOLVING MORE than two parties, dueling data can become a morass from which there is no hope of a meaningful resolution. That was the threat facing Francis E. McGovern, a professor of law at the University of Alabama, when he was called in to help resolve the final chapter of the Dalkon Shield litigation. To close out the bankruptcy of the shield's maker, the court needed information from a sample of the hundreds of thousands of women who were claiming shield injuries. Without the court's intervention, it was likely —inevitable—that the six competing interests in the bankruptcy proceedings would produce six different sets of self-serving numbers. The project was shaping up to be the largest piece of survey research in American legal history, and McGovern wanted to avoid the squabbling over data that would prolong the suffering of many. He decided to try to braid the six different interests into one strand of data.

Long before McGovern arrived on the scene, research had been shaping the destiny of the Dalkon Shield. Since most of the shield's twenty-year life was lived in court, clinical trials, epidemiological studies and reviews of the literature were produced by both sides. Doctors who had done

DALCON SHIELD (handwritten annotation)

studies (including one who said he had but hadn't) testified for and against women claiming injury. At each step along the way, research had reinforced with unshakable consistency the many antithetical interests.

A study by one of the shield's inventors, Dr. Hugh Davis of Johns Hopkins University, first proved that the device effectively prevented pregnancies without side effects. The time was the late 1960s, when the sexual revolution was sweeping a generation of young women into clinics and doctors' offices for birth control. The pill, an early favorite, had faded in popularity as studies began showing that users—especially smokers—risked possibly fatal blood clots. Intrauterine devices were impractical for women who had not borne children because their uteruses tended to expel them. Davis's breakthrough was to create an intrauterine device whose ten jagged prongs dug so strongly into the uterine wall that it could not be ejected. Davis's study was published in the *American Journal of Obstetrics and Gynecology* in February 1970 under the title "The shield intrauterine device: A superior modern contraceptive device." "Effective protection against pregnancy is achieved with a modern IUD without the actual and potential hazards of systemic medication for birth control," Davis wrote. "Taken altogether, the superior performance of the shield intrauterine devices makes this technic a first choice method of conception control."

As would someday become clear, Davis's study was deeply flawed. Although the results supposedly described the *FLAWS* (handwritten annotation) experiences of women over the course of a year, in fact most of Davis's subjects had worn the shield for less than half a year—not nearly long enough to judge a birth control device's efficacy. Furthermore, 640 subjects was too few to predict a pregnancy rate, especially in the range of 1 percent to 2 percent. Finally, Davis began the analysis of his statistics just three days after the study closed, almost certainly missing some pregnancies that would not be discovered until weeks, possibly months, later.

Several months after Davis's study was published, the A. H. Robins Company, which had one of the most aggressive sales forces in the country but no experience with contraceptives, bought the Dalkon Shield. Davis received $240,000, about a third of a 10 percent royalty and a $20,000-a-year consulting contract. Shortly thereafter, a Robins staff physician advised Robins's management that Davis was keeping inconsistent clinical data on his trials, resulting in different efficacy rates (99.22 percent or 96.9 percent) depending on the choice of data. Despite that, Robins's promotional literature continued to cite the better figure.

At the time the shield went on the market in February 1970, companies could sell medical devices like the shield—and silicone breast implants—without Food and Drug Administration approval. (Largely because of the shield, that changed in 1976.) Because the shield was distributed only through doctors, it carried the aura of medical approval and safety—all based on one study by the self-interested inventor. And Hugh Davis's study tested only the shield's effectiveness, not its safety. That would be tested on the public.

Intimations of trouble with the Dalkon Shield came almost immediately from doctors. "I have just inserted my 10th Dalkon Shield and have found that procedure to be the most traumatic manipulation ever perpetrated on womanhood," a doctor wrote to Robins. Another doctor called the shield "a veritable instrument of torture." Meanwhile, doctors began noticing episodes of quick, virulent and sometimes fatal septic abortions (miscarriages caused by infections), as well as pelvic inflammatory disease, in women who used the Dalkon Shield. Robins largely ignored these anecdotal reports. Over the next two years, evidence against the shield continued to build. Finally, in the spring of 1974, after months of bad publicity, Robins suspended sales of the shield in the United States. A year later, with at least fifteen women dead of septic abortions, Robins stopped worldwide sales of the shield.

Although the Dalkon Shield would never again be inserted in a woman, its story had only begun. The shield was still implanted in millions of women, and the company fought hard against a recall, claiming there was no solid proof against the shield and believing that a recall would imply legal liability. As a consequence, during the next thirteen years, thousands of women would file legal claims against Robins.

By 1985, it was clear that A. H. Robins could not pay

Bankruptcy

the mounting and threatened damages and would need to reorganize its debts with bankruptcy court protection. The very profitable company—maker of Chap Stick and Robitussin—had assets to be carved up, and many people wanted them. The injured women wanted their compensation, and so did the shareholders and other creditors. Under mounting financial and legal pressure, Robins had reluctantly put itself up for sale, and was bought by the American Home Products Corporation. That company, as well as Robins's former insurer, Aetna, wanted to pay the injured as little as possible. Before Robins could emerge from bankruptcy and become part of American Home Products, the court needed to know how much should be set aside to compensate current and future victims of the Dalkon Shield. It would need to estimate the total number of claimants, and how much each woman would collect.

Assets Bought

A veteran of other mass litigation, Professor McGovern had experience sampling big groups to assess damages. But the Dalkon Shield case was bigger and more complicated than most, and the warring parties even more vituperative. Knowing the potential for dueling data was high, McGovern decided to try to induce the adversaries to agree on a set of data they would not later attack. As the study was designed, every side—the company, the trade creditors, the equity committee, claimants, future claimants and Robins's insurer —would have an opportunity to try to influence the methodology to suit its own purposes. Once they had agreed to the process, however, they were bound by its results. "If they all didn't fully participate in the data collection and have the opportunity to say what they wanted, it would have been a terrible mess," said McGovern.

the parties

Even McGovern and the warring parties did not realize what a vast project this would turn out to be. By the time Robins filed for bankruptcy, there were already some 16,000 plaintiffs. Everyone suspected there could be as many as 30,000 to 50,000 potential plaintiffs. But when the company advertised for injured women to file shield claims, the total was close to 200,000. For most of those cases, the court had no information either about the strength of their allegations

# of plaintiffs

Problem: $ to pay each victim ??

—Could they prove they had used the shield? Could they prove they had been hurt?—or if they could prove they had been injured, how badly.

Using classic research technique, McGovern's survey would approach a small sample of the total universe of Dalkon Shield users by mailed questionnaire, put a value on their responses and then project the outcome onto the larger group. Once the court decided on the total amount to be set aside for the plaintiffs, it was fixed; no number of unexpected claims or injuries in the future could increase it.

The process of creating a massive survey research project from scratch and by consensus was, as McGovern said, "like building a plane as we flew across the country." It was also excruciatingly expensive and time-consuming, involving thousands of hours of conference calls among the competing experts. So prickly were the various parties about possible biases that when women called an 800 number to get help filling out the questionnaires, the answers came from scripts agreed upon by all sides.

As in any survey, preparing the questionnaire was the most complicated task, and it was here the various sides tried hardest to put their stamp on the methodology. It was in Robins's best interests to discourage women from responding to the survey. Little, if any, money would need to be set aside for nonrespondents, or so the company argued. If they could not do the relatively simple task of answering some questions and assembling their medical records, how likely would they be to embark on the arduous process of collecting money from the bankruptcy court? To keep the numbers low, Robins wanted a long and complicated questionnaire.

The claimants' committee, on the other hand, wanted the biggest universe possible, so it wanted to keep the questionnaire brief. In the end, the questionnaire was fifty pages long and consisted of eleven sections. "I got agreement by asking more questions than fewer," said McGovern. "That was a mechanism by which I got consensus."

Robins also preferred open-ended questions about the harm a woman was claiming from the shield, figuring that offering a list might encourage some to take a stab at it. The claimants' committee favored a quick and easy checklist. The compromise questionnaire contained both a checklist and open-ended questions about medical injury.

The biggest fight among the parties erupted over the question of whether women should be asked questions about their sexual histories. Robins, in line with its long-running defense of the shield as a scapegoat for sexual promiscuity, insisted on asking about sexual partners and practices. One question asked a woman to record the dates of the first and last times she had sexual relations with every sexual partner in her life before her injury occurred—and whether those people had sex with other people during that period. The claimants' committee violently opposed the sexual history questions, saying they were irrelevant and that they would bias the sample by discouraging participation. Naturally, both sides found doctors to testify either that the sexual information would be useless or that it was relevant. The bankruptcy judge, without explaining why, ordered the questions to be included. No use of the data those questions produced was made by experts from any side.

In all, 6,000 claimants were surveyed. Of the sample members who had been ruled eligible to make claims, about 65 percent returned the questionnaire. McGovern called that response "extraordinary," and it was, considering the complexities of the survey. But for most survey researchers, 65 percent is on the low side of acceptable.

Fourteen months and some $5 million later, McGovern had a set of data indicating how many women could make a case that the shield had injured them and how badly they were injured. Now it was time to manipulate the numbers. McGovern's survey had not usurped the parties' right to duel with data—it had only deferred it.

The ideal way to estimate the total cost of liquidating all the claims would have been to take a sample of the claims, liquidate them and then project the results onto the entire population. Instead of doing that, however, each interested party ran the group's consensual data through computers programmed with its own self-serving assumptions, creating six estimates for how much the injured would eventually collect. Robins estimated it would owe the women $1.2 billion. The committee of injured figured the company should put aside

$7,1 Bill

$7.1 billion. In the middle came the self-interested claims of the equity committee, the unsecured creditors and the insurance company.

How could the same set of data produce estimates with a fivefold difference? The answer is all in the assumptions. In computer models, assumption is the rudder that steers the boat, and someone has his hand on the tiller. A public health scientist who had tried to determine the future incidence of asbestos-related disease for Johns-Manville was asked about the assumptions he had made. "Were you requested at any time by Manville or its counsel to make assumptions in your estimates that would result in lower rather than higher resulting numbers?" he was asked in sworn testimony.

"I was asked . . . that whenever I had the chance to choose between two equally plausible assumptions, I should choose the assumption which led to the smaller number of cases of disease," the scientist replied.

In the shield survey, the assumptions would include how many women would have conclusive medical proof that they had used a shield and how many would be eliminated by statutes of limitation. Not surprisingly, each side used whatever assumptions would produce the right figure. Based on responses to the questionnaire, the company, the creditors and the insurer—those aiming for a low payout—assumed more than half the women would never file a claim or would receive little or no money. The company's expert put all the potential claimants through five screens he had devised, reducing the number of women who would get payments from 195,000 to less than 25,000. But the claimants' expert figured that given enough time and the incentive of a payoff, which the survey did not offer, every woman who was eligible would file a claim. This side also assumed that many more of the claims would turn out to be legitimate—that, for example, women would eventually be able to locate their medical records.

So far apart were the high and low sides that no compromise seemed possible. At a five-and-a-half-day hearing, fifteen medical and statistical experts for the competing parties testified about how they had arrived at their estimates. But as Richard Sobol pointed out, "The witnesses had no exper-

judge $2.475 bill

tise relative to [their assumptions], and no evidence or even opinion was offered in support of the assumptions that were made. The witnesses simply made the assumptions that would support the result favored by their employer." Although the judge hoped that the parties would be able to agree on a final amount, that did not happen. In the end, without disclosing his reasoning, the judge decided himself: $2.475 billion—more than double the low estimate, a third of the high. Even after the parties had agreed to the final figure, the judge would not explain whether his ludicrously precise figure was simply a compromise. McGovern, proud as he was of his survey, acknowledges that it may actually have delayed rather than speeded resolution of the case. Had all the sides known that they were going to have to reconcile themselves to a "high level of uncertainty," McGovern wrote, they might have resolved the case earlier.

◆

IN SURVEY RESEARCH, THE BIGGEST and best work generally shows up in unfair-competition and trademark litigation, where the adversaries, usually large companies, can afford top-quality surveys. These companies, which are often in food, drug or packaged goods businesses, can also recycle surveys prepared for court for market research purposes.

The boom in survey research in the courtroom began in the 1970s, as the television networks dropped their prohibitions against comparison advertising, and companies began naming their competitors rather than just calling them Brand X. Sometimes that comparative advertising, especially for products with little objective difference among various brands, like shampoo, aspirin or orange juice, involved consumer surveys, which became the "objective" measure for proving superiority. Because surveys can be so persuasive, showing with scientific trappings and apparent numerical certainty that one product is better or more popular than another, their proliferation brought a boom in lawsuits as well. "In shampoo tests with over 900 women like me," a model in an advertisement said, "Body on Tap got higher ratings than Prell for body. Higher than Flex for conditioning. Higher than

Sassoon for strong, healthy-looking hair." Vidal Sassoon sued Bristol-Myers. As it turned out, no woman in the test had tried more than one shampoo. Instead, groups of about 200 had tried one product and rated it. The court found this methodology "misleading."

All lawsuits alleging false advertising or unfair competition revolve around people's perceptions—what they *thought* a company was trying to say or convey. How else to measure them but with a survey?

In the case of the two diet entree giants locked in a legal battle, dueling surveys found that people either were or were not confused by one company's advertisements. Lean Cuisine, made by Stouffer Foods, had been running a series of advertisements aimed at people on Weight Watchers diets, showing them that Lean Cuisine frozen food was compatible with their Weight Watchers regimen. Weight Watchers said the ads were inaccurate and might confuse consumers, making them think Weight Watchers was endorsing Lean Cuisine. Weight Watchers sued, alleging trademark infringement and false advertising.

Both sides retained market-research experts. The Weight Watchers expert conducted mall interviews, screening people first for certain specifications (they looked for women between the ages of eighteen and fifty-five, for example). Then the interviewers showed the subjects three advertisements, among them one of Lean Cuisine's offenders, and asked such questions as whether they saw any "connection" between Lean Cuisine and Weight Watchers. If they did they were given six ways to describe that connection—for example, was there a business connection? Were the products interchangeable? Were both simply diet foods? Meanwhile, Lean Cuisine's researchers screened for males and females eighteen to fifty-five and showed the subjects three ads, all involving two products each. One was an ad proclaiming that a ticket on Japan Airlines would get you to Tokyo in fourteen hours, while an AT&T card would get you back to the United States in fourteen seconds. Another was an advertisement showing that Now cigarettes have less tar than Carlton. The third was the Lean Cuisine advertisement. The interviewers then asked questions about who sponsored or placed each ad.

*Court
Standards;*

Over the years, courts have developed several general criteria on the survey research they see. Survey researchers must select the right "universe"; draw a representative sample; design fair and correct questions; have experts at the helm; accurately report the data; work in accordance with generally accepted standards; do it independently of the lawyers; and employ professional interviewers who do not know for whom they are working. Since most surveys violate one or more of these standards, the courts must weigh the quantity and quality of each survey's violations against those of the other.

Perhaps the most popular area for judicial nit-picking of survey research is whether the right universe has been chosen. Selecting the right universe assures that the answers can be projected onto other people who were not surveyed. In the matter of universes, both the Weight Watchers and Lean Cuisine surveys were wanting. Weight Watchers researchers defined their universe as women who had bought a frozen entree in the past six months and had tried to lose weight through diet and/or exercise in the past year. That was too broad. Why not narrow it to women who had bought a *diet* frozen entree and tried to lose weight by dieting, not exercising? the judge wondered. The interpretation of the data was also faulty, overstating the number of people who were confused by the Lean Cuisine ad. Only people who believed the two had a "business connection" could be considered confused, ruled the judge, Michael Mukasey of the Southern District of New York. So while Weight Watchers had found that 63.5 percent of the people were confused, only 13.2 percent were legally confused.

But Weight Watchers got off easy compared to its adversary. Lean Cuisine also had a flawed sample—again not screening for people who ate diet frozen foods—and the questions were not a good measure of confusion. Worse, using the other two advertisements to adjust for "noise" factors, such as guessing or the confusion these respondents would feel looking at any advertisement, Lean Cuisine concluded that the level of confusion for Lean Cuisine's advertisements was "essentially zero." This conclusion assumes the other two ads set an acceptable level of confusion for ads that mention two products, and to be actionable an ad must exceed it. This "assures a party's control over a study's outcome by use of the control ads," Mukasey ruled. "I accord plaintiff's survey slight weight . . . I accord no weight at all to defendants' survey."

In the face of so much complicated and often sloppy research, the courts can be unpredictable and inconsistent, accepting methodology in one suit that is scoffed at in another. The defendant in a case involving competing lines of stuffed animals wanted to show that buyers had no problem distinguishing its product, the Goodtime Gang, from a competitor, Care Bears. No confusion would mean no trademark infringement. A group of girls aged six to twelve and a group of mothers of girls that age were shown four sets of animals. The girls were asked what they would request if they wanted each product, and their mothers were asked what they would buy if their children requested each product. But as the court noted, the stuffed animals were inside their original packaging, and so the names of each of the products could be easily read. "[T]his tested the participants' ability to read and little else," the court ruled.

Yet in another case, the researcher removed all tags and tabs from jeans before asking respondents for reactions; the court reduced the weight accorded the survey, ruling that the experiment did not replicate what shoppers really experienced.

◆

WHILE SURVEY RESEARCH WAS CRITICAL to the resolution of the Dalkon Shield claims, other kinds of research had played a major role in the litigation that delivered the company to bankruptcy court. As it made its millions of dollars of profits on the shield and then began fighting the first lawsuits, A. H. Robins coasted along on Hugh Davis's research and a few other small studies. Women who were complaining about getting pregnant with the shield in place were suffering from the luck of the draw; if they had pelvic inflammatory disease, maybe they were a little loose, morally speaking. Furthermore, their doctors may have inserted the shield improperly.

There was no evidence that the shield caused any particular woman's injury. All anyone knew for sure was that some women with shields happened to become pregnant and mortally sick. Despite the bravado, however, the avalanche of lawsuits against the company forced it to do something it had barely begun to do before: study the safety of its own device.

As the first shield cases came to trial, both sides struggled to find studies that would bolster their positions. No large-scale epidemiological studies of the shield had been done. Epidemiologists study groups of people and try to show correlations or associations between certain diseases and the habits, characteristics or exposures of those people—correlations that could not be attributed to chance alone. At this point it would be impossible to do prospective studies of the shield—studies that would track a group of people forward— because it would be unethical to implant the device. So any epidemiological studies would have to be retrospective, relying on the memories and medical records of a disparate group of women. In any population of women, some would suffer from pelvic disease, just as in any population there would be people afflicted by birth defects and lung cancer. What can be attributed to the use of a product and what to life itself? Other confounding factors, such as multiple sex partners and varying hygiene practices, would make it difficult to single the shield out for blame.

In the meantime, one of the few shield studies that did exist—Hugh Davis's—was becoming an issue in the various lawsuits against Robins. In 1974, Bradley Post, a Wichita, Kansas, lawyer representing a woman named Connie Deemer in a malpractice suit involving the shield, deposed Robins's detail man—the Robins representative who had peddled the product to the doctor—and got copies of the official material the company had been distributing to doctors, which included Hugh Davis's study. The promotional material "made the shield look so good it would practically be malpractice *not* to use it," Post said. Post quickly added Robins to the lawsuit as a defendant and went on conducting discovery. He found that in its promotional material to doctors, Robins had used the preliminary data from Davis's study showing a pregnancy rate of 1.1 percent. Later data from Davis's study showed the pregnancy rate to be five times higher. The revelation that the company knew about the final data but had not included it in its promotional material helped win Connie Deemer $85,000.

Without that, however, Deemer's chance of collecting any money was slim. Although a doctor could swear that in his or her opinion the shield had caused Deemer's perforated uterus, where was the proof of causation? In diseases or conditions that take years or even decades to develop, there may be hundreds, even thousands, of scattered cases before there is a pattern, and even then scientists may not be able to pin down exactly how it happens on a molecular level. It is almost inevitable that much of the courtroom science produced in the early years of an epidemiological battle, such as the association between asbestos and lung cancer, will turn out to be wrong. The judicial process tests the scientific truth prematurely. Not until thousands of people have used or breathed or drunk something millions of times does a pattern begin to gain a solidity approaching truth.

The gap between what is possible and what is true has long troubled the courts. In the often-cited suit of *Ferebee* v. *Chevron Chemical Company*, in which an agricultural worker claimed that long-term exposure to the chemical paraquat had caused his fatal pulmonary fibrosis, an appellate court in 1984 laid out the dilemma judges and juries face when confronted by dueling experts. "[A] cause-effect relationship need not be clearly established by animal or epidemiological studies before a doctor can testify that, in his opinion, such a relationship exists," the court said. The test for allowing a plaintiff to recover damages in a suit like this, the court continued, "is not scientific certainty but legal sufficiency."

In its defense against Dalkon Shield claims, A. H. Robins used studies and expert witnesses in two ways. It attacked the scientific expertise of its opponents, arguing there was no definitive proof that the shield caused harm. (Lack of a causal chain has persuaded some courts whose judges are uncomfortable with the uncertainties inherent in statistical associations.) Robins also commissioned its own studies in a way that gave the company sole discretion over whether the results would be made public. The company turned the administration of its research over to its law firm, which in turn commissioned outside investigators to do the trials. By running its research through its attorneys, Robins was able to claim that the studies were "work products" of the lawyers and so protected from discovery. Even so, in 1984 a judge ordered Robins to turn over several studies commissioned by Robins's lawyers—the "secret studies," as plaintiffs' attorneys called them because they had never shown up in court. Before all the studies were released, Robins filed for bankruptcy.

To the plaintiffs' lawyers, the idea that Robins was in charge of testing its own device was like the fox guarding the chicken coop. "When a company is on the line the way Robins was, they want studies that come out the way they want them to," said Douglas Bragg, a Denver lawyer who represented shield plaintiffs. "They try to run them in secret, they try to pick researchers they think will give them what they want, and they monitor the studies. If they start to come out badly, they terminate them."

Indeed, internal documents from Aetna made public in the late 1980s show just that. Scientists at New York University had implanted shields in baboons to test whether there was a higher incidence of pelvic disease among shield wearers than other IUD users. In a 1977 memo, an Aetna attorney said the study would be terminated if it found higher incidence of disease with the shield. The study, funded mostly by Aetna but partly by Robins, did, and it was halted.

While Robins could afford to commission its own exonerating studies, the plaintiffs were typically represented by small personal-injury firms that could not. A couple of small studies in the mid-1970s helped their case somewhat, but the plaintiffs had to wait until 1983 for a large-scale study. That year, the Centers for Disease Control in Atlanta published a study showing a higher risk of pelvic disease with the shield than without—and a higher risk with the shield than with other IUDs. The study was based on data from a 1981 study on IUDs and pelvic disease called the Women's Health Study, sponsored by the National Institutes of Health, which had found a higher incidence of pelvic disease across all brands of intrauterine devices but did not compare the different brands. The CDC study, for all practical purposes, ended the shield's life.

It was the data collected in the Women's Health Study that Richard Kronmal, the contrarian biostatistician, dismissed in his 1991 article in the *Journal of Clinical Epidemiology*. The article, called "The Intrauterine Device and Pelvic Inflammatory Disease: The Women's Health Study Reanalyzed," said the data behind the indictment of the Dalkon Shield were biased and incomplete. "The [Women's Health Study] was poorly designed, careless in its implementation and analysis and grossly over-interpreted," Kronmal wrote.

Like an increasing amount of modern research, Kronmal's study was simply a reassessment and recycling of data that had been collected earlier by someone else. As technology improves, it is hard to resist going back to old data and using more sophisticated techniques to analyze it. In 1990, a group of pathologists re-examined the fourteen-year-old slides of rat tumors that had formed the basis of a damning study of the chemical dioxin. The team, whose work was partly financed by the paper industry, concluded there were 50 percent fewer liver tumors than the original count had found.

Instead of producing any new data, Kronmal's shield study simply tried to discredit the earlier work, arguing with its methodology. For example, Kronmal said the Women's Health Study should not have excluded women who had a history of pelvic inflammatory disease from the sample. The Women's Health Study researchers believed these women would not be typical because, for example, their doctors might have recommended against an IUD because they had had the disease. Kronmal believed they should not have been excluded, because it had not been proven that a history of pelvic inflammatory disease altered IUD use. Kronmal also said the Dalkon Shield had been proven safe and effective in seventy-one clinical trials. Unfortunately, only sixteen of the trials noted whether users had suffered from pelvic inflammatory disease—the very condition at the heart of most Dalkon Shield litigation. The Women's Health Study, and others like it, Kronmal and his fellow authors concluded, caused

Robins's bankruptcy and the removal of most IUDs from the American market, resulting in hardship for many women.

Kronmal waited so long to release his study, he said, because it had originally been done, in 1983, for A. H. Robins, and he thought that might taint other scientists' perceptions of it. Indeed, Kronmal had approached A. H. Robins with his idea of reanalyzing the Women's Health data and asked for help. Before the study could be used in court, the company stopped mounting defenses in individual suits. Another author of the study, Stephen Mumford, was an expert witness for the equity committee in the hearings on the value of shield claims.

The authors of the Women's Health Study replied to Kronmal's criticisms in an article in the same journal. Calling it "replete with factual error, misrepresentation, and overstatement," the authors said that although their original study was imperfect, it contributed to an understanding of the IUD. Providing expert testimony on behalf of industry or individuals "does not preclude [investigators] from debating the scientific merits of research in peer-reviewed journals," they continued. "We are surprised that Kronmal *et al.* delayed for several years the submission of their manuscript, despite their concern that the Women's Health Study was seriously flawed and that its results were leading to loss of an important contraceptive method."

Kronmal's study, and other research questioning the association between shields and pelvic inflammatory disease, did have its use for the trust allocating the awards to injured women. Despite an understanding among plaintiffs and their lawyers that the trust would not argue causation, it did just that—contesting again whether the device was defective. All of the dozens of clinical trials, epidemiological studies and McGovern's massive survey had come to this: The women had research that proved the shield caused injuries, and the people with the money had research to prove that it did not.

◆

IN LEGAL ACTIONS WHERE THE issue is wider than the fate of one person or company, suits built almost entirely upon statistics

are becoming more common. Such suits—often in class actions alleging monopolistic practices or employment discrimination—put judges in the position of sifting through reams
of complicated statistical analysis—hypergeometric versus
binomial models; one-tailed tests versus two-tailed tests;
dummy coefficients and regression coefficients. No statistical
analysis can prove causation per se—the statistics simply
estimate the likelihood that the results occurred merely by
chance.

A typical Title VII (employment discrimination) dispute
involves two somewhat different but overlapping data bases
and two somewhat different but overlapping sets of variables
that are then subjected to regression analyses. Each side will
typically claim that the other's choices of data base and variables are misguided. The judge, who likely has no advanced
statistical training, must decide which data base and which
variables produce the truest picture of reality.

In one decision, in a race and sex discrimination suit
against a Texas bank, the judge devoted 80 of the 127 pages
of his decision to a review of regression analysis and an analysis of the experts' statistical evidence. The judge said he
and his clerks had taken a month off from their other duties
to devote themselves to understanding the issues and evidence before them. In the end, the judge's decision was felt
by many statisticians and lawyers to be a model of statistical
assessment. The judge himself, however, expressed doubts.
"I remain wary of the siren call of numerical display," the
judge wrote, "and hope that here the resistance was adequate; that the ultimate findings are the product of judgment,
not calculation."

One of the longest and most complicated employment
discrimination suits in history, the Equal Employment Opportunity Commission's action against Sears, Roebuck & Co.,
was fought largely with statistics. The suit involved an EEOC
claim that Sears, the largest private employer of women in
the country, discriminated against women in hiring, pay and
promotion. Rather than bring individual women into court to
testify, which EEOC lawyers said they had learned side-
tracked cases into debates about personal character, the
EEOC's entire case was presented in the form of statistics.

Sears's defense relied heavily on undermining the EEOC's statistics, although the retailer also put on the stand some experts and Sears managers to defend the company's policies. Together, the two sides' statistical experts produced 5,275 pages of trial testimony.

The Sears suit, like other sex and race discrimination suits of recent years, illustrates how difficult it can be to prove a case with statistics. No matter how obvious it seemed that something was amiss at Sears—in the five years before the EEOC started its investigation, fewer than 10 percent of the high-paying commission sales jobs had gone to women— the company could still effectively dispute the statistics demonstrating that disparity and produce its own surveys and studies showing that women simply were not interested in higher-paying jobs.

As an example of the kinds of variables statisticians have to wrestle with in suits like this, take the problem of determining how many women *wanted* high-paying commission jobs—selling such big-ticket items as refrigerators, auto parts, furnaces, roofing. The EEOC's statistician used the employment applications from 33,000 rejected applicants and almost 2,000 applicants who had been hired and compared the percentage of women who had been hired for commission sales jobs with the percentage of women in the applicant pool. Unfortunately, however, the applicants had not been asked whether they were interested in commission sales jobs or not; the EEOC made the sweeping assumption that anyone who had applied for a sales job was interested in a commission sales job. It was unlikely that every applicant for a sales job wanted a commission sales job—such jobs were, from a financial standpoint, slightly riskier and often involved working odd hours—and this worked heavily against the EEOC's case.

Sears did not do its own analysis, but rather attacked two assumptions in the EEOC's analysis—the assumption that women wanted the high-paying commission sales jobs and the assumption that women were qualified for such jobs. The company presented a string of witnesses—store managers, personnel managers and other store personnel—who said there was no discrimination; morale surveys of Sears employees; a study of the characteristics of commission salespeople; and other evidence from their files showing they were not discriminatory. Sears also said that because statis- tics showed men outperformed women in commission sales jobs in their first year after promotion, men must be more qualified for such jobs than women.

The EEOC lost in a federal district court, and then lost again on appeal. Writing a partial dissent, however, one judge criticized Sears and the courts for their conclusions about the interests and qualifications of women for commission sales jobs. "There is scarcely any recognition of the employer's role in shaping the 'interests' of applicants," wrote the judge. "Even the majority is willing to concede that lack of opportu- nity may drive lack of interest, but dismisses the matter as a 'chicken-egg' problem."

◆

SURVEYS ARE REGULAR FEATURES OF three other kinds of legal proceedings—obscenity suits, change of venue requests and jury selection. Sometimes the survey persuades the judge, and sometimes it does not. In a case in the 1950s, the NAACP hired the Roper Organization to poll several southern coun- ties in preparation for a change of venue motion for a black man accused of raping a white woman. The poll showed sig- nificant differences of prejudice among the residents of sev- eral counties, with the greatest prejudice being in the county where the trial was scheduled to be held. The prosecutor objected to the admission of the poll on the ground that it was hearsay. In the place of the poll, he put on the stand a parade of leading citizens, each of whom testified that the black man could get a fair trial in that county. The judge agreed and denied the motion.

In another change of venue request, the Rajneesh Foun- dation, defending itself in a civil suit against a former disciple who wanted her money back, requested that the trial be moved out of the Bhagwan's Oregon neighborhood because the locals were hostile to the growing and tax-free commune. The foundation was an arm of the religious cult led by the self-proclaimed prophet Bhagwan Shree Rajneesh. To prove that the potential jurors were biased, the foundation commissioned a poll, which showed among other things that 40 percent of county residents believed a Rajneeshee "would lie to protect Rajneeshee interests."

Judge Owen Panner was naturally interested in learning the methodological details of the poll, including its provenance, and he asked the Rajneesh lawyer to find out. In a letter to the judge, Swami Prartho Subhan began by saying that all the interviewers for the poll were "human beings and American citizens," but then acknowledged they were also all Rajneeshees. "The quest for truth and the courage to tell the truth are fundamental to Rajneeshees," the swami concluded, "who are perfectly capable of undertaking any scientific enterprise objectively." Connections between interviewers and litigants violates standard research procedure; that was one of the reasons Panner gave for throwing out the poll.

In jury selection, surveys are used to determine what attitudes or demographic characteristics might make a person most likely to condemn or acquit the defendant. In one case, a criminal action involving euthanasia, a survey was done in the community to test people's attitudes about it. To the surprise of the researchers, people's religions did not affect their feelings about euthanasia. Instead, age seemed to be a determining factor, with the young and old somewhat open-minded and the forty-five- to fifty-five-year-olds least sympathetic.

In obscenity cases, surveys are increasingly offered as a measure of the community standard, something many courts feel the jury itself represents. Here, too, the research is invariably designed to produce the outcome needed by the defense to show that its materials are not obscene and do not violate community standards.

In a 1988 Virginia obscenity case, a poll was commissioned by the defendants, who had been charged with racketeering in connection with the sale of raunchy videos and magazines with such titles as *Crotches*, *Tied Up*, *Wet Shots* and *The Punishment of Anne*. Perhaps wisely, the poller kept his questions about obscenity very broad. The introduction to the questions mentioned such specific practices as bondage, anal sex, group sex and others, but thereafter the questions referred simply to "nudity and sex." So, for example, respondents were asked if they agreed with the statement that adults who want to should be able to obtain and view materials depicting nudity and sex. The court found this to be totally unacceptable, saying "the term 'bondage' in the poll's definition of 'nudity and sex' simply does not adequately describe the sexual and physical abuse depicted" in the material at issue. "There are," the court continued, "no terms in the definition that inform the respondent that he or she is being asked questions about materials which show . . . a nude woman's breasts being repeatedly jabbed and punctured by pins while she hangs in chains."

The defense also tried to introduce evidence from an expert witness, something courts have frowned on in obscenity cases, reasoning that once the offending material is in evidence, the jurors can be their own experts. This expert, a sociologist, conducted an "ethnographical" study proving that the materials in question were acceptable to the adult community of Alexandria, Virginia, where the suit was tried. He did this primarily by going to bookstores and video stores of which some, but not all, sold adult books or tapes, and talking to the proprietors and customers about sexually explicit materials. He also called newspaper editors and asked them about letters to the editor they may have received about sexually explicit materials. He did not visit churches, community centers, garden clubs or Rotary Clubs.

◆

AN EVEN NEWER AREA WHERE survey research is beginning to be used—and manipulated by the opposing parties—is in trying to place a value on things that are not traded in markets, particularly in environmental cases. In several pieces of legislation, Congress has tried to force those who harm the environment to bear the economic costs of their mischief. But how that harm should be measured is complicated. The environmental damage may have wiped out a stream that provided a fisherman's living or a lake that brought vacationers to a resort. But Congress and courts have also recognized that a pretty stream or a clean lake may have value even to people who do not live near them. Those people might get pleasure just from thinking about that clean river, or they might think of the bubbling brook as a legacy to be passed to future generations.

One way of valuing natural resources, called contingent valuation, asks people directly how much value they would place on something: "How much are you willing to pay for preserving the remaining grizzlies in Yellowstone National Park?"

But contingent valuation is remarkably malleable, as parties to legal actions have quickly learned. Take, for example, the case of the Navajo Generating Station, a coal-fired power plant a dozen miles outside the Grand Canyon. Under pressure from the Grand Canyon Trust and the Environmental Defense Fund, the power plant had agreed to reduce sulfur dioxide emissions, which would improve visibility in the Grand Canyon. Three different studies were done to estimate the economic benefits of improved visibility.

One study, conducted for the Environmental Protection Agency and the National Parks Service, found through a survey that people would pay $95 a household a year to improve visibility to about 200 kilometers from about 150 kilometers. Another study, the "Preservation Value" study, also prepared for the EPA and the parks service, came to the conclusion that people would be willing to pay $1.30 to $3.60 a household a year. A third study, conducted for the owners of the power plant, found that people would be willing to pay between zero and fifty cents a household a year.

To illustrate how such a figure is arrived at, consider the surveys used for the "Preservation Value" study. The following question was mailed to 3,345 households in five states (with 1,647 usable responses): "What is the *most* your household would be willing to pay *every year* in increased prices and taxes to have average visibility improve from *Photograph C* to *Photograph B* at all national parks in the Southwest?" The subjects were given a choice in categories between zero and $750. The researchers then adjusted the figure to apply only to the Grand Canyon. Then some more adjustments were applied to arrive at the estimated range.

Contingent valuation is controversial for many reasons. One is that because people would not actually have to pay anything, their answers might be manipulated or exaggerated to nudge public policy in the right direction. Another is that most people would not have the vaguest idea how much a natural resource would be worth monetarily, and so their answers might be arbitrary. Still another is that people answer quite differently depending on whether they are asked how much they would pay to preserve a natural resource or how much they would sell it for. In most cases, people would be willing to pay much less than they would charge to sell, setting up a dispute among economists over whether the standard for assessing such damages should be "willingness to pay" or "willingness to sell."

This kind of research, like other kinds that appear in courts of law, contributes to a growing anxiety in the legal system that if everyone believes researchers are blatantly creating information with a specific goal in mind, their studies may lose potency. Skepticism about the conviction with which researchers hold their paid positions has led some lawyers to "talk deprecatingly of 'liars, damned liars and expert witnesses' in order of unreliability." Yet as the troubling alliance between science and law grows, studies commissioned for the courtroom push researchers into ever subtler ways of massaging data.

CHAPTER EIGHT

Solutions

◆

*Everybody gets so much information
all day long that they lose their
common sense.*

—GERTRUDE STEIN

Nuts May Lower Cholesterol, Study in Medical Journal Says, by the Associated Press, published in the *Washington Post*, March 4, 1993.

A study funded by the California Walnut Commission has found evidence suggesting that nuts in general, and walnuts in particular, lower cholesterol levels and thus are good for the heart.

Comment: *We know who funded it, We do not know if it is relevant, but we know the outcome was good news to the sponsor.*

"Including walnuts in the everyday diet may be an easy way to lower the risk of heart disease by improving the cholesterol profile," said Joan Sabate of Loma Linda University in California, who directed the latest study, published in Thursday's *New England Journal of Medicine*.

New England Journal *is better than many, but even it cannot be relied on to weed out all poor and tainted studies.*

The story began with a study of 31,208 Seventh-Day Adventists. Researchers questioned them about their consumption of 65 different foods. To the researchers' surprise, those who ate nuts at least five times a week had only half the risk of fatal heart attacks as those who had nuts less than once a week. That discovery was published last summer in the *Archives of Internal Medicine*.

Unfortunately, we do not know from this account how many of the sixty-four other foods were associated with a lower risk of heart attacks. We do not know if the nut eaters shared other characteristics besides eating nuts that may have explained their lower rate of fatalities. Seventh-Day Adventists do not smoke or drink, which makes them an abnormal population to study. And according to this account, the study was based on their memories, not observation.

This time, the researchers put 18 healthy volunteers on two carefully controlled diets for two months. One was a nut-free version of a standard low-cholesterol diet. The other was nutritionally similar, except 20 percent of calories came from about 3 ounces of walnuts per day.

While not a fatal flaw, eighteen subjects is a very small study. The subjects were put on a low-cholesterol diet, which means their cholesterol was going to drop no matter what. Think about eating three ounces of walnuts every day. It comes to more than fifty pounds a year.

On the no-nuts diet, the volunteers' cholesterol levels fell 6 percent. When they switched to the walnut diet, their cholesterol declined an additional 12 percent. Everyone's cholesterol dropped while eating nuts, and the average decrease was 22 points, from 182 to 160.

They lost me. Did all the subjects first eat the no-nuts, then the nuts regime? Or were there two groups, one starting with no nuts and one starting with nuts? Did the 22-point cholesterol drop include the decrease attributable to the low-cholesterol diet alone? How long did the study go on—that is, would the cholesterol level have continued to drop from the low-cholesterol diet with or without nuts? Those walnuts displaced other food—was the drop a substitution effect alone?

The reason for the drop is unclear.

More studies are needed. Do not start eating three ounces of walnuts a day.

◆

OF THE THREE CONFLICTS OF interest inherent in research—the sponsor's, the researcher's and the media's—only one, the sponsor's, is usually noted in news reports of studies, surveys and polls. That disclosure, many in the media believe, allows readers to decide for themselves if and how much the results have been compromised. The theory is that people will simply discount the information appropriately, like handicapping a horse race, and make an educated guess of how much to bet on it.

Unfortunately, that is impossible. The methodology and language of honest and dishonest research are indistinguishable. Self-interested researchers are just as intelligent as their colleagues, and just as articulate and persuasive. They deeply believe their work is not only right but untainted by its commercial underpinnings. If their studies are flawed, they note something every researcher knows—there is no such thing as a perfect study. Every study must be handicapped because of the unavoidable difficulties in measuring people. Is the deliberately bad much different from the accidentally bad?

But judging information based on its taint is very difficult. What is the proper formula? If a survey question seems a little slanted or a sample size too low or the results totally out of line with other research, should the information be discounted 10 percent, 25 percent or 75 percent? At what point does the balance tip from the research being mostly right to mostly wrong? At what point does the information become more damaging than no information at all?

If there is such a point, it would be impossible to find it without two major changes in the information system. First, the tools that allow people to make critical judgments about research must be widely distributed. Second, people must know how to use them.

Behind every piece of published research there is a methodology and a body of data on which the study and its results were based. In survey research, such information comes in the form of a technical index. Some researchers are generous with this material, some charge money for it, and some simply refuse to show it. The technical index is considered proprietary by most commercial clients, and neither they nor the researcher is under any legal or ethical obligation to produce it. But without it, there is absolutely no way of knowing whether the research has any value. "The minute they say the technical appendix isn't immediately available, you smell a rat," said Jack Honomichl, publisher of a marketing industry newsletter. Solomon Dutka, a veteran survey researcher, agrees. "If it doesn't have a technical appendix, toss it out," he said. "My point is, don't waste your time."

The technical index or other methodological details of any credible research must be available to news reporters or interested laymen. In physical science, to publish any experimental result while concealing the data on which it rests would be considered suspicious and improper.

Even with that information, however, most people would be ill-equipped to judge a piece of research. American schools, which have largely ignored the explosion of quantitative information in daily life, can and should teach people how to tell whether particular sets of numbers are believable. Learning information skills should be as important to high school and college as a working knowledge of literature, science, economics or communications. High schools should devote some of their mathematics curriculum to everyday statistics. College statistics departments should offer courses for nonmajors in the statistics of everyday life. All other university departments should incorporate into their courses training in the field's research methodologies and where and why they can go wrong.

◆

THERE ARE WAYS TO CLEAN up each part of the information stream and to restore, at least partially, people's faith in numbers, fact, reality and truth.

It is unlikely that government will save us from poor information. The government has largely refrained from trying to regulate research and its outcomes. Speech is protected by the First Amendment, and most information is speech of one kind or another. When state legislatures, Congress and federal agencies have tried regulating research, their efforts have mostly failed. No one relishes the idea of a government telling its citizens what they can or cannot know. But some regulators, troubled by the steady growth of unreliable information, have proposed small changes. They have tried to force pollers to disclose more of their methodology; that failed. They have tried to impose a national standard of ethics in biomedical research—also unsuccessfully. In survey research, legislators have tackled telemarketing, autodialers, call blocking, taxation and, especially, privacy. But in almost every case they have faced aggressive—and effective—opposition from researchers and their sponsors. For all practical purposes, there are few watchdogs overseeing the information business.

In the area of polling, a trade group called the American Association for Public Opinion Research tries to maintain order in the industry, but the group is largely toothless. When the question of mandatory professional standards arose at association meetings in the late 1940s, most of the membership was strongly opposed, and "quite frankly defended a 'let the buyers beware' position," said Angus Campbell, former director of the Institute of Social Research at the University of Michigan. In 1950, the association established an ethics code, and in 1968 it recommended standards of disclosure for published polls.

Disclosing what the association suggests pollers and the media should disclose would be an excellent way to start educating people about how to read polls. The association says the published report should say who sponsored and conducted the survey; how the questions were worded and whether interviewers and respondents got instructions or explanations; which population was being studied and how a sample was identified; how the sample was selected, including if self-selected; the size of the samples; a discussion of the precision of the findings; which results are based on part of the sample rather than the whole; and where, when and how the data were collected. In fact, television polls report almost none of these, and newspapers report whichever few they choose.

On the more commercial side of survey research, a trade organization called the Council of American Survey Research Organizations has a (voluntary) four-pronged code of standards: confidentiality of respondents, privacy, responsibilities to the client and responsibility in reporting to clients and the public. If researchers and the media followed the council's recommendations, it would be much easier to judge the quality of research. The council's standards suggest that researchers report:

- ◆ the exact wording of the questions, including interviewer directions and visual exhibits;
- ◆ the total number of people contacted;
- ◆ the number of people not reached;
- ◆ the number of people who refused to answer;
- ◆ the number of terminations;
- ◆ the number of noneligibles;
- ◆ and the number of completed interviews.

It is rare that such details trickle down to consumers, even when the results do.

The Food and Drug Administration and the Federal Trade Commission supervise various types of research and information. Both agencies are underfunded, undermanned and overburdened, and can tackle only the biggest cases.

Perhaps our best hope for improving research lies in the academy, where there is a tradition of commercial disinterest. In recent decades, however, universities have enthusiastically bargained away their independence for money. Today, corporate influence reaches into all levels of academia, endowing university chairs, awarding academic prizes, funding master's and doctoral theses and underwriting the construction of research labs. Academic and corporate America are so intertwined that it would take a huge effort to separate the two, if it could be done at all. "People say the universities have to do this because research money is drying up," says the historian and author David Noble. "What really happened is the faucets were intentionally turned off to force universities into that embrace. All you have to do to revive the autonomy of those institutions is to re-fund them." In the modern economy, that is unlikely to happen.

- ◆ Colleges and universities should take a long, hard look at what they are selling to private interests. They should try to insure that objective voices remain for public debates. No institution, but most importantly no institution that receives government money of any kind, should agree to a contract stipulating secrecy.

♦ Colleges and universities should create permanent committees to review their corporate relationships and to hear complaints about conflicts of interest. Every piece of work, whether published or not, that has been done by a university researcher should be subject to the scrutiny of this panel, whose interest would be only to perpetuate high standards in research. A disinterested outside review board should be available to hear appeals from insoluble intercampus disputes.

♦ Every institution, but especially public ones, should have a written conflict-of-interest policy and should require faculty and staff to disclose in detail their affiliations with commercial concerns. Those disclosures should be available to the public.

♦ Academic institutions should not invest endowment funds in companies that have relationships with researchers at that institution. Nor should officers of the university invest in any company for which university researchers are working. Universities should forbid researchers on their staffs from having an equity interest in any company for which they do research. They should monitor and perhaps restrict how and when academic researchers appear at company-sponsored news conferences or symposia. They should forbid their researchers from endorsing or seeming to endorse a product.

♦

IT WOULD BE COMFORTING TO think the media protect us from the flood of dubious information we face every day, but they do not and they never have. Asking the media to protect people from bad polls, wrote Michael Wheeler, "is as unrealistic as expecting that prostitution will die because of lack of customer interest." The media are willing victims of bad information, and increasingly they are producers of it. They take information from self-interested parties and add to it another layer of self-interest—the desire to sell information. For the media, news need not be favorable as long as it is exciting. In addition to distorting our individual facts, media self-interest also paints a world that is excessively dramatic, episodic and ultimately confusing.

Reporters, editors and publishers naturally want to produce the biggest news to fulfill their own ambitions, and they have never been above creating, embellishing and exaggerating stories. The famous, if apocryphal, exchange between an illustrator, Frederic Remington, who had been sent to Cuba in 1897, and the publisher who sent him, William Randolph Hearst, was evidence of that. "Everything is quiet. There is no trouble here. There is no war. Wish to return," Remington cabled Hearst. "Please remain," Hearst cabled back. "You furnish the pictures and I'll furnish the war."

After World War II, the big media threw themselves into the pursuit of objectivity, trying to wall off the opinions and motives of media owners from their news coverage. Balance, objectivity, accuracy were journalistic ideals. Reporters and editors were expected to be neutral, to get as close to "reality" as possible. Numbers and data, long favorite breeds of "fact," increasingly crowded out anecdotal information. Polls replaced the man in the street. Articles about food and health research squeezed out recipes. In stories about policy issues, surveys and studies spoke where passionate voices once debated. Expanding lifestyle pages needed research to give their soft columns ballast.

At the same time, biomedical researchers, who traditionally disdained the popular press, realized the usefulness of a friendly story. Scientists once assumed that "a record of accomplishment [was] sufficient to maintain research support," wrote Dorothy Nelkin. "Partly because of this assumption, information, the scientist's 'stock-in-trade,' has been directed primarily toward professional colleagues." Today, as more researchers pursue dwindling funding, researchers have become cozier with the media, using and being used by them. "When government money was easily available," an editor told Nelkin, "you couldn't get a story out of a molecular biologist. Today, I get copies of grant applications in the mail with this thing, 'single cure for blank,' or whatever the hell it might be, circled in red, saying, 'we need all the help we can get, fellers.'"

The media also contribute to the trivialization of information, publishing research that is so silly or obvious that it borders on self-parody. Magazines aimed at women (because women are thought to be especially naive about numbers?) are the worst.

♦ If you think you are in poor health, then you probably are, reported *Self* magazine. Data from several studies suggest that people who said their health was poor were seven times more likely to die in the next twelve years than those who said their health was excellent. The item ran under the shockingly irresponsible headline "Think Positive or Die." A more accurate headline would have been "People Know When They Are Sick."

♦ Sixteen percent of 1,500 chief executive officers surveyed were Scorpios, the most of any astrological sign, reported *Working Woman* magazine. Leos were in the basement, occupying only 4.9 percent of the executive offices. That must be because Scorpios are magnetic, creative risk takers, the accompanying article said, while Leos are intense, personal and too emotional. Actually, it is because chance alone virtually guarantees deviation from an average.

♦ If you want to give your baby daughter an advantage in the business world, do not name her something sexually ambiguous like "Shelby," reported *Working Mother* magazine in a recent study. The highest-scoring girl's name on the success scales: Jacqueline.

The media set our political and social agendas, narrowing a vast river of information into a stream by deciding which is important. Even among biomedical researchers, whose field produces thousands of esoteric journals, the mainstream media play a crucial role in the information flow. David Phillips, a sociologist at the University of California at San Diego, found that many doctors and scientists get their scientific and medical news first from the newspaper, then decide which journal articles are worth reading. "I started this research because I noticed that when the *New York Times* had picked up a piece of mine, I got a lot more scientific interest," Phillips said. "Science writers and editors are heavy hitters in the development of science. They are conveying information in two directions. We can see that the mass media are amplifying the transmission of medical information, but we don't know if they're also distorting it."

Without much effort, the media could upgrade the quality of information, simply by educating readers and viewers about it. The media could commit themselves to putting research into a historical and methodological context and clearly stating the numerous caveats inherent in any study. They could become more critical of it themselves, and stop depending on polls, surveys and studies to be the cheap raw material of entertainment. They could make an effort to separate the good from the poor instead of the exciting from the boring. The media should tell the real story of science by regularly publishing "negative" research. They should expand their concept of what is newsworthy in science, asking themselves, when they dismiss a report of a negative study, whether they would have dismissed the same study if it had produced positive results. Similarly, when they see a positive story, they should ponder the question of whether there could be negative results sitting in a file drawer somewhere.

The news media should also:

◆ teach their reporters and editors not only fundamentals of statistics but also how to be critical readers of many different kinds of research. One person on each staff should be a trained statistician, available to review research on deadline.

◆ demand that all research submitted for publication be accompanied by a technical index, and that the scientists involved in the research be available for interviews outside of carefully controlled news conferences. The media themselves should disclose methodological details and raw data for their own polls, as well as the price they pay for them.

◆ devote more space to describing the methodology of research. Every story about research should contain a paragraph describing other research on the same subject, especially if it contradicts the current work.

In poll stories, where some caveats are already published, though usually in a separate box, warnings should also appear in the text of the story not only about margins of error but also about question design and sampling. The exact text of the questions on which the story is being built should also be included.

Every story about research should disclose not only the sponsor but the cost of the research and the potential gain or loss the sponsor or researcher might have from the outcome of the research. If the researcher is a paid consultant to the sponsor, or has traveled at the sponsor's expense to medical symposia, the story should note that, too.

The media should not make promises that they will publish or broadcast—or give prominent placement to—polls and surveys in exchange for getting them exclusively.

The media should get out of the business of producing self-interested information. They should stop doing call-in and mail-in polls. If they can't break this lucrative addiction, they should stop describing them as polls. The media should also stop re-enacting actual events and staging situations for news programs, like NBC's exploding truck.

In the case of public opinion polls and surveys, the media should repeatedly note that public opinion can shift dramatically and quickly, and that it is risky to make long-term decisions based on surveys and polls.

The media should stop rushing to print or broadcast reports of studies they do not yet understand. They should take the time to review the research carefully and to get expert opinions of it.

(5) POLLSTERS

◆

POLLING, PERHAPS THE MOST WIDELY seen kind of research, especially during political campaigns, needs a broad overhaul. If pollers changed nothing about their business except to frequently warn readers and viewers of the inherent shortcomings of polls, that would be an enormous help. Wherever applicable, these suggestions should also be used by survey researchers who work for commercial clients.

First, and most important, pollers should stop approaching every question as though it were an election in which people can vote only for or against. Polls should tap into the richness of opinion, not reduce it to a binary choice. Pollers should slow down; instant opinions are unnecessary, and they exacerbate other shortcomings of polls. Most important, pollers and consumers should both take a test suggested by Michael Wheeler. To see if a question is a good indicator of public opinion, Wheeler wrote, ask yourself whether you would feel comfortable answering it. If you find yourself saying, "Yes, but" or "No, except," then do not ask the question, or disregard the poll.

The polling industry should form a governing body for the profession, like the bar association for lawyers or the Financial Accounting Standards Board for accounting. Both the polling and market research industries should institute some barriers to entry; if nothing else, aspiring pollers and market researchers should be required to have minimal training in proper methodologies and professional ethics.

Since it is unlikely that pollers will stop polling during election primaries, consumers should simply follow Wheeler's simple rule of thumb for reading them: Don't.

Pollers should stop doing polls in shopping centers unless they want to project their results only to people at shopping centers. Mail-in and call-in polls are also suspect—they are based on a self-selecting nonrandom group. Polls that solicit contributions should be ignored.

Pollers should stop selectively leaking their polls. Consumers should look skeptically at any poll that has been leaked because it means an undisclosed deal has been struck.

Consumers of polls should ask themselves the following questions, written by Wheeler, in assessing their value: Are the numbers right, and what do they mean? Have the numbers been adjusted? How was the poll conducted? Is it an election poll? If it is an issue poll, could you answer the question? What do the other polls say? What did the poller really ask? Who paid for the poll? Is it really a trend? How much do you know about the poll? The answer to any of these questions could justify ignoring the poll. As a general rule, the less information that is available about the way a poll was conducted, the less it can be trusted.

Neither America's leaders nor its citizens should make

decisions based on polls or surveys. Polls may serve as hints of a public mind, but they should never replace the experience, judgment and idealism of true leadership.

INDIVIDUAL RESEARCHERS

ULTIMATELY, THE JOB OF CLEANING up the research business rests in the hands of individual researchers themselves. They could push sponsors, media and universities toward higher standards. Although it would be better if researchers took no money from sponsors with a stake in the outcome of the research, it is naive to believe they will or could do this without a massive infusion of money from other sources. But it does not seem too much to ask that they personally not have a direct financial stake in the results of their research.

Researchers should fight against encroaching secrecy in their business. The purpose of secrecy is almost always to increase profit; its effect is almost always to stymie scientific progress. Researchers must insist on the right to share their work with colleagues.

Biomedical researchers and publications should stop the deterioration of the peer-review system. Scientists should treat their peer-review duties with the same seriousness they accord their own research projects.

Although the top biomedical journals insist that scientists disclose their financial affiliations with drug companies, scientists should do so even when it is not required, wherever and whenever their research is disseminated.

Researchers should not only disclose their sponsor but also whether the sponsor was involved in designing the protocol, collecting data, analyzing it or approving or revising the final article.

Researchers should state in advance what they are looking for over what period of time. Researchers should not report preliminary results of any study to a commercial sponsor.

Researchers should make public—even if they do not publish—the results of every study they do. Short of this, they should at least state in advance whether they will or will not publish the findings.

Researchers should insist on retaining some control over the way their studies are disseminated to the public. They should not let themselves be turned into shills for their sponsors' products.

Biomedical researchers should stop allowing their research to be published in journals sponsored by a single source. They should stop accepting junkets from pharmaceutical companies under the auspices of continuing education. To assure that they do continue to gather to discuss topics of interest, they should pool their money and let their trade associations sponsor the conferences.

⑦ US !   ◆

IT IS IDEALISTIC TO BELIEVE that academic institutions, researchers, pollers or the media will universally decide to stifle their self-interest and clean up the information industry. The task of managing information so that it is useful or, failing that, at least harmless falls to us, the consumers of research.

One of the unfortunate results of our obsession with numbers is that we allow them to supersede our eyes, our judgment and our common sense. Many people are afraid to try to pull apart statistics because they were not "good in math." The first thing consumers should do when they look at numbers is ask themselves if they seem right. That they do not seem right does not mean the numbers are wrong; the reverse is also true. But a little skepticism goes a long way to offset the intimidation of numbers. "My first reaction to anything like that [a study suggesting electric razors cause leukemia] is, 'Aw, come on,' " said Persi Diaconis, professor of mathematics at Harvard University.

It does not take a scientist to decide that some research makes sense and some does not. "Sometimes you can read a study and get a feel for whether there was a simple experiment behind it or massive data that was massaged," said Diaconis. "You can get a feel for whether there was a simple understandable comparison made, or a complicated mishmash of statistical adjustment. If it doesn't make sense, it probably isn't sense."

One study may hint at an emerging truth, and possibly

offer a diverting bit of entertainment, but in general that is all it is—a hint and a diversion. Unless and until a study has been replicated, it should be looked at with care—the experiments proving the existence of cold fusion, still unreplicated, being a good example. To establish something as widely accepted as the belief that smoking causes lung cancer took decades, and the evidence came from many different threads of research—animal studies, human studies, epidemiological studies.

Beware of research and researchers calling themselves independent. Independent often just means there are many paying clients instead of one; it does not mean that there is no financial incentive to provide agreeable results. Similarly, the word "nonprofit" means little in assessing the credibility of a study; nonprofit researchers still count on a regular paycheck.

The words "as many as" indicate hyperbole. It means that no one knows how many, and the reporter or researcher has taken the top of the range to make the problem seem more dramatic.

There are a few basic questions to ask about any study that will provide some clues about whether or how much to believe it. How many people were involved? Over what period of time? How was the study controlled for bias? What did earlier studies on the same subject find? How were results of the research disseminated? (Research papers presented at conferences may not have been as carefully screened as research papers published in peer-reviewed or refereed journals.)

Beware of the word "adjusted." Researchers use it as an all-purpose defense against challenges to their data. Adjustments are subjective decisions. Sometimes they are legitimate, and sometimes they are not.

◆

THE TACIT ACCEPTANCE OF UNTRUTH in daily life eats away at belief in right and wrong. If nothing is true, how can one solution be better than another? Progress stalls. "We should fuss, we should be indignant," wrote Ivan Preston about disinformation in advertising. "We should call the advertisers phonies, or bullshitters, or harassers, when we think that's what they are. . . . We should not allow our own silence to be one of the reasons why things stay the same."

If we do not do something about our information, it is almost inevitable that we will eventually lose our ability to cope with our problems. "When regard for truth has been broken down or even slightly weakened," wrote Saint Augustine some 1,500 years ago, "all things will remain doubtful."

It is time for us to reclaim our numbers, our truth.

NOTES

CHAPTER ONE: THE STUDY GAME

15   The 1840 Census was a cesspool: Patricia Cohen, *A Calculating People*, pp. 175–204.

15   Much of the battle over prohibition: Claude E. Robinson, *Straw Votes*, pp. 146–47.

15   America's Defense Intelligence Agency: *Triumph Without Victory: The Unreported History of the Persian Gulf War*. U.S. *News and World Report* staff. New York: Times Books, 1992.

16   "Fraudulent activities pervade": Jack D. Douglas, "Betraying Scientific Truth," in *Society*, November-December 1992, p. 76.

17   Ross Perot's straight-talking television commercials: David Wessel and Gerald F. Seib, "In Straight-Talking TV Spots, Perot Stretches the Truth to Make His Point," in *Wall Street Journal*.

17   "He mentioned a specific number": *New York Times*, September 12, 1992.

18   "Truth usually lies": Thomas E. Mann and Gary R. Orren, eds., *Media Polls in American Politics*, p. 10.

19   "As dupes we know": Sissela Bok, *Lying*, p. 13.

19   "[F]ew doctors accept that they": Michael D. Rawlins, "Doctors and the Drugmakers," in *Lancet*, August 4, 1984.

22   The researchers concluded: Charles K. West, *The Social and Psychological Distortion of Information*. Nelson-West, 1981, pp. 60–61.

23   In one survey, respondents: Herbert H. Clark and Michael F. Schober, "Asking Questions and Influencing Answers," in *Questions About Questions*, p. 33.

24   In 1947, a researcher: Stanley L. Payne, *The Art of Asking Questions*, p. 18.

24   "You sit in a lady's living room": Jean M. Converse and Howard Schuman, *Conversations at Random*, p. 27.

24   In one study, researchers: Barbara J. MacNeil, Stephen G. Paulker and Amos Tversky, "On the Framing of Medical Decisions." Origin unknown.

25   In one experiment on buffer questions: Norbert Schwarz and Hans J. Hippler, "Buffer Items: When Do They Buffer and When Don't They." Paper prepared for 1992 meeting of the American Association for Public Opinion Research.

26   A German research team: Michaela Wanke and Norbert Schwarz, "Comparative Judgments: How the Direction of Comparison De-

termines the Answer." Paper prepared for the American Association for Public Opinion Research convention, May 1992.

32 They may agree that it is easy: As quoted in Thomas E. Mann and Gary R. Orren, *Media Polls in American Politics*, p. 6.

34 "People are really": As quoted in Michael Wheeler, *Lies, Damn Lies, and Statistics*, p. 90.

34 The Republican poller: From *Money*, March 1988, p. 156.

CHAPTER TWO: THE TRUTH ABOUT FOOD

41 White bread will not make you: Diane Duston, "Wonder Bread Sponsors Research Defending White Bread," Associated Press, October 19, 1992.

42 Chocolate may actually: Barry Meier, "Dubious Theory: Chocolate a Cavity Fighter," in *New York Times*, April 15, 1992.

45 A person would have had to eat: "Oat Bran Cholesterol-Lowering Guide: Part II," from *Eater's Digest*, published by the Center for Science in the Public Interest, July-August 1989.

45 Yet when a food industry newsletter: "Oat Bran Heartburn," in *Newsweek*, January 29, 1990.

54 The National Aeronautics and Space Adminstration: Bob Davis, "Risk Analysis Measures Need for Regulation, but It's No Science," in *Wall Street Journal*, August 6, 1992.

56 After giving *60 Minutes* its exclusive: Peter Carlson, "The Image Makers," in *Washington Post*, February 11, 1990.

56 Excerpts from a self-congratulatory memo: Published in *Wall Street Journal*, October 3, 1989.

56 The industry hired its own: Peter Carlson, "The Image Makers," in *Washington Post*, February 11, 1990.

57 That study was later discredited: Warren T. Brookes, "The Wasteful Pursuit of Zero Risk," in *Forbes*, April 30, 1990.

57 Risk assessments "represent a best guess": Leslie Roberts, "Alar: The Numbers Game," in *Science*, March 17, 1989.

65 "If you want to get people": Sheri Roan, "Researchers Link Four Cups of Coffee to Heart Attack Risk," in *Los Angeles Times*, September 12, 1990.

67 As the beating of the warning drums: Larry C. White, *Merchants of Death*, p. 30.

67 Under the title "A Frank Statement": Ruth Brecker, *The Consumers Union Report on Smoking and the Public Interest*, p. 107.

67 In the minutes of a 1954 meeting: Joe B. Tye, "The Tobacco Industry's Research Ashtray." Unpublished article.

68 In June 1993, they sued: Michael Janofsky, "Tobacco Groups Sue to Void Rule on Danger in Secondhand Smoke," in *New York Times*, June 23, 1993.

CHAPTER THREE: THE NUMERICAL LIES OF ADVERTISING

71   In a 1615 case, a certain Baily: Dee Pridgen and Ivan L. Preston, "Enhancing the Flow of Information in the Marketplace," in *Georgia Law Review*, Summer 1980, p. 638.

72   A survey done in the mid-1980s: *Advertising Age*, March 5, 1984.

73   Until the government insisted: Robert Pitofsky, "Beyond Nader," in *Harvard Law Review*, February 1977.

73   "In markets where product claims": Pitofsky, loc. cit.

73   Each day, America's collective consciousness: Leo Bogart, "Strategy in Advertising," as quoted in Collins and Skover, "Commerce and Communication," in *Texas Law Review*, March 1993, p. 707.

74   "The World's Largest Van": *Consumer Reports*, April 1993.

75   The lesson here is clear: Bruce Buchanan and Doron Goldman, "Us vs. Them," in *Harvard Business Review*, May-June 1989, p. 5.

76   One of the most unbelievable: Bradley A. Stertz, "Ads Claim 'Import' Intenders Prefer Its Compact Cars to Japanese Competition," in *Wall Street Journal*, August 17, 1990.

76   A similar survey by New York City area: *Consumer Reports*, August 1992.

77   "One has to understand": Neil Templin, "Expanding Beyond Automobile Surveys, J. D. Power Defends Its Business Methods," in *Wall Street Journal*, September 5, 1991.

78   Almost a quarter of Americans: Bernice Kanner, "The Examined Life," in *New York*, March 1, 1993.

80   Without the caramel coloring: Ron Alsop, in *Wall Street Journal*, July 18, 1985.

84   "How can two lotions": Thomas Mohl, "Comparative Advertising: Who Wins?" Presentation to the National Advertising Division Workshop, April 29–30, 1991.

84   Deception "is often undertaken": Sissela Bok, *Lying*, p. 85.

85   Until the beginning of the twentieth century: Michael Schudson, *Advertising, the Uneasy Persuasion*, pp. 125–26.

86   Around the turn of the century: Dee Pridgen and Ivan L. Preston, "Enhancing the Flow of Information in the Marketplace," loc. cit., p. 647.

86   "Ironically, the drive for consumer protection": Pridgen and Preston, p. 648.

86   A very early example of this: Ivan L. Preston, *The Great American Blow-up*, p. 276.

88   "[Robert] McNamara is selling safety": "Carmakers Use Special Features to Push Product," in *Colorado Springs Gazette Telegraph*, July 24, 1992.

89   A Chrysler commercial showed chairman: Amy Harmon, "Auto Makers Driving Home Safety," in *Los Angeles Times*, June 26, 1991.

89   This was the same man who once said: Richard Cohen, "Over-the-Counter Lies," in *Washington Post*, March 3, 1991.

90 That is why in 1988: Jacob M. Schlesinger, "Is It Safe? Depends on Whom You Ask," in *Wall Street Journal*, August 29, 1988.

92 "The marketer decides what the claim will be": Bruce Buchanan and Doron Goldman, "Us vs. Them," loc. cit., p. 3.

93 "[N]either individual consumers": As quoted in Philip Gold, *Advertising, Politics and American Culture*, p. 167.

94 Marketers took deregulation: Stephen Gardner, "How Green Were My Values," in *University of Toledo Law Review*, Fall 1991, p. 33.

94 In the personal computing world: Jim Bartimo, "In Polls Ranking PCs, Everybody Wins," in *Wall Street Journal*, July 31, 1991.

96 An official of Vail ski resort: Marj Charlier, "Vail, Miffed at Loss of No. 1 Ranking in Skier Survey, Printed Fake Ballots," in *Wall Street Journal*, February 22, 1993.

Chapter Four: False Barometers of Opinion

100 Polling "is the purest form": As quoted in *Money* magazine, March 1988, p. 144.

100 The doubt inherent: George A. Lundberg, "Public Opinion from a Behavioristic Standpoint," in *American Journal of Psychology*, November 1930, p. 397.

103 The *Washington Post* and ABC News asked: *The New Republic*, September 30, 1985.

104 Between July 1 and November 3, 1992: "Putting Polls in Context," in *The Finish Line*, The Freedom Forum Media Studies Center, January 1993, p. 56.

104 After John Kennedy was assassinated: Michael Wheeler, *Lies, Damned Lies, and Statistics*, p. 102.

104 Similarly, the number of people: Lindsay Rogers, *The Pollsters*, p. 186.

105 But like any marketplace: Benjamin Ginsberg, *The Captive Public*, p. 37.

107 Real public opinion: George A. Lundberg, "Public Opinion from a Behavioristic Standpoint," loc. cit., p. 403.

107 The poller Daniel Yankelovich: "How Public Opinion Really Works," in *Fortune*, October 5, 1992.

108 "Twice as many": "A View from Britain," in *The Public Perspective*, November-December 1992, p. 17.

110 Whenever poll results: Benjamin Ginsberg, *The Captive Public*, pp. 61–65.

110 Indeed, James Fishkin: "The Deliberative Opinion Poll: A Dialogue," in *The Public Perspective*, May-June 1992.

111 "We [pollers] all know": Humphrey Taylor and David Krane, "The Polls and the 1992 Elections," in *The Public Perspective*, January-February 1993.

112 Question error can do far greater damage: Michael Wheeler, *Lies, Damn Lies, and Statistics*, p. 255.

112 It would be impossible to calculate: Wheeler, p. 247.

112 To show how much difference: David M. Wilber, "H. Ross Perot Spurs a Polling Experiment (Unintentionally)," in *The Public Perspective*, May-June 1993.

114 In America, democracy changed that: Benjamin Ginsberg, *The Captive Public*, p. 40.

114 These included "authentic facts": Patricia Cline Cohen, *A Calculating People*, p. 151.

115 "Statistics signaled America's rising power": Cohen, p. 169.

115 The early straw polls: Jean M. Converse, *Survey Research in the United States*, p. 117.

116 The 1948 polling debacle led: David Moore, *The Superpollsters*, pp. 70–71.

117 The government has taken several stabs: Michael Wheeler, *Lies, Damn Lies, and Statistics*, pp. 245–69.

117 The sociologist David Riesman: David Riesman and Nathan Glazer, "The Meaning of Opinion," in *Public Opinion Quarterly*, Winter 1948–49, pp. 638–41.

118 Pollers ask the questions: Benjamin Ginsberg, *The Captive Public*, p. 82.

118 In 1970, for example: Benjamin Ginsberg, *The Captive Public*, p. 81.

118 Lately, the trend in poll questioning: "Opinion Polls: Public Judgment or Private Prejudice?" in *The Responsive Community*, Spring 1992.

119 "The beliefs of those who care": Ginsberg, p. 64.

119 President Nixon used polls: Ginsberg, p. 66.

121 After ordering the mining: Michael Wheeler, in *Classics of Polling*, Michael L. Young, ed., p. 206.

123 In 1980, ABC let viewers choose: T. Keating Holland, "Margins of Error," in *Reason*, February 1992.

124 Perhaps the most infamous call-in poll: "The CBS News Call-In," in *The Public Perspective*, March-April 1992.

125 A few organizations also experimented with real-time polling: " 'Consumer' Journalism in the Electronic Age," in *The Finish Line*, The Freedom Forum Media Studies Center, January 1993.

126 Traditionally, as one said: Ibid, p. 48.

126 Worse, critics wonder: Ibid, p. 52.

127 "Isn't it reasonable to suppose": Philip Meyer, "Stop Pulling Punches with Polls," in *Columbia Journalism Review*, December 1991.

128 "I wonder how far Moses": David McCullough, *Truman*. New York: Simon & Schuster, 1992, p. 914.

CHAPTER FIVE: FALSE TRUTH AND THE FUTURE OF THE WORLD

131   "In the past year": Barnaby J. Feder, "Cloth Diaper Closings Set by Gerber," in *New York Times*, January 14, 1992.

131   "Who says it has to be neutral?": Gina Brisgone, "Questionable Questionnaires," in *Hartford Courant*, May 11, 1991. These two comments were made at different times in response to questions about the same cable television survey.

133   "Each group convinces itself": "Scare of the Week," in *Science*, April 7, 1989.

133   But from industry: Michael Wheeler, *Lies, Damn Lies, and Statistics*, p. 241.

133   And from a Connecticut representative: Brisgone in *Hartford Courant*.

134   In June 1991, the abortion warriors: Adam Clymer, "Abortion Foes Say Poll Backs Curb on Advice," in *New York Times*, June 25, 1991.

135   The National Association for Perinatal: Mickey Kaus in *The New Republic*, May 20, 1991.

136   "Even if congressmen discount": James L. Payne, The Culture of Spending.

136   The size of the homeless population: "Enumerating Homeless Persons: Methods and Data Needs," ed. by Cynthia M. Taeuber. Conference proceedings, issued March 1991.

137   "Arguments about numerical quotas": "Public Statistics and Democratic Politics," in *The Politics of Numbers*, p. 272.

138   " 'We've got to get Murray his inflation back' ": David A. Stockman, *The Triumph of Politics*, p. 96.

138   But the intricacies of human decision-making: EEOC vs. Sears Roebuck, 626 F. Supp. 1264, p. 1264.

140   One was Procter & Gamble's 1990 analysis: "Disposable versus Reusable Diapers: Health, Environmental and Economic Comparisons," a study issued March 16, 1990.

140   A 1988 study appraising: Carl Lehrburger, "Diapers in the Waste Stream: A Review of Waste Management and Public Policy Issues," a study issued December 1988.

140   A 1990 study sponsored by the diaper arm: "Energy and Environmental Profile Analysis of Children's Disposable and Cloth Diapers," a study issued July 1990.

140   A 1991 study: Carl Lehrburger, et al., "Diapers: Environmental Impacts and Lifecycle Analysis," a study issued January 1991.

141   Lifecycle analysis began: David Stipp, "Lifecycle Analysis Measures Greenness, but Results May Not Be Black and White," in *Wall Street Journal*, February 28, 1991.

141   It is helpful to know: Ibid.

145   Amassing data to advance a social agenda: Patricia Cline Cohen, *A Calculating People*, pp. 170–72.

145 The new scientific optimists: Robert Formaini, *The Myth of Scientific Public Policy*, p. 69.

145 "To be measured": Kenneth Prewitt in Alonso and Starr, eds., *The Politics of Numbers*, p. 270.

147 Co-opting experts without their knowing: As quoted in "Business Goes Back to College," by David F. Noble and Nancy E. Pfund, in *The Nation*, September 20, 1980.

147 The nonprofit Epilepsy Institute: "Miracle Drugs or Media Drugs?" in *Consumer Reports*, March 1992.

147 A study in large part funded by: Rory Van et al., "The Effect of Diaper Type and Overclothing on Fecal Contamination in Day-care Centers," in *Journal of the American Medical Association*, April 10, 1991.

148 The American Paper Institute's diaper group: "A Gallup Study on Disposable Diapers," August 22, 1990.

149 The final surrender in the war: *Garbage*, October-November 1992.

150 Risk assessment already guides: Bob Davis, "Risk Assessment Measures Need for Regulation, but It's No Science," in *Wall Street Journal*, August 6, 1991.

150 Using risk analysis: Ibid.

150 It was risk assessment, too: Much of this account was drawn from a detailed and fascinating recounting of the swine flu case, "Scientific Policy Meets Reality: The Swine Flu Episode" by Robert Formaini in *The Myth of Scientific Public Policy*.

153 That research suggests: Carolyn Lochhead, "Cradle to Grave," in *Insight* magazine, May 6, 1991.

153 Most of the study's financing came: Ted J. Smith and Melanie Scarborough, "A Startling Number of American Children in Danger of Starving," a case history of advocacy research presented to the May 19, 1992, conference of the American Association for Public Opinion Research. Used with permission of Melanie Scarborough.

CHAPTER SIX: DRUGS AND MONEY

161 In 1983, Cantekin approached his department chairman: Kathleen Hart, "Corporate-funded Research May Be Hazardous to Your Health," in *Bulletin of Atomic Scientists*, April 1989.

162 Because of an "oversight": "Are Scientific Misconduct and Conflicts of Interest Hazardous to Our Health?" Report by the House Committee on Government Operations, September 10, 1990.

162 Only one manuscript: "The Cantekin Affair," in *Journal of the American Medical Association*, December 18, 1991.

165 Had Cantekin's research been published: Hearings of the House Committee on Government Operations, September 10, 1990.

165 "[The center has] contracts: in *Washington Post*, June 13, 1989.

167   Bias, wrote T. C. Chalmers: As quoted in Roger J. Porter and Thomas E. Malone, *Biomedical Research*.

168   Study of a new epilepsy drug: Porter and Malone, p. 156.

168   A new product called Ricelyte: Jerry E. Bishop, "Test Finds New Bristol-Myers Product Superior to Abbott's for Infant Diarrhea," in *Wall Street Journal*, February 21, 1991.

168   Bald men are three times likelier: Glenn Ruffenach, "Bald Men, Objects of Jokes and Pity, Face Cardiac Risk," in *Wall Street Journal*, February 24, 1993.

169   The drug AZT prolongs: Marilyn Chase, "AZT Affects Races the Same," in *Wall Street Journal*.

169   A change in diet: "Study Casts Doubt on Ability of Diet to Lower Cholesterol," in *New York Times*, April 29, 1993.

169   Prescription drug prices are falling: Milt Freudenheim, "Study Says Prescription Prices Are Falling," in *New York Times*, March 31, 1993.

169   Davidson confirmed what he had suspected: "Source of Funding and Outcome of Clinical Trials," in *Journal of General Internal Medicine*, May-June 1986.

169   Researchers may become too attached: Roger J. Porter and Thomas E. Malone, *Biomedical Research*, p. 133.

170   It is difficult for young scientists: Porter and Malone, p. 137.

170   "All physicians who are conducting": Porter and Malone, p. 157.

172   When Max Gottlieb left academia: As quoted in John P. Swann, *Academic Scientists and the Pharmaceutical Industry*, p. 33.

172   Adopted in 1847: Swann, p. 30.

172   "Let me be the first to admit": Arthur Caplan, "A Question of Ethics," in *St. Paul Pioneer Press*, October 9, 1989.

174   Society is most vulnerable: Porter and Malone, *Biomedical Research*, p. 129.

174   The drug Retin-A had been used: An excellent overview of the Retin-A saga, from which much of this account has been drawn, can be found in "The Selling of Retin-A" in *Money*, April 1, 1989. Neither John A. Voorhees nor Barbara Gilchrest returned calls requesting interviews.

177   In addition to the $253,120 in research grants: "Are Scientific Misconduct and Conflicts of Interest Hazardous to Your Health?" A report from the House Subcommittee on Government Operations, September 10, 1990.

178   The so-called halo effect: Charles J. Sykes, *ProfScam*, p. 118.

178   "Despite this system, anyone who reads": Drummond Rennie, "Guarding the Guardians: A Conference on Editorial Peer Review," in *Journal of the American Medical Association*, November 7, 1986.

179   In 1991, the FDA took action: "Pushing Drugs to Doctors," in *Consumer Reports*, February 1992.

179   A 1986 survey: John P. Swann, *Academic Scientists and the Pharmaceutical Industry*, p. 178.

179   Verifiability is also no longer an effective deterrent: Robert L.

Engler et al., "Misrepresentation and Responsibility in Medical Re-search," in *New England Journal of Medicine*, November 26, 1987.

180   Agreements like that "come perilously": In *New York Times*, July 13, 1993.

180   Sheer volume of studies: Edward L. Petsonk, "Conflicts of Interest in Drug Research," in *New England Journal of Medicine*, Vol. 301, No. 6, 1979.

181   Leon Trachtman observed: As quoted by Anthony Schmitz in "Food News Blues," in *Health*, November 1991.

181   In 1991, the *Journal of the American Medical:* Gideon Koren and Naomi Klein, "Bias Against Negative Studies in Newspaper Reports of Medical Research," in *Journal of the American Medical Association*, October 2, 1991.

184   The results of the study: "Pharmaceutical Advertisements in Leading Medical Journals: Experts' Assessments," in *Annals of Internal Medicine*, June 1, 1992.

184   In 1982, Dr. Jerry Avorn: "Doctors Don't See Power of Drug Ads," in *Medical World News*, September 13, 1982.

186   Writing in the *New England Journal:* Alan L. Hillman et al., "Avoiding Bias in the Conduct and Reporting of Cost Effectiveness Re-search Sponsored by Pharmaceutical Companies," *New England Journal of Medicine*, May 9, 1991.

191   In studies conducted during the 1970s: Philip J. Hilts, "Strange History of Silicone Held Many Warning Signs," in *New York Times*, January 18, 1992.

191   "My advice to those patients": in *Washington Post*, June 23, 1992.

CHAPTER SEVEN: RESEARCH IN THE COURTROOM

193   In the spring of 1991: Lawrence K. Altman, "New Report Chal-lenges IUD Study," in *New York Times*, April 15, 1991.

194   Full disclosure is built: Stephen Fienberg, ed., *The Evolving Role of Statistical Assessments as Evidence in the Courts*, p. 149.

195   "I would go into a lawsuit": Blake Fleetwood, "From the Peo-ple Who Brought You the Twinkie Defense," in *Washington Monthly*, June 1987.

196   A Maryland expert broker promised: in *Wall Street Journal*, January 7, 1988.

197   "Junk science is any science": Natalie Angier, "Supreme Court Set to Decide What Science Juries Can Hear," in *New York Times*, January 2, 1993.

197   Surveys, the descriptive measure: Solomon Dutka, in *Harvard Business Review*, July-August 1980.

198   When a prosecuting attorney: Robert C. Sorensen and Theo-dore C. Sorensen, "Responding to Objections Against the Use of Opinion

Survey Findings in the Courts," in *Journal of Marketing*, October 1955, p. 136.

198 "The conclusions of market researchers": Fred W. Morgan, "Judicial Standards for Survey Research," in *Journal of Marketing*, January 1990, p. 68.

198 When a Sears, Roebuck store: Stephen Fienberg, ed., *The Evolving Role of Statistical Assessments as Evidence in the Courts*, p. 153.

199 John Henry Wigmore: R. J. Gerber, "Victory vs. Truth," in *Arizona State Law Journal*, Vol. 19, No. 3, p. 15.

199 Once a survey is introduced: Joseph G. Smith et al., "Legal Standards for Consumer Survey Research," in *Journal of Advertising Research*, October-November 1983, p. 24.

201 As would someday become clear: Morton Mintz, *At Any Cost*, p. 33. Morton Mintz of the *Washington Post* did a superb job covering the Dalkon Shield story over a number of years. I am indebted to him for his *Post* coverage, as well as his excellent book on the subject.

201 Several months after Davis's study was published: Mintz, in *Washington Post*, April 10, 1985.

202 Shortly thereafter, a Robins staff physician: Roger L. Tuttle, "The Dalkon Shield Disaster Ten Years Later," in *Oklahoma Bar Journal*, Vol. 54, No. 36, p. 2502.

202 Intimations of trouble: Mintz, in *Washington Post*, April 8, 1985.

203 By the time Robins filed for bankruptcy: Francis E. McGovern, "Resolving Mature Mass Tort Litigation," in *Boston University Law Review*, Vol. 69:659, 1989, p. 675.

204 The claimants' committee: Richard B. Sobol, *Bending the Law*, p. 171. Sobol has written an extraordinary book about the Dalkon Shield bankruptcy that was an invaluable aid to my reconstruction.

204 Robins also preferred open-ended: Francis McGovern, loc. cit., p. 684.

205 The ideal way to estimate the total cost: Richard B. Sobol, *Bending the Law*, p. 181.

206 A public health scientist: A. J. Jaffe and Herbert F. Spirer, *Misused Statistics*, p. 192.

206 "The witnesses had no expertise": Richard B. Sobol, *Bending the Law*, p. 181.

207 Had all the sides known: Francis E. McGovern, loc. cit., p. 686.

207 Because surveys can be so persuasive: Joseph G. Smith et al., loc. cit., p. 30.

213 Even so, in 1984: Richard B. Sobol, *Bending the Law*, pp. 18–19.

213 Internal documents from Aetna: Morton Mintz, in *Washington Post*, July 8, 1988.

214 In 1990, a group of pathologists: Jeff Bailey, "How Two Indus-

tries Created a Fresh Spin on the Dioxin Debate," in *Wall Street Journal*, February 20, 1992.

216   A typical Title VII dispute: Stephen Fienberg, ed., *The Evolving Role of Statistical Assessments as Evidence in the Courts*, pp. 28–29.

216   In one decision, in a race and sex: Fienberg, p. 25.

216   Rather than bring individual women into court: Susan Faludi, *Backlash*, p. 385.

217   In the five years before the EEOC started: Faludi, p. 379.

218   In a case in the 1950s: "Public Opinion Surveys as Evidence," an unsigned article, *Harvard Law Review*, Vol. 66, 1953, pp. 509–10.

221   "How much are you willing to pay": Frank B. Cross, "Natural Resource Damage Valuation," in *Vanderbilt Law Review*, March 1989, p. 315.

221   One study, conducted for the Environmental Protection Agency: Walter J. Mead, "Review and Analysis of Recent State-of-the-Art Contingent Valuation Studies." Presented at a symposium, Contingent Valuation: A Critical Assessment, in Washington, D.C., April 2 and 3, 1992. Mead's research, which is highly critical of contingent valuation, was funded by Exxon Company USA.

222   Skepticism about the conviction: *Introduction to English Law* by James, as quoted in Fienberg, ed., *The Evolving Role of Statistical Assessments as Evidence in the Courts*, p. 148.

CHAPTER EIGHT: SOLUTIONS

228   When the question of mandatory: Michael Wheeler, *Lies, Damn Lies, and Statistics*, p. 258.

230   Asking the media to protect people: Wheeler, p. 262.

231   Scientists once assumed: Dorothy Nelkin, *Selling Science*, p. 133.

231   "When government money was easily available": Nelkin, p. 141.

235   To see if a question is a good indicator: Michael Wheeler, in *Classics of Polling*, Michael L. Young, ed., p. 203.

SELECT BIBLIOGRAPHY

"Advances in Claim Substantiation." Proceedings of National Advertising Division Workshop III. April 29–30, 1991.

"Advertising and the Public Interest." Round Table held June 10, 1976. Sponsored by the American Enterprise Institute, Washington, D.C.

Alonso, William, and Paul Starr, eds. *The Politics of Numbers*. New York: Russell Sage Foundation, 1987.

Alsop, Ron. "Coke's Flip-Flop Underscores Risks of Consumer Taste Tests." In *Wall Street Journal*, July 18, 1985.

"Are Scientific Misconduct and Conflicts of Interest Hazardous to Our Health?" House Committee on Government Operations, September 10, 1990.

Blankenship, A. B. *Professional Telephone Surveys*. New York: McGraw-Hill, 1977.

Bok, Sissela. *Lying: Moral Choice in Public and Private Life*. New York: Pantheon Books, 1978.

Boorstin, Daniel J. *The Image: A Guide to Pseudo-Events in America*. New York: Vintage Books, 1992.

Brecker, Ruth. *The Consumers Union Report on Smoking and the Public Interest*. Mount Vernon, N.Y.: Consumers Union, 1963.

Brennan, Troyan A. "Causal Chains and Statistical Links: The Role of Scientific Uncertainty in Hazardous-Substance Litigation." In *Cornell Law Review*, March 1988.

Brower, Brock. "The Pernicious Power of Polls." In *Money*, March 1988.

Buchanan, Bruce, and Doron Goldman. "Us vs. Them: The Minefield of Comparative Ads." In *Harvard Business Review*, May-June 1989.

Buchanan, Bruce, and Ronald H. Smithies. "Taste Claims and Their Substantiation." In *Journal of Advertising Research*, June-July 1991.

Budiansky, Stephen, et al. "The Numbers Racket: How Polls and Statistics Lie." In *U.S. News & World Report*, July 11, 1988.

Clark, Herbert H., and Michael F. Schober. "Asking Questions and Influencing Answers." In *Questions About Questions*. Judith M. Tanur, ed. New York: Russell Sage Foundation.

Cohen, Patricia Cline. *A Calculating People: The Spread of Numeracy in Early America*. Chicago: University of Chicago Press, 1982.

Collins, Ronald K. L., and David M. Skover. "Commerce and Communication." In *Texas Law Review*, March 1993.

Converse, Jean M. *Survey Research in the United States: Roots and Emergence 1890–1960*. Berkeley: University of California Press, 1987.

Converse, Jean M., and Howard Schuman. *Conversations at Random: Sur-*

vey Research as Interviewers See It. New York: John Wiley & Sons, 1977.

Crespi, Irving. "Surveys as Legal Evidence." In *Public Opinion Quarterly*, Spring 1987.

Cross, Frank B. "Natural Resource Damage Valuation." In *Vanderbilt Law Review*, March 1989.

Douglas, Jack D. "Betraying Scientific Truth." In *Society*, November-December 1992.

Dutka, Solomon. "Business Calls Opinion Surveys to Testify for the Defense." In *Harvard Business Review*, July-August 1980.

Dutka, Solomon, and Lester R. Frankel. "Misuses and Abuses of Statistical Techniques in Market Research Surveys." In *Chance*, Vol. 3, No. 4, 1990.

Faludi, Susan. *Backlash*. New York: Crown Publishers, 1991.

Field, Mervin D. "Political Opinion Polling in the United States of America." In *Political Opinion Polling: An International Review*. Robert M. Worcester, ed. New York: Macmillan, 1983.

Fienberg, Stephen, ed. *The Evolving Role of Statistical Assessments as Evidence in the Courts*. New York: Springer-Verlag, 1988.

Formaini, Robert. *The Myth of Scientific Public Policy*. New Brunswick, N.J.: Transaction Books, 1990.

Gardner, Stephen. "How Green Were My Values: Regulation of Environmental Marketing Claims." In *University of Toledo Law Review*, Fall 1991.

Gerber, R. J. "Victory vs. Truth: The Adversary System and Its Ethics." In *Arizona State Law Journal*, Vol. 19, No. 3.

Ginsberg, Benjamin. *The Captive Public: How Mass Opinion Promotes State Power*. New York: Basic Books, 1986.

Gold, Philip. *Advertising, Politics, and American Culture*. New York: Paragon House, 1986.

Gray, Paul. "Lies, Lies, Lies." In *Time*, October 5, 1992.

Hardy, H. S. *The Politz Papers: Science and Truth in Marketing Research*. New York: American Marketing Association, 1990.

Hitchens, Christopher. "Voting in the Passive Voice." In *Harper's Magazine*, April 1992.

Huber, Peter W. *Galileo's Revenge: Junk Science in the Courtroom*. New York: Basic Books, 1991.

Jaffe, A. J., and Herbert F. Spirer. *Misused Statistics*. New York: Marcel Dekker, 1987.

Kaus, Mickey. "Facts for Hacks." In *The New Republic*, May 20, 1991.

Kintner, Earl W. "How Advertising Has Policed Itself." In *Advertising: Today/Yesterday/Tomorrow*. New York: McGraw-Hill, 1963.

Korn, Harold L. "Law, Fact, and Science." In *Columbia Law Review*, Vol. 66.

Lasch, Christopher. *The Culture of Narcissism*. New York: W. W. Norton, 1979.

Lavrakas, Paul J., and Jack K. Holley, eds. *Polling and Presidential Election Coverage*. Newbury Park, Calif.: Sage Publications, 1991.

Loftus, Elizabeth, and Katherine Ketcham. *Witness for the Defense: The Accused, the Eyewitness and the Expert Who Puts Memory on Trial*. New York: St. Martin's Press, 1991.

Lundberg, George A. "Public Opinion from a Behavioristic Standpoint." In *American Journal of Sociology*, November 1930.

Mann, Thomas E., and Gary R. Orren, eds. *Media Polls in American Politics*. Washington, D.C.: Brookings Institution, 1992.

McGovern, Francis E. "Resolving Mature Mass Tort Litigation." In *Boston University Law Review*, Vol. 69:659, 1989.

Mintz, Morton. *At Any Cost: Corporate Greed, Women, and the Dalkon Shield*. New York: Pantheon Books, 1985.

Moore, David W. *The Superpollsters*. New York: Four Walls Eight Windows, 1992.

Moore, Thomas J. "The Cholesterol Myth." In *The Atlantic Monthly*, September 1989.

Morgan, Fred W. "Judicial Standards for Survey Research." In *Journal of Marketing*, January 1990.

Nelkin, Dorothy. *Selling Science*. New York: W. H. Freeman, 1987.

Nisbet, Robert. "Public Opinion and Popular Opinion." In *Public Interest*, Fall 1975.

O'Neill, Harry W. "Conducting Legal Research: Do's and Don'ts." Address to the American Association for Public Opinion Research 47th Annual Conference, St. Petersburg, Florida, May 18, 1992.

Patterson, James, and Peter Kim. *The Day America Told the Truth*. New York: Prentice Hall, 1991.

Paulos, John Allen. *Innumeracy: Mathematical Illiteracy and Its Consequences*. New York: Hill and Wang, 1988.

Payne, James L. *The Culture of Spending*. San Francisco: ICS Press, 1991.

Payne, Stanley L. *The Art of Asking Questions*. Princeton: Princeton University Press, 1951.

Pitofsky, Robert. "Beyond Nader: Consumer Protection and the Regulation of Advertising." In *Harvard Law Review*, February 1977.

Porter, Roger J., and Thomas E. Malone. *Biomedical Research: Collaboration and Conflict of Interest*. Baltimore: Johns Hopkins University Press, 1992.

Postman, Neil. *Technolopy*. New York: Vintage Books, 1993.

Preston, Ivan L. *The Great American Blow-up*. Madison: University of Wisconsin Press, 1975.

———. *The Tangled Web They Weave: Truth, Falsity, and Advertisers*. Unpublished manuscript, 1992.

Pridgen, Dee, and Ivan L. Preston. "Enhancing the Flow of Information in the Marketplace." In *Georgia Law Review*, Summer 1980.

"Problems in Polling." In *Public Perspective: A Roper Center Review of Public Opinion and Polling*, March-April 1992.

"Public Opinion Surveys as Evidence: The Pollsters Go to Court." In *Harvard Law Review*, Vol. 66, 1953.

Riesman, David, and Nathan Glazer. "The Meaning of Opinion." In *Public Opinion Quarterly*, Winter 1948–49.

Robinson, Claude E. *Straw Votes: A Study of Political Prediction*. New York: Columbia University Press, 1932.

Rogers, Lindsay. *The Pollsters: Public Opinion, Politics, and Democratic Leadership*. New York: Alfred A. Knopf, 1949.

Schudson, Michael. *Advertising, the Uneasy Persuasion*. New York: Basic Books, 1984.

Siroky, Miriam L. "Criticisms of Consumer Perception Studies in Litigation." Address presented to National Advertising Division Workshop, April 29–30, 1991.

Smith, Joseph G., Wallace S. Snyder, James B. Swire, Thomas J. Donegan, Jr., and Ivan Ross, panelists. "Legal Standards for Consumer Survey Research." In *Journal of Advertising Research*, October–November 1983.

Sobol, Richard B. *Bending the Law: The Story of the Dalkon Shield Bankruptcy*. Chicago: University of Chicago Press, 1991.

Sorensen, Robert C., and Theodore C. Sorensen. "Responding to Objections Against the Use of Opinion Survey Findings in the Courts." In *Journal of Marketing*, October 1955.

Stockman, David A. *The Triumph of Politics*. New York: Harper & Row, 1977.

Swann, John P. *Academic Scientists and the Pharmaceutical Industry*. Baltimore: Johns Hopkins University Press, 1988.

Sykes, Charles J. *ProfScam*. New York: St. Martin's Press, 1988.

Tuttle, Roger L. "The Dalkon Shield Disaster Ten Years Later—A Historical Perspective." In *Oklahoma Bar Journal*, Vol. 54, No. 36.

Vreeland, Leslie N., and Mary Granfield. "The Selling of Retin-A." In *Money*, April 1, 1989.

Wheeler, Michael. *Lies, Damn Lies, and Statistics: The Manipulation of Public Opinion in America*. New York: Liveright, 1976.

Whelan, Elizabeth M. *Smoking Gun: How the Tobacco Industry Gets Away with Murder*. Philadelphia: George F. Stickley, 1984.

White, Larry C. *Merchants of Death*. New York: William Morrow, 1988.

Yankelovich, Daniel. "How Public Opinion Really Works." In *Fortune*, October 5, 1992.

Young, Michael L., ed. *The Classics of Polling*. Metuchen, N.J.: Scarecrow Press, 1990.

Zeisel, Hans. "The Uniqueness of Survey Evidence." In *Cornell Law Quarterly*, Fall 1959.

INDEX